Twinning Faith and Development

Twinning Faith and Development
Catholic Parish Partnering in the US and Haiti

■ ■ ■

Tara Hefferan

Kumarian
Press, Inc.

For Quinn and Connelly

Twinning Faith and Development

Published in 2007 in the United States of America by Kumarian Press, Inc., 1294 Blue Hills Avenue, Bloomfield, CT 06002 USA

The text of this book is set in 10.5/14 StempelGaramond.

Production and design by Viewtistic, Inc.
Proofread by Beth Richards.
Index by Viewtistic, Inc.

Printed in the United States of America by Thomson-Shore. Text printed with vegetable oil-based ink.

 The paper used in this publication meets the minimum requirements of the American National Standard for Information Sciences—Permanence of Paper for printed Library Materials, ANSI Z39.48–1984

Library of Congress Cataloging-in-Publication Data

Hefferan, Tara, 1972-
Twinning faith and development : Catholic parish partnering in the US and Haiti / by Tara Hefferan.
   p. cm.
   Includes bibliographical references and index.
   ISBN-13: 978-1-56549-236-3 (pbk. : alk. paper)
1. Church work with the poor—Catholic Church—Case studies. 2. St. Robert of Newminster (Ada, Mich.)—Charities—Case studies. 3. Notre Dame de la Nativité (Verrettes, Haiti)—Finance—Case studies. 4. Economic development—Religious aspects—Catholic Church—Case studies. 5. Economic development projects—Haiti—Verrettes—Case studies. I. Title.
   BX2347.8.P66H44 2007
   261.8097294—dc22

---

16 15 14 13 12 11 10 09 08 07   10 9 8 7 6 5 4 3 2 1   First Printing 2007

Contents

Acknowledgments

I owe an enormous debt of gratitude to the people of St. Robert and Nôtre Dame de la Nativité parishes. Without them, this project would not have been possible. I am grateful to the Haiti Committee at St. Robert, which has been supportive beyond measure, incredibly gracious, and generous in helping me gather data for this research, particularly Sister JoAn Brown, Anne Gruscinski, and Dennis Chamberlain. I also would like to acknowledge the assistance of Father Lou Stasker, Father Jean Francique, and Father Yvens Joseph. I reserve special thanks for Cassie Ellis, who went above and beyond the "call of duty" time and again to provide me with information, interpretations, and kindness— and who, even after reading the criticisms I raise herein, has been incredibly supportive of this work.

Several other people in twinning networks have been of invaluable assistance. For kindness and support big and small, I thank Theresa Patterson, Adeline Marcelin, Father Jean-Salomon Vincent, Father Mackenzy Célestin, Father Apol Martin, Father Gustana Valcourt, Father Rosemond François, Father Alexis Robinson, Sister Judy Vollbrecht, Tim Ryan, Pat Abner, Amy Marsh, Gaston Cherichel, Mathieu Pierre, Valerie Mossman, Jean-Rony Jean Baptiste, and Wilsi Merisca. I especially thank Bill and Char Baker and Tom Braak for companionship and assistance in Haiti. To Doug Porritt, a trusted friend and committed advocate on behalf of Haiti, I send special heartfelt thanks and deep gratitude.

This work is based on dissertation research carried out while I was a student at Michigan State University. I benefited enormously from the expert guidance of my dissertation committee, made up of Drs. Laurie Kroshus Medina (Chair), Anne Ferguson, Rita S. Gallin, and Andrea Louie. I thank each of them for their unending support over these many years, as well as for their suggestion that I get the dissertation into book form immediately. I benefited from many other relationships at Michigan State University, each of which has contributed to my ability to undertake this research. For these, I thank Drs. Lynne Goldstein, Fred Roberts, Bill Derman, Rob Glew, and Laurent Dubois. Thanks, too, to Pascale Pierre and Terri Bailey and to the staff of the Women and International Development program.

For preparing me to study at Michigan State University, I thank Dr. Tracy Bachrach Ehlers, and for preparing me to study in Haiti, my thanks to Beverly Bell. Dr. Erica Bornstein read and commented on an earlier draft of the book, for which I am most grateful. Various aspects of this research have been presented at conferences over the years; I appreciate the comments and suggestions I have received from co-panelists and discussants—particularly Drs. Sangeeta Kamat and Nina Glick Schiller. Thanks also to Tawney Fuhrmann for her wonderful assistance in preparing this manuscript for publication.

The research was supported by an International Predissertation Fellowship awarded by the Social Science Research Council and the American Council of Learned Societies, with funds provided by the Ford Foundation; a National Science Foundation Ethnographic Training Grant awarded by Michigan State University's Anthropology Department; and a Ford Predissertation Travel Grant awarded by the Center for the Advanced Study of International Development and the College of Social Science at Michigan State University. Advanced language training in French and Haitian Creole was made possible by three Foreign Language and Area Studies Fellowships awarded by the Center for the Advanced Study of International Development and the Women and International Development program at Michigan State University. I thank each of these funders for their generosity.

I want to end with special thanks to my family. My mother Kimberly Engelman Hall pushed me to follow my heart and do what I love: anthropology. Quinn Hefferan Nordlund and Connelly Hefferan Nordlund, my daughters, shaped the course this research took, including its interpretation and write-up. I thank them for allowing me to work, even though they would prefer that I play. And most especially, I am grateful to my husband, Jerry Nordlund. His unconditional support has enabled me to research and write over the years. This project would have been impossible without him and his encouragement. Thank you.

CHAPTER ONE

Introduction

Critics of conventional development—as both ideology and practice—have charged that one of its primary effects has been the depoliticization of poverty, which serves to quell "Third World" resistance to global inequity and economic marginalization. Indeed, some have argued that development is really about controlling people in the global south by labeling them "poor" and promising them a better life through northern intervention in their economies and cultures (Crush 1995; Escobar 1995a, 2000; Ferguson 1994; Rist 1997; Sachs 1992). This control is operationalized through the development apparatus, a global network of interconnected ideas, funding channels, organizations, and development professionals ("experts") that disseminates notions of progress and modernity. But a crisis in foreign aid, combined with intensifying globalization and government privatization, has recently led to radical transformations in international development. Foremost among them has been a shift in development away from governments and toward nongovernmental organizations (NGOs). On the surface, at least, the hegemonic "development apparatus" appears to be mutating into new, fractured, and privatized forms.

This book explores these shifts in development by looking at one increasingly important manifestation of development's privatization: citizen-to-citizen networking. In particular, this work considers the expanding linkages between Catholic parishes in North America and those in Haiti, as individual parishes form local grassroots partnerships that focus on creating and implementing development in Haiti. Motivated by philanthropy, religion, and/or belief in social justice, lay men and women without training or experience in international development are bypassing the formal dimensions of the aid industry as they directly attempt to "develop" what we know as the Third World. One question immediately arises: What is development—what does it mean, how is it constructed, what are its goals—to these increasing numbers of noncredentialed "lay" developers? That is, how do nonexperts understand, define, and design international development projects? Another question also emerges: How are private, nonprofessional initiatives related to the entrenched institutionalized development apparatus that antidevelopment scholars have criticized as depoliticizing, bureaucratic, and managerial? And finally, do these lay efforts constitute "counterdevelopment," or are they extensions of the hegemonic discourses and practices of conventional development?

Such questions stem from a development studies literature concerned with the relationships between power and knowledge and with their operation within the development field. Building from the work of such theorists as Michel Foucault, Antonio Gramsci, and Pierre Bourdieu, anthropology of development studies, in particular, have examined how the crafting of "professional" knowledges is an exercise of power that at once builds and legitimizes the "cult of the expert." By setting limits on what people are able to think about the world and its operations, professional discourses create spaces, particularly within institutions, where only some people—those deemed experts—have authority and legitimacy.

From this perspective, the knowledge upon which development is founded and practiced has not been discovered in a scientifically neutral or politically disinterested way. Rather, development knowledge—like all knowledge—has been created as an exercise of power. Power in this sense is "dispersed, indeterminate, heteromorphous, subjectless, and productive," says Foucault (Best and Kellner 1991:48–49). That is to say, power is not a thing but a force that flows through institutions, formulates knowledge, and produces norms and technologies that discipline and "normalize" individuals and populations.

Knowledge and power, then, are intimately interwoven and mutually reinforcing fields that—together with notions of "truth"—configure discourse and practices (Foucault 1990). These discourses affect people, shaping their understandings of the world, the ways they experience particular phenomena, the languages they use. In essence, experts—often by crafting knowledge that is "measurable, specific, and calculable" (Cruikshank 1999:40)—shape discourses that define the terms upon which something can be known, spoken about, or experienced. They "set the rules of the game" by stifling competing discourses and "locking out" those who are unable to achieve and demonstrate appropriate expertise (through earning a diploma or sometimes accumulating experience) (Escobar 1995a). The "knowers," or specialists, are in positions of power and privilege that "structure the possible field of action by others" (Foucault in Cruikshank 1999:41). Those who are not deemed experts are thwarted in their efforts to institutionalize discourses of their own, so they are thought either to buy into (or, more recently, to "accommodate, rework, and resist") the views of the world that the experts put forth.

This is admittedly an oversimplified rendering of a complex set of theoretical arguments, but I raise it here to ask, "What about the many development programs being created, led, and implemented by average folks? Just how do such programs affect our thinking about the power/knowledge helix?" These questions assume that the development field indeed can be divided into a camp of experts and a camp of nonexperts. I make the distinction as a way of separating people for whom development is a career from those who engage in development as a voluntary activity,[1] those who have specialized training or education in development from those who do not, those who participate in the professional dimensions of development work (for example, conferences, publications, research) from those who do not, and those who "do" development with outside funding and grants from those who do not. Although I recognize that such distinctions are less than clear in practical application, I adopt them as a way to compare what I term conventional development—that is, development done by professionals/experts—from lay development done by nonprofessionals/nonexperts. Or, to put it bluntly, I attempt to understand how a group of middle-class Americans with no formal experience with international development discourses and practices seemingly comes to adopt, engage, rework, and deploy them. As the text will suggest, international development may owe less to the creation of exclusionary expert discourses than to the generalized experience of middle-class Western modernity[2] that permeates development in its multiple forms.

With the devolution and deconcentration of development away from state experts and toward NGOs, a relatively novel space has opened to those, such as Catholic parishioners, who are interested in international development but lack the desire or willingness to engage in such work as a career. The perceived need for action exists, because the gap between the world's richest and poorest is expanding, warfare increasingly is targeting civilians, natural disasters such as tsunamis in Indonesia and Hurricane Katrina in Louisiana, are becoming more frequent, and global health epidemics such as the avian flu and SARS are spreading across national borders. Yet, at the same time that these headline-grabbing realities seep into the American public's collective consciousness, governments worldwide are privatizing and cutting back on the social services they provide. The traditional experts, as some in my study suggest, seem unable or unwilling to battle these dehumanizing forces. As I discuss in Chapter Three, this perceived gap between the needs of the poor and downtrodden worldwide and the willingness or ability of professionals to care for (or "manage" them) has helped fuel voluntary action such as Catholic parish twinning.

Although it is situated in these gaps born of state neglect, incompetence, and predation, twinning—I argue—is not a libratory project; rather, twinning might be understood as a new form of "transnational governmentality"[3] (Ferguson and Gupta 2002) that operates via the goodwill and volunteerism of its participants. By this I mean that twinning—like NGO-ization more broadly—in many ways is a "new modality of government, which operates by creating mechanisms that work 'all by themselves' to bring about governmental results." It does this via the "devolution of risk onto the . . . individual . . . and the 'responsibilization' of subjects who are increasingly 'empowered' to discipline themselves" (Ferguson and Gupta 2002:989).

The key people in this study—American lay Catholics, for the most part—have been "responsibilized" to become developers, even though they are not trained in state-led or nongovernmental conventional development (Lacey and Ilkan 2006). This is one point of departure from traditional development studies, where those targeted for aid—the developed—tend to be the objects of examination. Even where studies have focused on the developers, they most often have examined development bureaucrats or bureaucracies (for example, Ferguson 1994; Gardner 2000; Moore 2001; Rew 1997) rather than volunteers or voluntary organizations (Korten 1990; Lacey and Ilkan 2006; MacDonald 1995).

A second point of departure from traditional development studies is the focus here on faith-based initiatives. Until the mid-1990s, few works considered religion's importance to economic development, except insofar as religion was thought to help or hinder economic "progress" (for example, Weber 1958 [1920]). But as NGOs in general began to rise in number and profile, so too did faith-based NGOs. While the study of NGOs has become a burgeoning field in development studies (Bebbington and Thiele 1993; Carroll 1992; Fisher 1997; Lewis and Wallace 2000; Riddell and Robinson 1995), the more focused study of faith-based NGOs is only beginning to emerge (for example, Belshaw, Calderisi, and Sugden 2001; Bornstein 2005; Candland 2000; Mayotte 1998; Occhipinti 2005; Tomalin 2006). This may be because, broadly speaking, spirituality and religion themselves remain largely undertheorized and unacknowledged in the development literature. Analyzing the contents of three mainstream development publications between 1982 and 1998, Kurt Ver Beek found that spirituality and religion were "conspicuously under-represented in development literature and in the policies and programmes of development organisations" (2000:36; see also Selinger 2004).

That said, studies examining development institutions—in both the governmental and nongovernmental sectors, with both secular and faith-based orientations—have tended to focus on the experts. The people in this study constitute a second, much less studied group: faith-based *lay* developers. They are the volunteers, the nonprofessionals, those without formal training or practical experience in development who nonetheless are designing, funding, implementing, and evaluating international development programs. This book focuses on these folks to explore how programs such as Catholic parish church partnering might enhance our understanding of the links between conventional and lay, secular and faith-based, development.

The book does this through an ethnographic case study of a partnership established in 1995 between St. Robert parish in Ada, Michigan, U.S.A., and Nôtre Dame de la Nativité[4] parish (referred to hereafter as "Our Lady") in Verrettes, Haiti. Matched by the national nonprofit organization the Parish Twinning Program of the Americas (PTPA), the two parishes have an active partnership—called a "twinning"—focused on supporting children and education in Haiti. Through regular transfers of money, intermittent travel, and occasional correspondence and telephone calls, St. Robert and Our Lady have crafted a vision for developing Verrettes by educating its people. The vision has been operationalized through the founding of a vocational school, a "Sponsor a Student" project to pay school fees for 200 students, and a feeding project to provide hot meals to 1450 children three times a week. St. Robert also funds a microcredit project, as well as forestry and agricultural extension in Verrettes. Taken together, the many projects that St. Robert funds and Our Lady administers in Haiti look very much like conventional development, and many of the challenges that both parishes encounter as they carry out these activities echo those identified by scholars and practitioners as characteristic of development initiatives more broadly. To consider whether, in fact, this religious grassroots programming is simply another manifestation of "development as usual," this book explores the extent to which nonprofessional, or lay, programs reflect, challenge, or render obsolete dominant development discourses and practices.

I carried out research for this project both in Michigan and in Haiti over periods between 2000 and 2004. Described in detail below, fieldwork included three research trips to Haiti (July–August 2000; May–June 2001; January–March 2002) to assess the scope and details of twinning programs in Point-à-Raquettes, Seguin, Ennery, and Verrettes, Haiti. In Haiti, I talked with priests, nuns, and others active in twinning about their programs, their relationships with U.S. parishes, and their ideas about development. I was a participant–observer in parish life (for example, masses and social events), in twinning projects (for example, vocational school), and in a mission trip of U.S. participants to Haiti. I also administered a survey questionnaire to participants of the vocational school at Verrettes to investigate their ideas about development, job training, and hopes for the future.

Because the focus of this project is on the developers rather than on the developed, the bulk of my research was Michigan-based; it was carried out over two research periods, July–December 2001 and July 2003–August 2004, largely in the greater Grand Rapids area. I gathered information from several Michigan parishes, including Holy Trinity, Sacred Heart, and Holy Spirit, and I was a participant–observer in many Grand Rapids twinning activities (for example, Creole language classes and fundraising events). For the most part, the data presented and discussed in the book come from my work with St. Robert, specifically. I conducted semi-structured interviews with a sample of members of the St. Robert Haiti Committee, and I was a participant–observer in the weekly mass, Haiti Committee meetings, and other, related parish events (for example, potlucks and "Know Your Parish" weekends). I conducted a brief survey of Michigan parishes active in church partnering, gathering data on programming, budgets, travels, and the like. The project also draws on archival materials, including parish bulletins at St. Robert, twinning promotional materials, and correspondence between St. Robert Haiti Committee members and Haitian priests and others. I discuss my research methods in more detail in Chapter Two.

∎ What Is Twinning?

Haiti is the poorest country in the Western Hemisphere, yet it is virtually in the backyard of the richest. Over the past century, the U.S. government has many times intervened in Haiti's economy and political life (Farmer 1994; Heinl, Heinl et al. 1996; Schmidt 1995), but the rise in individual and "Third Sector" activity in Haiti is more recent (Morton n.d.). Coinciding with an opening of Haiti to outside economic interests under Jean-Claude "Baby Doc" Duvalier, as well as with the growing *ti-legliz* liberation theology[5] movement in Haiti (Greene 1993; Mathieu 1991), the first official church-to-church partnering between Haitian and American Catholic parishes began in 1978 under the name "Adopt a Parish."

The movement began in Nashville, Tennessee, as a personal crusade by three Catholic parishioners—Harry and Alice Hosey and Theresa Patterson—who believed that their parish had resources and talents to share with the poor of Haiti. In fundraising speeches, informal chit-chat, and promotional materials, Theresa, cofounder and director of what is now called the Parish Twinning Program of the Americas (PTPA), offers the following account of how she became involved in Haiti. Inspired by stories told by Harry and Alice, missionaries long active in Haiti, as well as by parishioners at her church—St. Henry—in Nashville, Theresa made her first trip to Haiti in 1978. She describes the trip as long, difficult, and both physically and emotionally taxing. But the experience was in many ways life-changing for her. She experienced a profound recognition, she says, of the universality of the Catholic Church—that even though her life in the United States was so very different from the lives of those she was meeting in Haiti, together they shared a common faith that bridged chasms of social and physical location. Theresa also felt that her parish had many economic advantages to share with the Haitian parish, while the Haitian parish had spiritual richness to impart to hers. And she was thunderstruck by a question: What if U.S. parishes joined forces with those in Haiti to exchange their respective gifts with each other? In 1978 her parish, St. Henry, initiated a formal partnership with a parish in Beauchamp, in northwestern Haiti, after a series of droughts had devastated the area. The relationship was sanctioned by the bishops of each diocese after Theresa requested their permission by letter.

For the next few years, Harry and Theresa together increasingly promoted the idea of "twinning" to other parishes in their diocese. As twinnings grew in number locally and expanded to dioceses in other parts of the United States, and as Harry's health deteriorated, the Haiti Parish Twinning Program (HPTP) formally organized as a nonprofit in 1992, and Theresa took over as director. She chose to rename the program HPTP—emphasizing "twinning"—to capture the coming together in close relationships of participant parishes. In 1998 HPTP was rechristened the Parish Twinning Program of the Americas (PTPA), to reflect the expanding of twinning into other countries of the Caribbean, as well as into Central America and South America (see Figure 1.1).

In reality, linkages between parishes in Mexico, Jamaica, and elsewhere already had been established by Harry, but the renaming accom-

1978 known as *Adopt a Parish*
1992 known as *Haiti Parish Twinning Program* (HPTP)
1998 known as *Parish Twinning Program of the Americas* (PTPA)

FIGURE 1.1   CHANGING NAMES OF CATHOLIC CHURCH PARTNERING

panied an administrative division in the organization between twinnings focused on Haiti and those elsewhere in the region. The twinning movement has mushroomed in the years since its founding and now includes over 660 parishes and programs in North America and Haiti.

As noted in PTPA's mission statement (see Figure 1.2), the focus of twinning is to "serve those in need in Haiti" by creating direct, grassroots-level linkages between parishes. These linkages are to become "bridge[s] whereby the love of God flows in both directions as parishes learn to care, share and pray for one another" (HPTP promotional materials, n.d.). At an organizational level, this mission stems in part from the roots of Theresa Patterson's thinking in social justice, particularly liberation theology. Liberation theology attempts to address and reform the political and economic conditions underpinning human suffering. As Michael Zweig (1991:4) explains, liberation theology understands religious teaching as a call to action in support of social justice. Thus liberation theology

> is a theology that prods religious institutions to serve as active agents for social change, on behalf of and in conjunction with the poor, the oppressed, and working people who experience injustice as a daily fact of life. It is a theology that seeks to address and change social institutions, not just individuals.

Citing Christ's work on behalf of the poor and downtrodden, liberation theologians call for the Catholic Church to return to its original mission of confronting authority and injustice (Greene 1993). Although liberation theology has been a critical framework for Theresa Patterson and the development of twinning, it is not a guiding principle for the majority of those participating in St. Robert's twinning program.

In discussions with me, Theresa separated the Catholic Church into "conservatives" and social justice advocates, categorizing the priests in Haiti as advocates on behalf of their parishes and Haiti's bishops as responsible, in part, for the collapse of the liberation theology movement in Haiti. With little support or funding, the priests are largely responsible for locating financial aid or parish expenses and programming. The twinning program, in its mission to be sensitive to differences in power and wealth, emphasizes the right of the Haitian priest to direct how money coming from the U.S. twin is disbursed. That is, priests play the central role in initiating, maintaining, and directing twinning activities in Haiti.

In contrast, U.S. parishes are encouraged to establish Haiti committees to facilitate the twinning. These committees are peopled and generally led by lay parishioners rather than priests. Priests can be—and often are—a part of these U.S. committees, but the leaders are typically laity who are particularly interested in and committed to Haiti. Haiti committees work directly with Haitian priests to sustain the relationships, and they also serve as intermediaries between the Haitian priest and the

---

The mission of the Haiti Parish Twinning Program is to serve those in need in Haiti by:

- Encouraging *linkages* between Catholic parishes, institutions and individuals in the United States and Canada and parishes and institutions in Haiti.
- Developing *models* for parish actions.
- Encouraging *prayerful solidarity* with our sisters and brothers in Haiti.
- Providing *resources* and *support* in religious, educational, medical and economic areas.
- Promoting an *awareness* among Catholics of the injustices present in Haiti and our Gospel call to respond.

FIGURE 1.2 HPTP'S MISSION STATEMENT

U.S. parish. In short, then, twinning is predicated upon the central role of the priest in Haiti and the importance of laity in the United States.

If the primary mission of twinning is to serve those in need in Haiti by building direct linkages between Catholics in Haiti and in the United States, what is the nature of these relationships? That is, once two parishes are joined together, how does the relationship play out? Although developing cultural understanding and building personal relationships are important "voiced/ideal" aspects of twinning, the U.S. parish is expected to provide, first and foremost, some sort of financial assistance to its Haitian twin. The amount of money that parishes send varies considerably. In a 2001 survey of twenty-four Michigan parishes and programs participating in PTPA (response rate, nine parishes), I found that all send money to Haiti regularly, with a range of $1200 to $18,000 a year.[6] Some parishes (three of the nine responding) send money simply to supplement their Haitian twin's budget, without specifying how the money should be spent. But most send money to support specific projects or activities, and education is a high priority both in twinning promotional literature and in the Michigan twins' practice. Six of the nine parishes explicitly list supporting education (by providing student "sponsorships," supplementing staff salaries, and/or sending school supplies) as a priority activity. Promoting better health is also a main concern. Sending medicines is something that five of the nine parishes regularly do. Medical missions—whereby U.S. medical teams travel to Haiti to work in clinics and dispensaries—are becoming increasingly frequent. One of the nine Michigan parishes sent a medical mission in 2001 (the year of the survey), and 40 of the 330 participating PTPA parishes nationwide did so (Patterson, personal communication).

Twinning is predicated on mutuality, a notion that each party has something to offer the other. Respect and solidarity are supposed to characterize the relationship, and one way this is thought to be fostered is through frequent communications with one another, as well as through travel. That is, through development of a first-hand understanding of one another's "culture, customs, and needs," the distance between the parties is thought to be mediated, maybe even eliminated. In short, by getting together and talking, these "sister parishes" are supposed to bond and to take on aspects of the committed, heart-felt relationships of familial love. Practically speaking, when Americans travel to Haiti to visit their twins, they are most often shocked by the poverty and "difference" there, a reaction that is thought to translate into a deeper commitment to and greater understanding of Haiti and Haitians. Accordingly, when a church decides to join PTPA (usually having heard of twinning via word of mouth, from those already active in the twinning program sharing stories of their involvement), members are immediately encouraged to visit their Haitian twin, a prospect made less daunting by Theresa's active participation. PTPA not only maintains a lovely (and secure) guesthouse in Port-au-Prince but also arranges for in-country transportation, provides interpreters, and makes preparations for the stay with the Haitian twin. Moreover, Theresa usually travels with a group the first time it visits Haiti. In a nutshell, PTPA deals with the practical issues that travelers otherwise might face in trying to navigate Haiti alone, allays their concerns about security, and creates a sense among travelers that they are in good—and experienced—hands.

Traveling is something the Haitian priest is expected to do, as well. Priests are to visit their U.S. twins with some regularity, often once every year or two. To my knowledge, PTPA usually is not active in arranging the priest's travel, presumably because traveling to the United States is thought to be less intimidating and troublesome for Haitian priests than traveling to Haiti is for U.S. parishioners. Indeed, many of the Haitian priests I know have relatives living in the United States, so they travel there with some regularity. The U.S. parish generally assumes the responsibility of arranging and paying for the priest's travel. Unlike visits to Haiti, which are typically undertaken in groups, priests usually come to the United States alone or with foreign (U.S. or British) nuns, who serve as interpreters. Because of restrictive U.S. travel policies, obtaining a visa for any Haitian other than the priest is virtually impossible. Learning about U.S. culture (for example, attending hockey games, visiting museums, and seeing local attractions) is often part of the Haitian priest's experience, but the priest's visit is also explicitly about fundraising, communicating to the U.S. parish the needs of those in Haiti, and providing an accounting of how the monies sent are being spent.

Twinning, then, is both an idea—that parishes in the United States and Haiti have something to offer one another, can learn from one another, can benefit each other—and a practice—networks of travel and money, projects, prayer. PTPA claims it is the largest citizen-to-citizen network linking the United States and Haiti, a fact that has enabled the program "to generate over $10 million in *direct transfers* to aid parishes, nutrition centers, orphanages, hospitals, catechetical work, education, and economic development programs in Haiti" (PTPA n.d.). In the years it has been in operation, PTPA has gradually expanded its reach and its scope, most recently by beginning construction on a hospital in one rural region. It has organized a series of conferences, bringing together twinned parishes from across the United States and Canada to share their insights and experiences. Again, the program has greatly expanded in size; over 660 parishes and programs now participate. This means that three-quarters of Catholic parishes in Haiti are currently twinned with at least one U.S. parish or program. (McGlone 1997).

St. Robert of Newminster Parish

St. Robert is a wealthy parish located in Ada, Michigan, an especially prosperous community just outside Grand Rapids. Ada residents earn comparatively large salaries and live in more expensive homes than others in the local Kent County area.[7] This relative affluence also characterizes St. Robert, which the Grand Rapids Diocese classifies as a "top tier" parish—meaning it is among the largest and wealthiest parishes in the area. As a whole, St. Robert is a very active parish. It has 8534 registered parishioners, most of whom are white and—judging by the types of vehicles in the parking lot, the designer clothing worn, and the assessments of the priest, nun, and others—middle- to upper-middle-class. They fit with Ehrenreich's (1990:45) notion of what it means in a "cultural sense" to be middle-class: home ownership, the ability to put one's children through college and to enjoy family vacations.

As we have noted, St. Robert has been twinned with Our Lady of the Nativity parish in central Haiti since 1995. The twinning was spearheaded by Cassie Ellis after she attended a local diocesan function on behalf of one of St. Robert's other outreach programs. There she met Doug Porritt, who at that time was volunteering as a PTPA facilitator at the Grand Rapids diocese. Sparked by Doug's enthusiasm and drawn to Haiti for its French heritage (Cassie has studied the French language), Cassie approached the priest and nun at St. Robert. Both were receptive, despite the fact that until then, St. Robert had had an unwritten policy against working outside of Kent County. The parish felt it was important to address local needs first, but even though the decision to work in Haiti departed from this philosophy, it was justified because the "needs there were so great."

At the invitation of Our Lady, St. Robert sent a delegation of five people, led by Doug and Cassie, to Haiti in January 1996. They spent a few days at the PTPA guesthouse in Port-au-Prince before heading to Our Lady parish. During that time, the delegation asked the priests at Our Lady to come up with a wish list that could be presented to St. Robert. They did, and the list was compiled and later published in St. Robert's weekly parish bulletin. It included a generator, religious education books, stipends for catechists, additional salaries for the parish school teachers, money for two parish support groups, money for a student sponsorship program, a motorcycle for the priests, a school lunch program, and some office equipment. From there, the Haiti Committee—led by Cassie—forged a plan of action for Our Lady of the Nativity. Now, nearly 10 years later and with an annual budget of around $60,000 a year, the twinning includes a mix of projects and exchanges, which I describe in more detail below.

Our Lady of the Nativity Parish

Our Lady is a sprawling, 200-year-old parish in Haiti's Artibonite Valley, and it includes 55,000 people, 21 chapels in addition to the main church, as well as 6 parish schools.[8] The main church is located in a town of about 8000, and the chapels are in the mountains surrounding the town. Most people in the parish are farmers, have an average income of $60 a year, and live without running water or electricity.

At the urging of their bishop, a French priest assigned to Our Lady approached PTPA in 1994, asking to be twinned with a U.S. parish. As the priest wrote, "this parish has never been twinned and does not benefit from financial support for its pastoral activities. [The priests who will be replacing me] are young Haitian priests who receive no aid whatsoever. Therefore, the problem is very serious and urgent." By the time the twinning was established in 1995, Our Lady indeed had three new priests. Father Jean Francique was now leading the parish, and he was very eager to establish the twinning with St. Robert. To launch the relationship, he invited the St. Robert delegation to Haiti in 1996. He was careful not to ask St. Robert for anything, he says, other than to come for a visit.

Between 1995 and 2001—when he was transferred to a new parish—Father Jean was the primary contact for St. Robert; he was the person charged with communicating the needs of his parish, maintaining ties with St. Robert, processing the twinning payments, and entertaining Haiti Committee members when they came to visit. Cassie and Father Jean had a close working relationship, and other members of the Haiti Committee felt confident that Father Jean was a good steward of the twinning money. Father Jean told me that although communication problems often plagued the twinning, he felt that the "relationship between our church and St. Robert is a gift from God." Before the twinning, Our Lady didn't raise enough money from the weekly collections "to do anything," but since twinning, a number of programs had been implemented and sustained.

The Programs

As we have noted, St. Robert's aid especially focuses on children in Haiti, and its largest single project is the school lunch project, which feeds 1450 students a day, 4 days a week, and had a budget of $33,000 in 2005. This project was suggested by Father Jean, who during his visit to St. Robert in 1996 spoke often of the need to help the children in his parish. His message was conveyed to St. Robert in the weekly parish bulletin of October 27, 1996, which announced, following Father Jean's visit,

> These children walk two to three hours one way to attend the parish schools (the government does not provide schools in the mountain areas) without breakfast or lunch. Since hungry children have difficulty learning, Father wants to feed the children lunch. Rice and beans are the staples of the Haitian diet. In order to feed the children, it is necessary to have the pots and

pans to cook the food and dishes with which to feed the children. Father hopes to use the money that was given this weekend to begin the project.

He did, and the school lunch project is now the largest project that St. Robert's sponsors. As Father Jean wrote in English in a letter to St. Robert, "Thanks to you, the food program that was a dream becomes reality." Because it is meeting "such a basic need," as one committee member said, it's the project "we feel most pleased with." St. Robert buys most of the food for the lunch project locally rather than getting "lesser quality, but cheaper foods" elsewhere, because the committee feels that local buying "helps the local economy." Father Jean has appointed one woman who is responsible for buying all the food for the project. Each school has a committee of four to six people, who work together with the schools' principals to prepare the food.

Sponsoring students is the second-largest project, with a budget of about $20,000 a year. St. Robert provides students, who apply through Our Lady, with money to pay for tuition, school uniforms, and books. Pictures and "profiles" of students who need sponsors are made available to St. Robert's parishioners, who are asked to donate $100 a year for elementary and $200 for secondary students. Those who are interested arrange sponsorships through Cassie.

St. Robert also contributes $6000 a year to augment the pay of the forty teachers working in the parish schools. The priests at Our Lady have suggested that the parish teachers are likely to leave their employ unless raises are given, because public schools pay their teachers more than private schools. These programs also were developed at the suggestion of the head pastor, Father Jean.

St. Robert also founded and now supports a vocational school in town. This school cost $120,000 to build, and it teaches three programs, which were administered by volunteers from Switzerland under the direction of Our Lady's priests. The largest and most important project is auto mechanics, the second is masonry, and the third is sewing and cooking. The vocational school was the brainchild of one of Our Lady's former assistant priests, Father Alexis Robinson, who is now stationed at a parish about 20 miles from Our Lady. An automotive aficionado and trained mechanic, Father Alexis was the impetus behind the automotive project, which, like the masonry project, has a 3-year curriculum. The 2-year sewing and cooking project was initiated by St. Robert's Haiti Committee, who felt the school should offer something "for the women." The programs are intensive; the mechanics and masonry students are in class 20 hours a week, the sewing students 15 hours a week. Despite the investment of time and energy, however, graduates of the vocational school are unable to find jobs locally. Perhaps a little defensively, Father Jean is quick to emphasize, "Our job [at the vocational school] is to give information, not find jobs. But, if people have information, it will be easier for them to find jobs." Indeed, with formal sector unemployment hovering around 70 percent for the past several decades (CIA World Factbook 2005), it is not surprising that vocational school graduates are not finding jobs.

After meeting with people at Our Lady who recounted the demise of the town's previous small-loan project, St. Robert's Haiti Committee decided to start their own microcredit project for the area. With an initial budget of $10,000, the microcredit project primarily targets women, who take out loans of less than $100 to begin or augment their small businesses. There are typically eighty women borrowers at any one time. The project began in 2000, after Cassie spent several months researching how to run a microcredit project. While the Haiti Committee at St. Robert pushed to establish a low-interest project, Gerard, the parishioner in Haiti charged with running the project (who was selected by Father Francique for his ability to speak English and interact with the Americans), also spent many months researching loan programs. He pushed for a relatively high interest, modeling the project on regular bank loan applications and procedures. Eventually, Gerard and an assistant priest came up with a formal application (written in French), an interest rate of 1¼ percent a month, and procedures (including an assessment of creditworthiness) for securing a loan. St. Robert wanted to offer women start-up money for small businesses and to provide the area's farmers with access to credit. Cassie has been very vocal about her desire for farmers to have access to the loan funds. Gerard, on the other hand, did not want to offer credit to the farmers, fearing that farmers would not be able to repay. Ultimately, he says, the farmers did not want the loans anyway, and he is glad about that. "For the past two years, [the farmers] have had no harvest. One guy I talked with said he had to sell a cow to pay a loan. We don't want that. We want them to have a goat. . . . Farmers want credit, but not for farming. They want it for business."

St. Robert also partially funds an agriculture and forestry project in the parish, Faith in Action International (FIAI). FIAI is an explicitly Christian NGO founded and headed by Tom Braak, an American Protestant who says he was "called" to Haiti by God. Through a mutual friend, Tom and Cassie came together over their interest in Haiti. When Tom decided to travel in Haiti in 1997, Cassie urged him to consider working in Our Lady parish. While Tom traveled throughout the northern half of Haiti, staying at most 3 to 4 days in any one location, he stayed with the priests of Our Lady parish for over a month. During that time, aided by the priests, he made contacts that shortly thereafter led him to settle permanently in the town. St. Robert continued to pay for Tom's travel and lodging expenses while he established himself and his project in the area.

Although predicated on religious faith, FIAI is a conventional development NGO, in that Tom works full-time as its director and employs two full-time staff. Together, they attend development conferences and interact with other development groups in the country. The group is registered as a U.S. nonprofit, holds regular board meetings back in the United States, and produces a quarterly newsletter. FIAI has several programs, including a tree-planting project, agricultural extension, soil conservation, some tapping of wells, and microcredit. Cassie researched forestry projects and corresponded with several people in Haiti about appropriate and desirable trees to plant in Our Lady's region of Haiti. Her work lay some of the foundation for FIAI's current tree project.

St. Robert considers Tom's program to be an extension of its twinning activities, because it makes an annual contribution of $6000 to FIAI's budget. Tom is in regular contact with Cassie and has helped resettle St. Robert's parishioners Bill and Char Baker, who now spend 6 months out of the year in Haiti, helping Tom with his project, as well as administering certain aspects of the twinning projects, including student sponsorships. Tom, however, does not see FIAI as connected to St. Robert or to its twinning program. When I asked him how FIAI relates to St. Robert's program, he said, "Hmmm. I don't know that it does. We're obviously working in the same community, with the same people. But [FIAI is] working with adults. [St. Robert] more [with] the students."

■ The Context

To understand how and why faith-based movements—including twinning—have such traction in the mid-2000s, it is important to examine their social, historical, and political underpinnings. What emerges from this examination is a story of increasing levels of service and volunteerism in the United States, of shifting social service delivery from governmental to nongovernmental entities, and of radical changes in Catholicism that encourage lay men and women to become involved in leading their parishes.

Looking at the "episodic and cyclical pattern" of civic service in the United States, James L. Perry (2004:168) defines four policy cycles in the evolution of U.S. civic service. In the 1930s and early 1940s, cycle one was a response to the Depression (the 1930s to 1942). Civic service was government-supported and focused on providing employment opportunities for the unemployed, through organizations such as the conservation corps. During and after World War II, civic service levels dropped in the United States. The 1960s gave rise to what Perry sees as cycle two—the response to rising poverty, including to the founding of the Peace Corps and other poverty alleviation programs. In the 1970s, a third cycle emphasized a more decentralized and individualized approach to service, whereby federally funded programs increasingly were administered through community-based projects. Finally, Perry defines policy cycle four as one of civic service retraction and subsequent re-engagement. In the 1980s, as neoliberal[9] governments reduced spending on social services, financial and ideological support for federally funded civic service programs waned. However, in his 1989 inaugural speech, President George Bush reinvigorated the idea of service in his call for a "thousand points of light," which was envisioned as "all the community organizations that are spread like stars throughout the Nation, doing good." This idea was given weight with the passage of the National and Community Service Act of

1990, which funded the Points of Light Foundation to "engage more people more effectively in volunteer service."

President Bill Clinton continued Bush's service agenda because "fiscal shortages demanded innovative solutions to growing . . . social problems," says Perry (2004:171). The government was no longer able— or at least no longer willing to try—to staunch the flow of "social problems" on its own. It was calling explicitly on citizens to fill in the gaps, to take up the government slack. To encourage this, the National and Community Service Trust Act of 1993 expanded the 1990 law to create a national-level umbrella for service activity. The shift in cycles three and four, then, is one of decreasing government funding for social services and an increasing reliance on citizens to address social problems—such as poverty—through volunteerism, service, and charity.

This trend continues into the 2000s, though with a more explicitly religious tenor. Calling attention to the good work that religious organizations do, President George W. Bush in 2001 highlighted what he saw to be a fundamental contradiction in U.S. social services delivery. In his estimation, the best and most efficient purveyors of services—faith-based organizations working with low overhead and often through volunteers— frequently were overlooked or bypassed for government funding. Resting on assumptions about the inefficiency of governmental bureaucracy versus the comparatively focused and effective approach of nonprofit organizations, Bush explicitly set a goal to "strengthen and expand the role of FBCOs [faith-based community organizations] in providing social services" (Office of the Press Secretary 2001:webpage). He did this in 2001 by establishing the Office of Faith-based and Community Initiatives to support faith-based organizations' work as providers of social services.

In the last decades of the twentieth century, then, the political climate in the United States has been very favorable to the development of nongovernmental social service delivery programs and engagement in civic service. At the same time, however, these political trends have called forth—or, more precisely, called upon—a patriotism couched in middle-class values. For example, reflecting the values of the middle class and their economic status, President George H. W. Bush (1989:webpage) said, in his inaugural address,

> My friends, we are not the sum of our possessions. They are not the measure of our lives. In our hearts we know what matters. We

cannot hope only to leave our children a bigger car, a bigger bank account. We must hope to give them a sense of what it means to be a loyal friend, a loving parent, a citizen who leaves his home, his neighborhood and town better than he found it. . . .

America is never wholly herself unless she is engaged in high moral principle. We as a people have such a purpose today. It is to make kinder the face of the Nation and gentler the face of the world. My friends, we have work to do. . . .

The old solution, the old way, was to think that public money alone could end these problems. But we have learned that is not so. And in any case, our funds are low. We have a deficit to bring down. We have more will than wallet; but will is what we need . . . . We will turn to the only resource we have that in times of need always grows—the goodness and the courage of the American people. I am speaking of a new engagement in the lives of others, a new activism, hands-on and involved, that gets the job done.

As later chapters will demonstrate, this ethos characterizes twinning, as well, where material comforts are viewed as insufficient for creating rich and fulfilling lives. Instead, being engaged and committed to creating a better world, to making a difference in the lives of those heretofore unknown frames twinning and motivates participants.

The milieu from whence twinning sprang in the 1960s, then, has become increasingly vociferous about serving others, volunteering, pitching in to make the world a better place. And these public exhortations have been framed in terms of self-sufficiency, as ways of "giving back" to society by offering opportunities for people to wean themselves from dependency on governments. Moreover, they have drawn on middle-class views of the world as divided into material (read: "possessions") and moral (read: "goodness") realms, where service to others is a type of currency to buy goodness/fulfillment.

As we will see in Chapter Four, twinning also must be understood in relation to Catholicism. As a religious act, charitable service is something U.S. Catholics (and, as Bornstein [2005, 2001a, 2001b] points out, Protestants too) have done for at least the past two centuries. Indeed, for much of its history, the U.S. Catholic Church has been especially attuned to issues of poverty, particularly among the urban poor (Oates 1992). But a more expansive drawing together of churches from the global north and south is fairly recent, owing in part to Pope John XXIII's 1961 call for increasing missionary work in the global south. The coming together of diverse congregations also owes much to the radical changes that swept through the Catholic Church following Vatican II. As detailed in Chapter Four, among the many significant changes Vatican II brought to the Church, the most significant for this project is the increasing importance of the laity to church life. Coinciding with an exodus of priests and nuns from their vocations, in many parishes lay men and women were encouraged to become deeply involved not only as active participants in mass, but also in ministry and leadership roles. It was in this context of openness, change, and focus on laity that twinning emerged.

Twinning is hardly a unique phenomenon, then. Volunteerism, charity, and the impulse to "do good" are tightly interwoven with religion in the United States. In the United States, there are 350,000 congregations, which claim 135,000,000 members (Ammerman et al. 1998). More people belong to congregations than to any other type of voluntary organization, and more financial support is given for the work of these religious communities than for all other philanthropic causes combined (Ammerman et al. 1998:8). As the global environment encourages more civic involvement in social welfare and less on the part of states, faith-based NGOs have been especially well poised to transfer their organizational and financial strengths into development practice. Jeff Haynes (2001:143) argues that these "transnational networks of religious actors . . . [facilitated by globalization] form bodies whose main priority is the well-being and advance of their transnational religious community." In the case of twinning, it has created a climate where Catholics in the United States become interested in the fate of their co-religious in Haiti and can translate that concern into practical action.

■ Conclusion

Twinning provides an intriguing entrée into the study of international development's current state. Although much analysis of development has focused either on the impact of development in local beneficiary communities or on the formal dimensions of the aid industry—and particularly on the discourses guiding them—far fewer works have considered how development is understood, produced, or practiced by developers outside the dominant development apparatus, particularly those for whom development is a voluntary rather than a professional activity. And yet, nongovernmental initiatives such as parish twinning are increasing both in number and in profile, for reasons discussed in Chapter Three. Clearly, they merit study and understanding.

By looking at development's increasing privatization through parish-to-parish twinning, this book examines how development plays out among lay practitioners, how lay initiatives compare to more conventional approaches, and whether efforts such as parish twinning constitute counter-development vis-à-vis hegemonic discourses and practices.

To this end, Chapter Three addresses the larger forces at play in what I call formal or conventional development, as well as their anthropological critiques. What is development? What discourses have guided it? How has development been differently understood across economics and anthropology? In examining these questions, I am especially interested in this particular "moment" in development—the crisis in aid, increasing privatization, and neoliberalism.

Chapter Four looks in detail at St. Robert, its Haiti Committee, and some individual twinning participants to consider several questions: Who are the people engaging in twinning? How do they participate? What motivates them? What do they get out of it? In what ways do they think about Haiti and twinning?

Chapter Five considers how parishioners at St. Robert construct development, how they think about it, and what they hope it will do for Haiti. Chapter Five asks: What does development mean at St. Robert? Why is it thought to be needed in Haiti? How do parishioners move from development theory to practice? How do they conceive of their efforts in Haiti, as development or as missionization?

Chapter Six presents an integrated look at both formal and lay development to consider whether, and if so in what ways, the two share similar discourses and practices. By comparing and contrasting these apparently different approaches to development, I will consider whether lay development represents a new mode of development or is simply an alternative manifestation of the dominant development apparatus. In what ways do lay and professional initiatives overlap, converge, and/or diverge from one another? What is the relationship between the entrenched, hegemonic discourses that post-structuralist development scholars suggest exist—discourses that are institutionalized and implemented by development experts—and the discourses and practices of those who stand outside the "development machine"? Is twinning counter-development or an extension of more conventional initiatives?

■ Notes

1. I understand that this is not necessarily a clear distinction. For example, a clear divide between volunteer and paid service activities breaks down when we look at people who choose to work in low-paying, social services careers, in effect donating labor that would be compensated at much higher levels in other sectors.

2. As Arce and Long (2000b) convincingly argue, modernity is a contested and locally contingent concept. The "modern" I refer to here includes capital accumulation, consumption, education, self-determination, concern for the individual, concern for expertise, good health, and belief in science.

3. Michel Foucault suggested that governmentality is "where technologies of domination of individuals over one another have recourse to processes by which the individual acts upon himself and, conversely . . . where techniques of the self are integrated into structures of domination" (Abrahamsen 2004:1459).

4. I have decided to call Nôtre Dame de la Nativité Paroisse "Our Lady parish" for two reasons. First, given that this is a study from the perspective of the developers, I wanted to use the terminology they themselves employ in referring to their Haitian twin. That is, St. Robert calls its twin "Our Lady," so I adopt that usage here. Second, the priests in Haiti rarely refer to their parish as Nôtre Dame de la Nativité Paroisse in correspondence with St. Robert, instead signing letters as "Our Lady," "Paroisse des Verrettes," or "Parish of Verrettes."

5. Despite a long history of conflict with the Haitian peasantry, the Catholic Church in Haiti allowed a more liberation-based theology following Vatican II, the 1968 Latin American Bishop's meetings (CELAM) in Medellín, Colombia, and the 1979 meeting in Puebla,

Mexico. Manifested in *ti legliz* (little church) movements and emphasizing human rights, community development, education, and the like,
liberation theology in Haiti gained momentum, eventually culminating
in the ouster of Jean-Claude Duvalier in 1986 (Greene 1993). Despite
the popular election to the presidency—and subsequent overthrow—of
former priest and *ti legliz* leader Jean-Bertrand Aristide in 1991, the
Catholic Church in Haiti has tempered its activism and become increasingly conservative. Underscoring this orientation, unlike most nations
in the world, the Vatican formally recognized the *junta* regime that had
launched the coup d'état against Aristide in 1991.

6. St. Robert of Newminster—the case study for this book—did not
respond to the survey. Its annual budget of approximately $60,000 per
year dwarfs those of other churches in the area.

7. The median household income in Ada Township is $83,357 per year,
compared to $45,980 for the greater Grand Rapids / Kent County area,
making Ada one of the highest-earning communities in the region. The
median housing value in Ada Township is $198,100, compared to
$111,600 for the area as a whole (U.S. Census Bureau 2000).

8. These figures are estimates. I have been told that the number of parishioners may be as high as 80,000, with as many as twenty-eight chapels
and schools. These inconsistencies also occur in the documentation and
correspondence exchanged between St. Robert and Our Lady. I have
chosen to present a mid-range estimate.

9. "'Liberal' in the classic sense of lack of state control and reliance on
markets and price mechanisms; 'liberal' in the contemporary sense of
concern for victims, but 'neo-' in that suffering is [assumed to be] an
inevitable consequence of reform and efficiency" (Peet and Hartwick
1999:53).

CHAPTER TWO

Studying Twinning
and Development

One purpose of this research is to explore how lay initiatives such as twinning compare to conventional development. To do this, I selected one set of twinning partners for an in-depth case study. Looking at the "operation of the international development 'apparatus' in a particular setting" (Ferguson 1994:17), my interest is in the "dailiness" (Abu-Lughod 1993) of twinning—in what lay developers are doing, particularly in relation to dominant development discourses; how they understand Haiti, Haitians, and (under)development; and what they intend for twinning to accomplish in their lives and the lives of the Haitians with whom they have partnered. This intensive look at local-level discourses and practices—particularly as they are crafted by the developers rather than by those to be developed—is not intended to produce scientific "truths" or generalizable laws. Rather, it is an in-depth investigation of how people give their lives—and others' lives—meaning, as well as how they act and react in attempting to make the world a better place through twinning. A variety of data collection methods were used, including content analysis of archival data and organizational literature (for example, correspondence, meeting minutes, and promotional materials), participant–observation, questionnaires, and interviews. This investigation is a study of the "particular" (Abu-Lughod 1991) intended to capture what is happening "on the ground" (Arce and Long 2000;

Fisher 1997) at one particular place and one moment in time. Thus the stories and findings presented here may or may not reflect the goings-on in other twinning programs. Indeed, they do not necessarily reflect the program as it is currently practiced at St. Robert. Instead, what is explored here is important for its localness, for its examination of the connections and interactions between the "development machine" and individuals seemingly outside its reach. According to Escobar (1995:109), "a local situation is less a case study than an entry point to the study of institutional and discursive forces and how these are related to larger socioeconomic processes." This is how I conceive of this project: as an entry point to the study of (dis)continuities and connections linking and separating professional and nonprofessional development initiatives.

■ Understanding Twinning: The Reverse Mission

My research into these questions began through a preliminary study of Haitian migrants to the Grand Rapids, Michigan, area.[1] Engaging in participant–observation at a local Haitian church and interviewing a handful of Haitian migrants about their lives in the United States, I discovered strong connections between the Haitian community and Doug Porritt, then the diocesan director of the Haiti Outreach Project (HOP). HOP, I was later to learn, was the local-level liaison and coordinator for PTPA in the Grand Rapids area. The Grand Rapids Diocese was unique in having a staff person devoted to promoting and supporting twinning at the diocesan level, which helped explain why Grand Rapids—with seventeen—is second only to Nashville in number of twinned parishes.

I contacted Doug to learn more about twinning, how churches became involved, and what the features of these relationships were. In May and June of 2000, I began participating in HOP-sponsored activities, such as pancake breakfast fundraisers and Creole language classes. I learned of a "reverse mission" trip planned for August 2000, and I asked Doug, in his capacity as HOP director and leader of the reverse mission, for permission to accompany a newly twinned parish, Holy Trinity of Grand Rapids, as it visited its partner, Pointes-à-Raquettes parish in Haiti, for the first time. Reverse missions are central to twinning, because they enable U.S. participants to travel to Haiti and bear witness to the challenges Haitians confront and the gifts they possess. Such travels are called reverse missions because they are intended to be moments of spiritual growth and learning for those traveling to Haiti, rather than moments of evangelization for Haitians.

I attended all preliminary meetings in Grand Rapids to prepare for the reverse mission, and I met up with the Holy Trinity group in Port-au-Prince in August 2000.[2] I participated and observed all aspects of the trip, visiting orphanages, schools, and hospitals, as well as attempting (though failing) to meet with then President Jean-Bertrand Aristide. (Reverse missions occasionally include such an opportunity.) These service aspects of reverse missions are particularly powerful and meaningful experiences for participants. Coming from relative affluence, reverse missioners have a visceral reaction to the "rows and rows of metal cribs" holding sick and malnourished infants; they feel compelled to hug and comfort the babies and kids. They bring lotions and nail polish to massage and beautify the elderly and dying. Such interactions with especially vulnerable and marginalized Haitians introduce participants to the struggles they face and serve as points of contrast for missioners' experiences in the United States. In the evening, missioners would gather on the rooftop of the guesthouse to sing Catholic songs, pray, and talk about their experiences. Feeling very subversive, in the evenings I also would break out my bottle of Haitian rum to share with my "roommates." Such interactions created bonds and familiarity among the missioners, many of whom were traveling to Haiti for the first time with people they did not know.

The purpose of this trip was for Holy Trinity to make initial contact with Pointes-à-Raquettes parish, located on the island of La Gonave. This was a "getting to know you" trip to establish ties between the two parishes. The small rectory could not accommodate us all, so the group was housed in separate quarters. The inadequacy of the shower, lack of electricity, and summertime heat were frequent topics of conversation, but so was the hospitality we experienced. The Holy Trinity parishioners truly felt welcomed by the priest and parishioners at Pointes-à-Raquettes, and many felt humbled by the generosity they extended. The priest took us by boat to an incredible beach one afternoon, where we spent the day swimming and feasting. This offered the missioners a glimpse of a different side of Haiti, one that harked back to a time when Haiti was a tourist destination. For me also, the experience was eye-opening. Most travelers knew little or nothing about Haiti or its history, yet they were excited and animated in their discussions about how Haiti might be "developed." One man in particular, a successful and wealthy entrepreneur from Grand Rapids, was continually speculating on ways in which Haiti might develop: guava production, increasing agricultural efforts, enhancing factory output. Equally animated were discussions among twinning participants responding to the question "Are you missionaries?" Several participants were adamant that they were not. For example, after the long ride back from Pointes-à-Raquettes to the guesthouse in Port-au-Prince, as we swam in the small cement pool, three women discussed being surprised by the persistent question of whether they were missionaries. Doug, they agreed, was a missionary, but they were in Haiti "to help, to do something useful." Indeed, one woman was very vocal about feeling rather useless on the trip. She wanted to roll up her sleeves, to build something, to do something tangible. For her and for others I would later encounter, the spiritual dimensions of twinning were an interruption or distraction from getting things done. At the end of the reverse mission, I felt perplexed. I knew I wanted to study twinning in greater depth, but I was not sure exactly how to classify it. Was twinning about religion, about missionizing, about development, or about cultural exchange?

▪ Finding Parish Partners and Projects

Over the next year, as I refined my research proposal, I stayed in contact with Doug and participated in the occasional HOP-sponsored event. In summer 2001, I again worked with Doug to identify which PTPA-HOP churches would be good candidates for research leading to a better understanding of twinning and its relationship to development. I drafted a letter of introduction and invitation to participate in the research, which Doug sent to the seven churches that, together, we had identified as having both stable and active twinning programs. Three responded that they would be interested in working with me, and I arranged with them to visit their Haitian twins during May and June of 2001.[3] Working with Theresa Patterson, I also arranged to spend two nights at Visitation House[4] in Port-au-Prince. There, I interviewed her about PTPA's history, goals, and structure.

I spent a week in each of the three twinned Haitian parishes: Verrettes, Ennery, and Seguin. In each of the parishes I participated in masses, talked with priests and other clergy, visited schools, talked with parishioners, and located projects supported by each Michigan parish. I was hoping to understand what twinning looked like in Haiti, what projects are typically sponsored, and how "locals" in Haiti see twinning.

The parishes at Verrettes, Ennery, and Seguin were very different from one another. I began in Verrettes. Father Jean Francique picked me up from the PTPA guesthouse in Port-au-Prince in the truck St. Robert bought for him. Verrettes is a fairly large town that is now accessible by a paved highway. It has a grand Catholic church, a large rectory, and lots of other centralized businesses and buildings: bank, gas station, schools, market, stores. There are many dirt streets tucked off the main road and lots of tidy houses in good shape, many with brightly painted cement and tin roofs. In general, Verrettes has an air of relative affluence.

The rectory in Verrettes sits next to the church and is surrounded by a gated wall that blocks it from the view of the street. Three priests were assigned to Our Lady parish in 2001: head pastor Father Jean and two assistant pastors. Although Father Jean was always exceedingly cordial, his assistants made me distinctly uncomfortable. The four of us would take dinner together, and my lack of table manners—not knowing how or when to stand to pray, or the proper way to manage the sophisticated inversion of bowls and cups to keep them clean, for example—was met with sidelong glances and disdain, particularly by one of the priests. The assistants did not initiate conversation with me, and they were reluctant when I engaged them. I do not know why they greeted me with such reserve, but I would speculate that it had something to do with my status as a student/researcher, because others active in twinning did not report similar experiences.

By contrast, Father Jean had an almost exaggerated cordiality. He was clearly at ease entertaining American visitors, and he went out of his way to try to make me comfortable. He would ask what "project" I had for the day and try to help (for example, by arranging a guide or interview). He offered refreshments, made sure I felt relaxed in my room, sat with me on the veranda, and helped me practice my Creole by talking slowly and with clear pronunciation. In short, Father Jean was very courteous, and he expressed an interest in my research project, including a willingness to host me as a long-term researcher in the future.

The variety of projects established in Verrettes was impressive: the vocational school, microcredit program, student sponsorships, and forestry extension. During this initial trip to Verrettes, I became acquainted with them all. I was able to talk with participants and get a sense of what the programs did and how they worked. Overall, I felt quite comfortable in Verrettes, excited by the range of U.S.-sponsored programming under way there, and sanctioned by Father Jean to return.

Father Gustana Valcourt from Ennery came to pick me up from Verrettes. Father Val is gregarious and cheerful, almost jolly. Rather than sneering at my obvious etiquette incompetence, Father Val merrily taught me how to cut mango and eat it delicately. I spent a lot of time laughing while I was with him, and he likewise seemed at ease with me. Ennery is a smaller town than Verrettes, but it has a hospital (no patients were in evidence during my two visits), schools, and small stores. The church and rectory sit across from the market. The rectory is quite lovely and, like the rectory at Verrettes, is surrounded by an enormous cement wall, although this one was capped with broken bottles. A balcony runs the entire second story. With just two priests—Val and his assistant—the parish in Ennery is smaller than the Verrettes parish. The church itself is probably one-third the size.

Father Valcourt has a close working relationship with Sacred Heart parish, its Michigan twin. Both he and Pat Abner, the U.S. Haiti Committee chair, exuded genuine warmth when talking about one another. Even though Father Valcourt enthusiastically spoke of anthropology—whose history he traced to theology—he was less interested in the research dimensions of my trip. He was a great entertainer and was eager to play dominoes with me, his cook, and the other "help" who live in the rectory. And Father Val did help me to explore the community. I was a member of his procession—he had me carry the cross—as he and his assistants walked through town to administer last rites in the homes of the sick. I helped him transport a sick and bloodied man to the hospital. And he spoke to me about and showed me projects that he has created with Sacred Heart. With money sent by Sacred Heart, the parish at Ennery has dug wells, supported a medical clinic, sponsored students, and built housing (Pat likened this project to Habitat for Humanity).

Father Val also spoke of projects he would like to initiate: an activity center and an eye clinic. He asked whether I knew of anyone who could come and work on people's eyes. I did not. Father Val spoke of the problems of the aged in Haiti. In the United States, he said, the state will take care of the old; not so in Haiti. He said that in Haiti, people spend their lives working, only to be cast aside once they are no longer able to contribute their share. I enjoyed Ennery and Father Valcourt, but he was less interested in my research than Father Jean, and overall there were fewer established projects to explore there.

My third stop was Seguin, which sits in the mountains high above Jacmel and feels very much off the beaten path. In fact, when I first arrived, the "town" felt deserted, the town being the rectory, market, church, dispensary, and nearby elementary school, along with a few rows of houses. The church was small and doubled as the school; indeed, it struck me more as a chapel than as a main church because it was so tiny and nondescript. The priest—Father Rosemond François—was not there, nor was he expecting me, said his housekeeper, Magaly. (Before arriving in Haiti, I had had trouble getting in touch with Father Rosemond, but I thought I had confirmation that he was expecting me.)

While I waited for Father at the rectory, I was welcomed by lots of people—mainly women and children, who were both shocked and delighted that I spoke Creole. They showed me around town and brought me with pride to the new rectory—under construction—which sits on a hill overlooking the current rectory. The contrast between the two rectories was stunning. Whereas the current rectory consisted of three very small rooms—one bedroom for Father, one for Magaly, and one sitting/dining area, the new rectory included four bedrooms and four bathrooms. Whereas the current "kitchen" was a fire-pit in the yard, the new kitchen was enormous and inside the house. Two large balconies overlooked the particularly beautiful terrain. Compared to the two rectories where I had just stayed, this rectory was enormous and opulent—even though it was "in the middle of nowhere." My gut reaction was that the new rectory was ostentatious and scandalously extravagant. I was told it was large in order to accommodate visitors from Michigan comfortably. Father Rosemond later told me that when Holy Spirit parishioners first visited Seguin, he had wanted them to stay nearby at an upscale bed and breakfast on the edge of a national forest. They declined those accommodations in favor of staying with the priest, where they could be more a part of parish life.

Constructing the rectory was the largest project under way at Seguin. Holy Spirit had also sent medical missions to Seguin, and they were particularly interested in bettering health locally. This was one reason why they were interested in working with me, so that I could follow up with the patients they had treated at the clinic. The local dispensary was closed while I was there, but Magaly said that Holy Spirit was going to send her to school in Port-au-Prince to become a nurse and to staff the clinic.

During the time I spent in Haiti, I felt most a part of the community in Seguin. The people were especially warm and conversational, perhaps because the rectory was not walled off from the community. People could call to me from outside the window. I was more accessible and so interacted more with parishioners than with the priest. I spent hours listening to Magaly and her friends singing hymns. I would record the songs on my cassette player and play them back, to the delight of the singers. We laughed as they flipped through the Holy Spirit directory and pointed out people who had visited previously, laughing at what they remembered of the visitors' quirks and peculiarities. But in contrast to the friendly attitude of the people in the community, Father Rosemond was especially distant. Perhaps his genuine surprise at finding me waiting for him in his house was off-putting. Or maybe he did not fully understand why I was there or trust my intentions. At any rate, he was absent for most of the week I spent in Seguin. He took me on a "tour" of the area, but nearly every morning he left in his truck before dawn, sometimes returning later in the morning, sometimes not. When he was there, Father was not overly talkative, and I certainly did not feel he was pleased by my presence. In the end, I decided not to work in Seguin because there was simply not enough programming to investigate. Holy Spirit sent money to Seguin and occasionally medical missions, but actual projects were not directly sponsored. Moreover, although I enjoyed my time with Magaly and others in the town, I did not get the sense that Father really wanted to work with me on the project, even though he said that he would.

Having gained a sense for the range of twinning activities in the three locations, I decided to work with the St. Robert and Our Lady (Verrettes) parishes. In particular, Father Jean expressed a willingness to host me and facilitate my research. In retrospect, I think his invitation might have stemmed from a rational calculation about the costs of declining (alienating St. Robert, who wanted me there in Verrettes) versus the benefits of working with me (appeasing St. Robert and staying on friendly terms). Of course, like the other two head pastors I considered working with, Father Jean had no particularly compelling reason to want to invest time in this project. The project, it might be construed, could potentially expose elements of money handling, favoritism, or the like that their U.S. parish twins had been unaware of, for example. But from my perspective, I hoped that my project could be useful to the Haitian parishes. In my preliminary research, I had come across a variety of negative views about Haitians held by U.S. participants—I discuss them in more detail later in the book—that I hoped my project could undo. I saw the imbalances between those who have money to give versus those who are in need of receiving, and I wanted to shine a light on the problematic aspects of this. And I wanted to give the Haitian parishes useful research by conducting a parallel study on their U.S. parish partners that would be constructed around their research questions. I stated this to the priests, and Father Jean seemed most receptive to my projects. I also chose to work with Our Lady and St. Robert because two St. Robert parishioners—Bill and Char Baker—were preparing to "retire" to Verrettes to help administer St. Robert's projects. This meant that I would have a front row seat to observe how key players in the St. Robert and Our Lady twinning negotiated their relationships. Finally, Cassie, Haiti Committee chair at St. Robert, was especially enthusiastic about the research project and vocal in her desire to work with me.

Upon my return from Haiti, I attended St. Robert Haiti Committee meetings, stayed abreast of committee correspondence via their email list, and attended occasional mass services. I also worked with Cassie to come up with a set of questions she would like my research to address. The St. Robert Haiti Committee was particularly interested in assessing the impact of their projects in Haiti: Were vocational school students finding jobs upon graduation? Were microcredit borrowers increasing their wealth? Were sponsored students really attending schools and how were they doing? During this time, I also conducted the brief survey previously mentioned, which I sent to the twenty-four Michigan parishes active in the twinning program, to collect data on programming, budgets, goals, and the like.

■ Research in Verrettes, Haiti

I returned to Verrettes, Haiti, in January 2002 to explore the range of programming sponsored in Haiti by St. Robert, and in particular to examine the ways in which "beneficiaries" negotiated such programming and understood development more broadly. As is not uncommon in ethnographic research, I experienced some difficulties in carrying out the proposed research, in part because a new set of priests had been installed at Our Lady after my visit the previous summer. Father Jean was no longer in Verrettes, and his invitation to me to conduct research at Our Lady no longer stood. The new priests—head pastor Father Yvens Joseph and his assistant, Father Jean-Salomon Vincent—were reticent about helping me arrange research access at the various project sites. Father Yvens explained that, like me, he had arrived only in January; he told me that he wanted time to learn more about the projects himself before allowing me access.

While the groundwork I thought had been laid during my previous visit shifted beneath me, I felt caught off guard. I no longer felt welcome at the rectory, and Father Yvens, in particular, was cool toward me. I emphasized that my research was intended to be useful to him, that I wanted to investigate questions that he thought were important and that would help St. Robert understand more clearly life in Haiti and in the parish. In retrospect, I realize how naïve my interest in conducting "participatory" research must have sounded. Of course, I understood his reticence; Father did not know me, nor did he know what my intentions were. Knowing the dynamics between Our Lady and St. Robert, I understood that Father might think I was there to spy on him, to provide surveillance on behalf of St. Robert. I tried to ease these apprehensions by suggesting that I wanted to help St. Robert better understand life in Haiti and at Our Lady. I wanted, in essence, to help Our Lady move toward greater autonomy from St. Robert and be more appreciated by its twinning partner. Although Father Yvens asked how he could help, he was cautious and did not overtly sanction my research or go out of his way to provide help.

My first order of business while in Haiti was to explore the Sponsor a Student program. The St. Robert Haiti Committee had asked me to help them update their records by locating the sponsored students, taking their pictures, and having them fill out a brief form (which they had written in English) thanking their Michigan-based sponsors. I approached Father Yvens with the list of students St. Robert had provided me and asked for his permission to visit the parish schools to talk to the students. Father said no, that I was not to visit the schools until he talked with the supervisors, who then would tell the teachers to expect us and make sure the kids were there. There was a "structure" to the school system that must be worked through, Father said. There was no need to rush, he said; I felt quite the opposite, given the limited time I had to spend in the community. Because there had been a recent administrative division in the parish, some schools formerly tied to Our Lady had been absorbed by a nearby parish—Des Armes—headed by Father Mackenzy Célestin. Father Salomon suggested I talk with Father Mackenzy about visiting those two schools first.

Like Father Yvens, Mackenzy was hesitant about assisting in the research, saying that he was new to the area and did not have sufficient knowledge to share with me yet. But Father Mackenzy went on to caution me about the difficulty I would face carrying out my "intellectual study" with people in the mountains. Such people, he said, would not be able to give me the information I was looking for. For my project, he suggested, it would be best if I gathered my information from the priests, who could "reflect on and assess things." Father Mackenzy said I could take pictures of the children: "No problem. That will be easy." But for more than that, I should ask the priests.

Thinking I had authorization, with a Haitian friend and my husband, I visited two schools, Allaire and Majen, in search of sponsored students. I had no success. At the first school, the director said that Father Yvens told him to expect us. I asked whether we could visit with the students whom St. Robert sponsors and maybe take pictures of them for their St. Robert sponsors. The director said that the sponsorship money went directly to the school, not to individual students. I asked whether he had a book listing the students at the school; even if the scholarships were not individualized, I could cross-reference his list with mine. He brought out a thick, student-style notebook containing the handwritten names, dates, and amounts paid by the students. There were no matches. Looking at my list, the director pointed out names he recognized and said those students were at other schools, including Majen. He suggested that I go there, since it was only a few minutes down the road.

The school at Majen was empty because the students had only a half-day of instruction that day. But I found the director, and he seemed confrontational about who we were and what we wanted. Explaining that the director at Allaire had sent us, I said we were looking for students sponsored by St. Robert and asked if he would look over the list of students I had and tell us which might be his. He abruptly said no. He told me that he did not want to provide me any information until he talked with Father Mackenzy. He told us to return in a few days.

I immediately returned to Verrettes to meet with Father Mackenzy myself. Greeting me wearing a blue "I souled myself to Jesus" t-shirt, Father Mackenzy flashed immediate irritation when I told him about the visit to Majen. He told me that I should not return to Majen because he wanted to talk first with Yvens, who—it turned out—had unexpectedly left for the United States and would not be available anytime soon. My research into the sponsorship program stalled here. *Stonewalled* was the word I used in my field notes to describe how I was feeling about the research at this point.

Although I never did receive authorization to locate the remaining sponsored students, I did carry out other facets of the research plan. With Father Yvens's permission, I was a participant–observer at the vocational school, where I sat in on all classes for training in auto mechanics, masonry, and sewing. I was closely associated with Nicholas, the newly appointed Swiss director of the vocational school. A white *blan* (foreigner), Nicholas had arrived in Verrettes in January, as I had. Moreover, he authorized my presence there, allowing me access to the classrooms and students, apparently without first asking the professors. He accompanied me into each of the classrooms, and as I self-consciously stood at the front of the class, he introduced me as "Madame Tara" to the students and professors and told them they should help me with my research. I was later to learn that Nicholas was acutely disliked by both students and faculty at the school, and I think working my entrée into the school through him was a mistake, even though it was the path the priests laid out for me.

The vocational school students, for the most part, reacted to me in two ways: They ignored me or they mocked me. In the masonry and auto mechanics classes, the students tended to ignore me. They would occasionally talk to me, often to ask questions that would ordinarily be considered rather rude: Could they come to my house? Would my husband be jealous? What would he say? The sewing and cooking students were more vocal about their distaste for me. They would talk loudly among themselves about the *blan*—and much of what they had to say I simply could not understand. But I understood enough to know that they resented me and my presence in their classes. I understood their reservations about me, and I never was able to feel welcome during my time there.

I was in Verrettes from January to March of 2002. Although I had data from interviews with the priests and others, field notes from participation in the school, masses, and other local events, and the survey of the vocational school students, I did not accomplish what I had hoped in Verrettes. I did not collect the information about student sponsorship that the St. Robert Haiti Committee asked me to gather. The priests in Haiti did not invest in my research and were not interested in collaborating with me to design a project that might be useful to them. I did not feel welcomed by the community or the parish. But what I *did* have at the end of my stay was a grounded understanding of the difficulties of administering twinning in Haiti. I gained a sense of the pressures that priests feel and their fear of external discipline and "big brother" scrutiny. I understood how important "white folks" are to the continuation of programs as they currently exist at the parish, and I recognized the resentment those in Haiti feel that this is the case.

■ Research in Ada, Michigan

After a 16-month partial sabbatical,[5] I undertook research with St. Robert parish from July 2003 to August 2004.[6] I conducted in-depth, taped, semi-structured interviews with twenty-one of the most active members of St. Robert's Haiti Committee.[7] The interviews explored notions of Haiti, Catholicism, twinning, and development (see Appendix), and they ranged in length from 45 minutes to 4 hours; most interviews lasted about 90 minutes. All participants were informed of their rights as research participants, and each signed a letter of consent to be interviewed. Most "didn't care" whether direct quotations were attributed to them by name, but two of the twenty-one interviewees requested confidentiality. Given the small number of people participating on St. Robert's Haiti Committee, I have chosen not to use individual names when providing direct quotations, except in situations where the speaker would be recognizable or where knowing the source of the quotation was important. All interviewees mentioned by name have given consent to be identified. Omitting just the names of the two interviewees who requested confidentiality would be insufficient, because anyone familiar with the program would be able to deduce who was "missing" from among those identified. When speaking of the program generally, however, I have chosen to name those who were most active in the twinning program. They are the "public faces" of twinning at St. Robert, so these key players' identities are already known by those in the program. To attempt to conceal their identities through the use of pseudonyms would be pointless.

I was active on the St. Robert Haiti email list, the medium through which the committee most frequently corresponds. All such correspondence was indexed in a MS Word file. I also engaged in participant–observation at weekly masses, as well as at Haiti Committee meetings, writing notes "at the scene" of conversations, activities, and other goings-on. Again, direct quotations generally are not attributed here by name, except when it is important to know who is being quoted or when it would in any case be obvious who the speaker was. Cassie, founder and former chair (now co-chair) of the Haiti Committee, provided me with many written documents (including correspondence, meeting minutes, budgets, photographs, and the like) that record the development of the Haiti program from its inception until my joining the committee in 2001. Finally, Anne Gruscinski, St. Robert's business manager, compiled a wide array of reports, financial data, parish bulletins, and other records documenting the administration and growth of the St. Robert Haiti program.

Throughout the book, I provide direct quotations taken from interviews, committee meetings, masses, correspondence, and the like. These quotations generally are presented verbatim. However, in the interest of clarity and to reduce the repetitions and redundancies that characterize oral speech, I have occasionally edited wording, being careful to maintain the original content and meaning. (See Abu-Lughod 1993:31–36 for discussion about the politics and constraints of editing oral narratives.)

■ Notes

1. Grand Rapids is home to about 500 Haitians, most of whom left Haiti following the violence of the 1991 coup d'état. Unlike Detroit-based Haitian migrants—many of whom migrated during the Duvalier era— Haitian migrants living in Grand Rapids have been the subject of few studies (for an exception, see Verna 2000). This preliminary research was intended to make contact with the Haitian community in Grand Rapids and to assess what kinds of questions my research might answer for them.

2. I was already in Haiti when the Holy Trinity group arrived, because I was participating in a language program to study French. I was a participant in the University of Massachusetts' "Haiti Today" program based in Montrouis, Haiti. I have studied French for several years, having earned a bachelor's degree in French, as well as a certificate in French Studies from Université de Droit, d'Economie et des Sciences in Aix-en-Provence, France. I also have studied Haitian Creole intensively for 2

years as a Foreign Language and Areas Studies Fellow at Michigan State University, as well as with a tutor in Haiti.

3. Actually, a fourth parish also expressed interest, but only after my itinerary and research plan had been crafted around the other three parishes. Thus I chose not to do further exploratory research with the fourth church.

4. Following the controversial exit of the previous manager, the guesthouse was renamed Matthew 23.

5. "Partial" in the sense that I was still participating in occasional HOP and St. Robert activities, as well as receiving HOP and PTPA correspondence and St. Robert email.

6. Although my collection of primary data ended in August 2004, I continued to take part in Haiti committee meetings, receive correspondence, and otherwise participate in the Haiti committee at St. Robert through May 2005.

7. The Haiti committee is rather amorphous. For example, anyone who has traveled to Haiti with St. Robert is considered a part of the committee, as are several people who have simply demonstrated an interest in Haiti. But since beginning research with St. Robert in 2001, I have identified a "shifting core" of approximately sixteen people who attend the committee meetings and provide consistent feedback on programming. These people are the key players who shape St. Robert's twinning. The remaining interviewees are those identified by Cassie as people who are consulted on Haiti matters, travelers to Haiti, and members of the email list, including Tom Braak and Doug Porritt. That is to say, the remaining interviewees are important to the Haiti program, even though they are not the most active in meetings or travel.

Development's Theory and Practice

Chapter Three explores two questions: What is international development? How has it been differently understood by economists and anthropologists? By looking at development as a historical process currently undergoing seemingly radical transformation—in "crisis," according to some (for example, Grant and Nijman 1998)—this chapter considers the different ways in which scholars have attempted to understand the parameters of development and also sets the stage for investigations into how and why nonexperts now have opportunities to engage in development.

■ What Is Development?

Development is a contentious term, not only because scholars have a hard time agreeing on exactly what it is,[1] but also because it implies that a group or nation is somehow deficient or abnormal and requires outside intervention in order to "fix" it. I am less interested in finding a single definition of development that I prefer than in exploring development as a product of history, as the result of the production of knowledge, and as situated within networks of power and privilege. That is, the overall focus of this book is to explore other people's concepts and practices of development—particularly those within

St. Robert's twinning program—rather than to advance a new or revised model of development. This chapter begins the exploration of development by looking at literatures produced by two groups of scholars: economists and anthropologists.

The Organisation for Economic Co-operation and Development (OECD)[2] defines official development aid as "flows of official financing administered with the promotion of the economic development and welfare of developing countries as the main objective" (OECD 2006). To be considered aid, these flows must be concessional and must contain a grant element of at least 25 percent (OECD 2006).

Broadly speaking, aid is classified in two ways. First, there is multilateral aid, which is administered through international organizations—such as the World Bank—for reallocation to recipients. Second, there is bilateral aid, whereby resources are directly channeled from donor to recipient governments (Bauer 1995:359). On average, 70 percent of OECD aid is bilateral (Grant and Nijman 1998).

In his tome tracing the history of development thinking, John Martinussen (1999:37) argues that although no general agreement on how to define economic growth or development exists, there is wide consensus that economic development is "a process whereby the real per capita income of a country increases over a long period of time while simultaneously poverty is reduced and the inequality in society is generally diminished." An important feature of this definition includes its focus on growth as measured by rising per capita incomes.

Indeed, as a "post World War II phenomenon" (World Bank 1998a), development has since its inception been propelled by belief in growth, progress, and social engineering (Grant and Nijman 1998; Rist 1997; Escobar 1995). Arising in a context of decolonization and cold war ally-making—and as outlined in President Truman's "Four Point Message" (Truman 1949)—development has rested on assumptions that the global system is divided into centers of modern "progress" and peripheries of traditional "backwardness" (Peet and Hartwick 1999). The "modern" is characterized by industrialization and democracy, as well as by specialization of economic activities and occupational roles, the growth of markets, urbanization, mobility, education, rationality, weakening of traditional elites, secularization, high mass consumption, the importance of commodities, technology, exploitation of nature, and the emergence of an intelligentsia (Peet and Hartwick 1999; Rist 1997). The "backward" is not only lacking each of these characteristics but also marked by disease, poverty, and scarce education. The frequently stated goal of development, then, has been economic growth to move people from backwardness to modernization on the Western model, even when the precise meaning of modernization is elusive (see Arce and Long 2001).[3]

Following World War II, as the gap between the rich in the industrial north and the poor in the south widened, a sense that poverty was reversible—or at least manageable—emerged. Drawing inspiration from the obvious success of the Marshall Plan in rebuilding worn-torn Europe, institutions such as the United Nations invested ideologically and materially in social and economic engineering—a notion that with the proper inputs, poverty and its associated evils (malnutrition, disease, ignorance) could be ameliorated.

The implementation of such inputs—for example, infrastructure, health programs, education—was seen to be the logical role of states. Thus, in the early days of development, states and their agencies were to play central roles in developing their countries. Throughout the 1950s and 1960s, the UN, the World Bank, and other large development institutions loaned and gave money to states for large-scale development projects, such as constructing dams, highways, power plants, and other symbols of technology and progress. The assumption driving such approaches was that poverty was caused by ignorance, low productivity, and disease, so it could be eliminated by transferring knowledge and technology from the rich to the poor.

But despite such inputs, by the 1970s it was clear that development was not "progressing" those in the global south (Escobar 1995; Sachs 1992a). Disparities in wealth between the world's richest and poorest expanded, both within individual countries and between those in the global north and south. One explanation for this failure focused on development's heretofore overly "macro" orientation. That is, by concentrating on large infrastructural projects and macro-level policy, development inputs had ignored and neglected micro-level processes and needs. To be successful, development would have to be reformed, to focus more on meeting "basic needs" and incorporating "popular participation" at the local level (Gardner and Lewis 1996; Gardner 1997). Thus some of the focus for development shifted away from states, encouraging a more decentralized and locally generated development agenda (Gardner 1997:134–139). This shift was reinforced by neoliberal policies of the 1980s and 1990s that called for smaller governments less narrowly focused on social welfare provision. Concomitantly, such policies encouraged governments to take supportive, rather than "dominant," roles in development (World Bank 1998a:10; Farrington and Bebbington 1993:178). The "New Right" policies of neoliberalism stressed self-reliance, decentralization, and the ideal of civilian participation in development rather than government control (Gardner 1997). The emphasis since has been on shrinking the size of the state and lowering its expenditures.

In the 1990s, the U.S. Treasury, the United States Agency for International Development (USAID), the International Development Bank, and several other large development institutions came together to outline the ways they collectively agreed that development should proceed. What emerged came to be known as the "Washington Consensus." The principles it espoused are summarized by Williamson (1993) as fiscal discipline to reduce government budget deficits; public expenditure priorities on health, education, and infrastructure; tax reform; financial liberalization so that interest rates are market-determined; reduction in barriers to the entry of foreign firms, in order to promote foreign direct investment; privatization of state enterprises; trade liberalization; deregulation of restrictions against competition; and secure property rights (Williamson 1993; Peet and Hartwick 1999). In brief, neoliberalism encourages a reduction in the role and size of states, but it also emphasizes that states should support market institutions with "good policies"—that is, those that encourage trade (Kothari and Minogue 2002).

The policy conclusions resulting from the Consensus were the following. States that want development need to open their borders "and let change in." They must integrate into the existing global system and "should welcome, indeed encourage multinational corporations, advanced technology, and export-oriented economic activities" (Peet and Hartwick 1999). States also should limit aid and privatize their economies. Finally, the market should be free to "discipline" national economies, to reward those with "good" policy environments and punish those with bad ones (Peet and Hartwick 1999). Not surprisingly, these reforms have resulted in decreased government spending on social services.

In much of the development literature, globalization is largely equated with both neoliberalism and modernization (Fisher 1997; Kothari and Minogue 2002; Rist 1997), key elements of the Washington Consensus. There is certainly debate about whether the state is, in fact, collapsing under the weight of globalization and neoliberalism. Some (for example, Putnam in Salomon 2001) have suggested that the rise of states "'crowded out informal voluntary activity and left it without a clear social function,'" whereas others (for example, Salomon 2001) contend that "two epic foes" are engaged in a battle over social organization: states and their agencies versus citizen self-organization. And, in Salomon's (2001) estimation, the "global associational revolution"—the incredible expansion in private voluntary action—indicates that self-organization is becoming increasingly important. A third interpretation posits that the "revolution" reflects not so much a fissure separating the state from "civil society" but, rather, their convergence in managing and producing "citizen subjects," as I describe below (Cruikshank 1999).

As disputes over the status of the state continue to rage (for example, over whether the nation–state is an increasingly weak element in world economic and political processes [Friedman 1994] or a continuing powerful and hegemonic force of social organization and welfare provision [Zaidi 1999]), a practical question faces development theorists and practitioners: If states are decreasingly promoting development, who is? With development economists working through institutions such as the World Bank and the International Monetary Fund to decentralize and deconcentrate states, space has been created for nongovernmental organizations (NGOs) to become increasingly important players in development design and delivery (Fisher 1997; Gardner and Lewis 1996; Lewis and Wallace 2000).

NGOs are often considered to be part of "civil society," or the "sphere of social relations and institutions that exists between the sphere of government and the sphere of for-profit market oriented organizations" (Wuthnow 2004:22). Over the past two decades, there has been steady growth of northern NGOs and a veritable explosion in the numbers of southern NGOs, with substantial amounts of multilateral and bilateral funds being diverted through them for development purposes (Fisher 1997; Gifford 1994; Riddell and Robinson 1995; Zaidi 1999). Riddel and Robinson (1995) identify three reasons for the growth in NGOs: (1) increasingly positive attitudes by donors and host governments toward the NGO sector; (2) growing availability of funds from foreign donors, both NGOs and governments; and (3) retreat of government provision of welfare services as a result of cutbacks in public expenditures and a weakening of state legitimacy in the wake of pressures for democratization.

Salomon (1993) outlines a different set of reasons to explain why the NGO revolution is unfolding now. He points to "four crises and two revolutions" that, combined, have created space for NGO involvement in traditionally state-led activities: (1) a crisis in the modern welfare state, whereby states are overburdened and unable to meet the demands of citizenry, as well as a sense that too much state welfare breeds dependency, stifles initiative, and undermines personal responsibility; (2) a crisis in development (detailed below), which he attributes to the oil crises of the 1970s, the recession of the 1980s, and skepticism about the role of the state as a capable agent of social change; (3) a global environmental crisis, prompted by wasteful overconsumption in the north and poverty in the south, which has mobilized citizens for action; (4) the collapse of communism, which further cemented ideas about the inability of governments to meet human needs as well as free markets; (5) a communications revolution, which made even the most remote locations accessible and allowed collective action across wide geographical distances; (6) the rise of a new global bourgeoisie, which wanted more political participation and economic opportunity, following the recession of the 1980s.

Taken together, the various explanations for the rise of the NGO sector point to a growing set of concerns on the part of ordinary citizens, development experts, and states. In the early years of development thinking and practice, optimism fueled state-level interventions into disparate economies around the globe, but pessimism prevailed in later years as poverty and its associated "lack of freedoms" (Sen 1999) persisted. Moreover, a growing disillusionment about development's potential to eradicate poverty coincided with monumental changes in the organization of the globe, both politically and economically.

NGOs, then, can be understood as the response and—according to some—the solution to the myriad crises besetting the world at the dawn of the twenty-first century. To be sure, some have viewed NGOs as part of an "alternative development paradigm" capable of remedying traditional state-sponsored development's failures (Adam 1993; Edwards and Hulme 1996; Zaidi 1999). Many development professionals held the belief — "NGO-lore"—that compared to traditional state-led initiatives, NGOs allowed wider and more diverse notions of development, exhibited greater sensitivity and responsiveness to local needs and opinions, and could foster alternative visions and discourses (Farrington and Bebbington 1993:180; Grillo 1997). Many also believed that NGOs were more participatory, community-oriented, democratic, and cost-effective and were better at targeting the poorest of the poor than traditional state-led approaches (Tvedt 2001). In sum, NGOs were supposed to "do" development very differently than states (Tvedt 2001; Zaidi 1999). This was important to those disenchanted with conventional initiatives, given their lack of faith that the state, its institutions, and public policy could address underdevelopment effectively (Tvedt 2001; Zaidi 1999). But the reality is that NGO interpretations and practices vary widely, making it nearly impossible to generalize about whether NGOs are better at development than other institutions (Grillo 1997). In fact, Lewis and Wallace (2000) go so far as to say that the label NGO is itself "in many ways a virtually meaningless label," because it encompasses such a disparate array of organizations and agendas.

More recent works have approached NGOs from a different perspective: as manifestations of governmentality, which—drawing on Foucault—has been described as the "everyday relations of power extending beyond the central state, micro-institutional relations of power that order societies and make human beings into subjects, i.e., subjects to government by others and to self-government" (Merlingen 2003:366). "The developed" are both the targets of a normalizing power and its effect; "the modern self is both the object of improvement and the subject that does the improving" (Abrahamsen 2004:1459). NGOs in such analyses are "new strategies of discipline and regulation" that produce subjects capable of governing themselves (Ferguson and Gupta 2002:989, 990).

For scholars such as Abrahamsen (2004), Ferguson and Gupta (2002), and Lacey and Ilcan (2006), the rise in the number of NGOs does not signal a weakening of government or a more "democratic" sphere but a "new modality" of government (Paley 2002). "NGOs both result from and produce a 'decentering of power' into more diffuse sites, where 'new mechanisms and techniques of auditing, accounting, monitoring, and evaluation' link state and non-state systems of rule" (Abrahamsen 2004:1459). Thus, for example, in Barbara Cruikshank's (2002) study of welfare in the United States, "empowerment" of the poor does not result in their freedom from oppression or poverty. Rather, being "empowered" signals the creation of a certain subjectivity—the "citizen" who acts on her or his own behalf. "Democratic governance cannot force its interests but must enlist the willing participation of individuals in the pursuit of its objects" (Cruikshank 2002:39). The result: citizen–subjects who can self-govern and self-discipline.

Even though the study of NGOs is a burgeoning field in development studies (Bebbington and Thiele 1993; Farrington and Bebbington 1993; Fisher 1997; Lewis and Wallace 2000; Riddell and Robinson 1995), religious voluntary projects such as twinning are rarely considered (Occhipinti 2005). This may be partly because "faith-based" development undertaken by nonprofessionals does not easily fit within the broader debates in the NGO literature (Are NGOs "better" at development than states? What role should NGOs play vis-à-vis state-led development?) Twinning and initiatives like it are not a part of the "formal development world" (Lewis and Wallace 2000). They do not provide "jobs for the middle-class" (Townsend 1999), nor are they led by credentialed experts in the field. Instead, they are spearheaded by ordinary citizens with little to no training in development theory or practice. These initiatives typically do not incorporate as organizations separate from the larger parishes in which they are located. In brief, lay initiatives exist largely outside conventional development "NGO" parameters, and this may be one reason why they are largely ignored in the development literature. Another reason may be their very association with religion. As one development scholar told me while dismissing the importance of this project, twinning was not worthy of study because it was simply "old wine in new bottles"—that is, an extension of larger missionary activities that religious organizations have long undertaken.

This response raises a legitimate question: To what extent are these parish-to-parish relationships simply relics or holdovers of past missionary activity, rather than something new? Parallels certainly can be made. For example, in critiquing the U.S. missionary surge to Latin America, which began and peaked in the 1960s, McGlone (1997:114) suggests that many missionaries had more zeal than skill or training.

> Often they lacked . . . adequate tools for deep understanding of the cultures in which they were ministering. In relation to that, the very generosity that impelled them could also be expressed or interpreted as an attitude of cultural superiority.

As discussed in more detail below, I have similar concerns about twinning, where most St. Robert's participants do not speak French or, more important, Haitian Creole, where visits are brief and "buffered" by priests and other gatekeepers, and where the rhetoric of cultural sensitivity is voiced but often not realized.

However, as this book will make clear, twinning is not simply a manifestation of "missionization as usual." Unlike the Catholic missionary surges of the past, twinning rests not with the priests or other clergy but with lay practitioners. And although religious motivation undergirds some participants' commitment to twinning, most engage in twinning not to "convert the heathens," so to speak, but to put their Catholic faith into practice. Moreover, most are explicit—their goal *is* to "develop" Verrettes, or at least those within Our Lady parish. That is, development is one purpose of St. Robert's twinning, rather than a byproduct of some larger project of evangelization.

▪ The Crisis in Aid: Conventional Development

Many development scholars and practitioners (for example, Duffield 1994; Grant and Nijman 1998; Salomon 1994) suggest that development is in crisis. In short, the crisis includes declining official development assistance[4] (ODA), as well as a sense that development aid has been ineffective. To put it more bluntly, "aid has failed" (The North–South Institute 1996). After 50 years of the aid regime, "most countries of the world have failed to develop in the modernist sense" (Grant and Nijman 1998:6). That is, they have been unable to replicate the Western development experience or "stages of growth" (Grant and Nijman 1998:4; Rostow 1960). This malaise is captured in a quote by Senator Patrick Leahy, who in 1992 suggested that the U.S. foreign aid program is

> exhausted intellectually, conceptually, and politically. It has no widely understood and agreed set of goals, it lacks coherence and vision, and there is a very real question whether parts of it actually serve broadly accepted United States national interests any longer. (in Nijman 1998:29)

In light of declining official aid levels, aid's failure to develop the global south, and the current political malaise, we will now consider a few explanations given by economists for the current crisis: the end of the cold war; the history of giving aid to countries with "bad governance"; and aid's flawed underlying assumptions. The next section serves two purposes. First, it looks at how economists have responded to the crisis. Second, it offers an economic prescription for how development needs to proceed in the future. Rather than giving an exhaustive overview of economic development thinking, which can be found elsewhere (for example Rist 1997; Martinussen 1995), this next section—which details the aid crisis—reveals some of the assumptions and biases guiding what I have referred to as conventional economic development thinking in the late 1990s and early 2000s.

End of the Cold War

Foreign aid during the cold war was often used to promote and strengthen geopolitical alliances: "foreign aid was used as an instrument of *realpolitik*: it served to keep certain countries within the donor's sphere of influence and out of the camp of the opposition" (Grant and Nijman 1998:184). More about politics than about development, foreign aid was justified to taxpayers as essential for cold war security. As a result, the end of the cold war has in many ways set the stage for the current questioning of the purpose of aid and of whether it is really necessary to continue pouring money into the "rat holes" of the world, as Jesse Helms infamously put it (Bates 1995:webpage). The communist threat has ended, so why should states continue to pursue political alliances via development aid?

Yet despite widespread perception of "aid fatigue"—coinciding with or fueled by the end of the cold war—public opinion surveys completed by the United Nations Development Program demonstrate that support for foreign aid did not significantly diminish in the 1983–1995 period (in Garrison 1998:26). That is, Garrison argues that "aid fatigue" does not really exist; citizen support for foreign aid has remained at about the same level, or even has slightly increased, in most OECD countries (Garrison 1998.). This suggests that although states' motivations for undertaking foreign aid may have shifted away from security concerns, the end of the cold war may have had little impact on citizens' understandings of the need for aid. At the same time, however, the report suggests that most people prefer that aid go to refugees and victims of disasters.[5] Aid for improving health and for protecting the environment is also popular. There is far less support for long-term development assistance, in part because governments in developing countries are viewed as dictatorial and corrupt (Garrison 1998).

In sum, the end of the cold war has signaled a new era in development aid. With the fading of the "communist threat," a redefinition of states' foreign policy priorities and goals has been required.

Money "Wasted" on Countries with Bad Institutions

Development aid should be targeted only to countries with "good institutions," some argue. Historically, there has been no correlation between a country's performance and the amount of aid it receives. The "random" nature of aid flows has been both inefficient and ineffective in promoting development (Burnside and Dollar 1998, 1997). Such arguments rest on assumptions that aid can and will work only in good policy environments. Without such environments, aid will be (and has been) little more than extra income for government expenditure.

Burnside and Dollar argue, in contrast, that when a country has good economic management—as outlined in the Washington Consensus—aid stimulates growth and improvements in social indicators. Like the World Bank (1998a), they suggest that although aid should be targeted to countries with strong economic policy environments, bilateral donors' strategic interests—including cold war concerns—traditionally have "overwhelmed" the effort to reward good policies with aid (Burnside and Dollar 1997:3). As a consequence, bilateral aid most often has a strong positive impact on government consumption but no positive effect on growth (1997:3–4). They argue that if aid is to have a large impact on growth and poverty reduction, it must be directed to countries with sound economic policies (Burnside and Dollar 1997:4).

Building on the good policy arguments, some economists go further to suggest that aid is a real detriment to the poor living under bad governments. "By subsidizing political irresponsibility and pernicious policies, foreign aid ill serves the world's poor" (Bovard 1986:webpage). Indeed, surveying the impact of aid on the African landscape, Van de Walle (2001:189) argues that aid to Africa has slowed "the process of policy reform . . . protect[ed] and sustain[ed] weak governments . . . and has actually exacerbated the neopatrimonial tendencies" of government decision makers. That is, aid does not simply allow governments to live beyond their means but also provides governments with a ready-made red herring—"the World Bank made me do it"—to blame for government irresponsibility and Washington Consensus–styled retreat from service delivery.

Similar observations have been made by Bauer (1995:365): "Unlike *manna* from heaven, aid does not descend indiscriminately on the population at large, but goes directly to the government. Because aid accrues to the government, it increases its resources, patronage, and power in relation to the rest of society." In this way, the history of giving aid to countries with poor institutions is problematic not only because it is money wasted but also because it has had the effect of sustaining those states' poor policies, while further concentrating the states' power.

If poverty reflects government failure (Boone and Faguet 1998:19), then attention must be on government reform. Only the government, not donor aid, can create "development." Instead, long-term aid has been used to increase the size of governments and civil services (Boone and Faguet 1998:17). Furthermore, governments do not require aid to develop. To illustrate this, Boone and Faguet cite Cuba, China, and Kerala (India) as governments that have exhibited dedication to reforming basic human development (as measured through human development indicators contained in UNDP,[6] including infant mortality). Boone and Faguet (1998) make the point that if governments were really interested in development, they would prioritize basic health. They argue that such programs are not costly—3.1 percent of GNP in low-income countries—and could bring life-expectancy and infant-mortality indicators of low-income countries almost to OECD levels (Boone and Faguet 1998:19). As an interesting aside, Boone (in Boone and Faguet 1998:19) found no evidence that liberal democracies used aid more effectively than other regimes. Hence, we might conclude that for some economists, "good policy" is not the exclusive domain of democracies.

Boone and Faguet (1998) and Feyzioglu et al. (1998) also argue that in most cases, aid is highly fungible, except when small countries receive a large amount of aid. Therefore, governments can simply interchange aid money for government money. For example, aid intended for crucial social and economic sectors often simply substitutes for spending that governments would otherwise have engaged in themselves (Devarajan and Swaroop 1998). The "extra" money that has been freed up can then be used for "unproductive" expenditures, such as military spending (Feyzioglu et al. 1998:29). In practice, then, most development aid goes to fuel consumption, and little is invested in promoting economic development. As a result, aid has no significant impact on a country's growth. "The factors causing high investment and growth in developing countries neither correlate with foreign aid receipts nor are engendered by them" (Boone and Faguet 1998:15). Accordingly, some economists charge that aid allows "bad" governments to sustain themselves, and their high levels of consumption, without "advancing" their countries toward development via economic growth. Generally speaking, despite perceptions that a country "needs" to be developed, those that stagger under poorly run governments should be passed over for aid.

Faulty Assumptions

Some economists believe the crisis in aid may stem from its very roots—that is, the assumptions underlying the whole aid enterprise are faulty. Bauer contends that the "Third World" is merely an invention of the aid industry and that "developing" countries do not really exist. "The Third World is the creation of foreign aid; without foreign aid there is no Third World" (Bauer 1995:87). In his view, the great diversity of the Third World, including socioeconomic, geographical, cultural, linguistic, religious, and political differences, makes foreign aid the only thing that Third World countries have in common. Bauer further suggests that aid "diminishes" the global south by implying that recipient countries cannot achieve "development" on their own, as the West did. To Bauer, aid is predicated on the perceived inferiority of the global south. In contrast, he argues that many parts of the global south have progressed rapidly; those that have not, he is convinced, have had limiting "factors that cannot be overcome by aid, and are indeed likely to be reinforced by it" (Bauer 1995:363).

In a different vein, some have argued that the logic of aid is itself flawed. If aid is targeted to the poor, there is little incentive for governments to reduce poverty (Svensson 1997). That is, because governments are able to collect revenues based on the poverty of their citizenry, reducing that poverty limits their access to these external resources. But if aid patterns are indeed random, as suggested above, it seems unlikely that the poorest countries are disproportionately benefiting from excessive aid flows. Indeed, Israel, which is classified as a high-income country, historically has received the largest percentage of U.S. aid. Nonetheless, Svennson's (1997) suggestion is to "tie" aid, or to delegate part of the aid budget *not* to governments but to an international agency with less incentive to keep poverty levels high, a suggestion he maintains is against conventional wisdom.

Is There Really a Crisis?

The Overseas Development Institute (ODI) argues (1994:5) that there is wide consensus among OECD countries that the "aid crisis" is really simply a transition to a new pattern of global development. That is, declining aid flows and a sense of aid's ineffectiveness are not so much a crisis as an opportunity for redefinition and revitalization of development cooperation. This redefinition, ODI suggests, will have three components. First, the rationale will shift to a "human development and security" agenda to promote not only economic growth but also democracy, institution building, and the like. Second, it will focus more on a "partnership approach," with member rights and responsibilities, and mutual accountability. Third, guidelines for resource allocation—that will focus separate additional funds for new claimants and global problems—will exist alongside official development assistance as "real aid" that is poverty-reducing, untied, unpolluted, participatory, and the like. Most important for this book, I argue that this transition also includes the increasing importance of ordinary citizens—not development professionals—in designing and delivering development. Within this context, nongovernmental organizations have emerged as an alternative to conventional development aid, which has traditionally been funneled through states.

▪ Locating the "Aid Crisis" in the Caribbean

Within the wider context of diminishing aid flows, official development assistance (ODA) to the Caribbean dramatically decreased in the 1990s, owing in part to its declining geopolitical importance with the end of the cold war. Aggregate data for ten Caribbean countries show that net ODA peaked in 1991 at U.S.$688 million. By 1997, flows had dropped to U.S.$212 million (Caribbean Development Bank 2000:1). These rates of decline are among the highest in the world, and they reflect primarily cuts in bilateral funding (Caribbean Development Bank 2000:2). In tandem with these lower aid flows, private flows in the form of foreign direct investment (FDI) have exploded—from U.S.$154 million in 1990 to over U.S.$1 billion by 1996 (Caribbean Development Bank 2000). Just three countries—Trinidad and Tobago, Jamaica, and Guyana—have received 77 percent of this FDI, however.

Small countries, such as those of the Caribbean, experience more volatile growth rates and are more dependent on trade than are larger countries (Brautigam and Woolcock 2001). This means that small countries are highly vulnerable to rapid fluctuations in the global economy.

Some suggest that because small countries are more vulnerable to external shocks, the quality of their governmental institutions is even more important than in larger countries (Brautigam and Woolcock 2001). Even so, aid flows typically are concentrated on small countries with what economists consider poor economic policy environments. That is, "considerable sums of aid money are being *wasted* in small poor countries that do not have the institutional infrastructure in place to use it effectively" (Brautigam Woolcock 2001, italics added).

In assessing claims such as these, the Caribbean Development Bank (2000) draws on the work of Guillaumont and Chauvet (1999) to posit that the most important determinant of aid's effectiveness is the recipient country's vulnerability to external shocks and natural disasters. Aid helps recipient countries overcome these shocks, which then enables them to create better policy environments. This is important to note, they argue, because six of the world's ten most vulnerable countries are in the Caribbean. Their implicit argument: Despite what some might consider poor policy and government, Caribbean states should continue to receive aid.

Yet, in reality, owing to the end of the cold war, the increasing importance of "good governance" in aid distribution, and attacks on aid's fundamental underlying beliefs, the Caribbean is experiencing drastic cuts in aid flows. Will foreign direct investment compensate? It appears that, given the targeting of FDI to only a few countries, others in the Caribbean are likely to suffer overall budget reductions. These decreasing flows are accompanied by the dissolution of preferential markets for Caribbean exports. Currently, producers for preferential markets are otherwise uncompetitive in the wider global market (Demas 1997). As a consequence, when preferences are lifted, their ability to sell exports is drastically reduced, further weakening Caribbean economies.

As the World Bank (1994) notes, "Caribbean countries have in common a number of stubborn structural problems, including uneven economic diversification away from agriculture and preferential markets, poor macroeconomic management in the three largest MDCs, high levels of unemployment, and an inadequate education system." These problems, combined with the vulnerabilities—to vagaries in international markets, changes in donor policies, and natural disasters—that plague small (island) economies make me pessimistic about the Caribbean's potential to "develop" itself. As later chapters will show, this is the same conclusion reached by those involved in parish twinning.

■ International Development and Anthropology

The previous section introduced some "conventional" economic under-standings of international development aid; this section explores some of the ways in which anthropologists have approached development. Anthropology has long engaged with, and has often criticized, economic development theory and practice. The primary focus of this section is on recent debates at the intersection of anthropology and development: debates about power, discourse, and professional knowledge. But first, to provide the context for understanding current debates within the anthropology of development, I want to provide a brief accounting of anthropology's concern with development.

As outlined above, notions of development often rest on assump-tions of evolution along a continuum, where stages of progress are mapped with the "backward" at one end and the "modern" at the other. To be modern is often taken to mean a group is secular, relies on science, is educated, has a complex division of labor, is urban, and the like. To be backward means to be lacking in these characteristics. Those considered developed are modern; those who are undeveloped are backward.

At a basic level, such evolutionary thinking would be repugnant to most anthropologists working today, but early scholars of anthropology heavily invested in ideas of social evolution. Seminal theorists such as Lewis Henry Morgan and Edward Tyler specified scales of progress, whereby "primitives" could be measured against western European "civilization" (Langness 1993:48; Kuper 1988). Equated with children or neurotics, so-called primitives were imagined to be somewhat less than fully human—to be evolving in the direction of European civilization, but not quite there yet (Langness 1993).

Such blatant evolutionary thinking was largely undermined by anthropologists working in the United States in the early part of the twentieth century, although more palatable forms of evolutionary thinking were retained by scholars such as Leslie White, Julian Steward, and Marvin Harris, as well as certain "development anthropologists." For example, Allan Hoben (1982:353) suggests that in the early days of development, anthropologists were heavily involved in "applied" development work, and from the perspective of development institutions, this work was to "facilitate the diffusion of improved technology by overcoming resistance to change grounded in traditional values, institutions, and practices." Many development anthropologists of the 1940s and 1950s believed in and promoted "modernization" (Little and Painter 1995). The International Cooperation Administration (the precursor to USAID) was once the largest employer of anthropologists (Hoben 1982:354). Yet many anthropologists resented working under the conditions prescribed for them in this applied setting. They felt their roles were not broad enough, that there was not enough time to conduct projects, and that their advice was often ignored. So, over the 1950s and 1960s, most anthropologists left applied development and policy work (Hoben 1982).

By the 1970s, however, a coherent theoretical concern with development on the part of anthropologists re-emerged. This new interest—in light of Project Camelot and the aftermath of the Vietnam War—reflected a newly critical orientation in anthropology attuned to the "questioning of accepted dominant structures and ideologies" (Rylko-Bauer et al. 2006:181). This new consciousness extended to anthropological assessments of development and included a concern with growing poverty in the global south as a consequence of the capitalist world system (Hoben 1982). From the mid-1960s through the early 1980s, anthropological development theory frequently was framed in Marxist and neo-Marxist terms (Peet and Hartwick 1999; Gardner and Lewis 1996), and it often invoked world systems theory (Wallerstein 1974) and dependency theory (Frank 1967) to assess (under)development in relation to a global system structured to benefit the few and exploit the many.

By speaking to concerns raised by dependency theory and world systems theory, anthropologists attempted to account for a "political economy" structuring "the production and distribution of wealth within and between political entities and the classes composing them" (Wolf 1982:9). But their concerns moved beyond the "structural forces" affecting people (things like their position in the capitalist system and their lack of control of or access to certain resources) to account also for local-level agency and action (for example, Peoples 1978; Smith 1978; Morgan 1987). That is, anthropologists attempted to combine a concern for structural forces impacting local people with concern for particular circumstances, social location, and what people actually did.

Within this general climate, anthropologists crafted a litany of "highly critical" appraisals of development. Little and Painter (1995:603), for example, point to charges levied by ecological anthropologists (for example, Galaty 1988; Posey 1985; Richards 1985) concerned with "the imposition of environmentally destructive, Eurocentric models of monocropping and range management in agricultural development schemes." They also highlight the challenges raised by feminist anthropologists (for example, Ehlers 1990; Gladwin 1991; Guyer and Peters 1987) worried about the ways in which development can particularly harm poor women.

Peter Little in later works (for example, 2000) distinguished between development *theory* and development *approaches*. He says that concerns like those just raised are theory, in that they stem from and contribute to broad understanding of concepts such as "institutions, power, gender, and economy" (Little 2000:127). By contrast, development "approaches"— for example, those that focus on community participation or on the relationship between gender and development—attempt to apply theory to particular activities or sectors. That is, approaches are concerned with the application and practice of development. Little raises this point in response to what he sees as the "demise of grand paradigms" that accompanied the postmodernist turn in anthropology in the 1990s and 2000s.

Postmodernism in many ways signaled and was the response to a "crisis" in the social sciences, generally speaking. Concerned with power, authority, and knowledge, and critical of Enlightenment principles such as science, objectivity, neutrality, and expertise, *postmodernism* presented a radical challenge to social science as usual. And it particularly shaped the work of development anthropologists, who were simultaneously facing the "crisis in aid" detailed above. Together they generated a *post-structural* deconstruction of development thinking and a call for the "death" of development practice, as discussed below.

In the context, then, of two crises—in development and in the social sciences—a particularly controversial set of development critiques arose. These critiques, as Rutherford and Nyamuda (2000:840) point out, focused mainly on "analyzing power through the lens of discourse[7] and power" (for example, Crush 1995; Escobar 2000, 1995, 1988; Ferguson 1994; Peet and Watts 1996; Rist 1997; Sachs 1992a; Slater 1992). Specifically, this new literature examines the "institutional forces, restriction of 'voices,' and arrangements of control within the development industry," while considering the ways in which "the people targeted by development are strongly shaped by the identities through which they are imagined within development, even as those targeted (try to) subvert and resist these terms" (Rutherford and Nyamuda 2000:840).

Post-structural analyses are particularly concerned with the "development discourse," which they contend is "socially produced to confer meanings to people and their material worlds." Significantly, for post-structuralists, "discourse is not just words. . . . Discourse is not the expression of thought; it is a practice, with conditions, rules, and historical transformations" (Escobar 1995:216).

Drawing on Foucauldian understandings, these analyses understand power to be productive; it creates knowledge, discourse, and subjects, which simultaneously (re)produce and sustain power, working in a circular spiral of ever-increasing concentration. Thus power operates not so much through physical force as through the "hegemony of norms, political technologies, and shaping of body and soul" (Best and Kellner 1991:49). In this way, development discourse defines what is rational, "true," and sane; those who speak outside of these defined parameters are marginalized and excluded.

For example, Escobar (1995:40–41) suggests that to understand development (and how its statements are reproduced), we must look at the system of relations within the development apparatus. He argues that the relations among institutions, socioeconomic processes, forms of knowledge, technological factors, and the like collectively define the ways in which objects, concepts, theories, and strategies can be incorporated into the discourse. That is,

> the system of relations establishes a discursive practice that sets the rules of the game: who can speak, from what points of view, with what authority, and according to what criteria of expertise; it sets the rules that must be followed for this or that problem, theory or object to be named, analyzed, and eventually transformed into a policy or plan. (1995:40–41)

Here, discourses are used to create and control knowledges, which in turn support the further increase of power.

Applying discourse analysis to development theory and practice, scholars such as Escobar (1995), Rist (1997), and Sachs (1992b) conclude that development has been constructed as an object of knowledge. Moreover, according to Escobar (1995:44–45), development was a post–World War II "response to the problematization of poverty," rather than

> a natural process of knowledge that gradually uncovered problems and dealt with them; as such, it must be seen as a historical construct that provides a space in which poor countries are known, specified, and intervened upon.

That is, Western models of development resulted from the creation of a constructed and specialized knowledge about the global south, one predicated upon notions of poverty and the need to correct its "abnormalities" (for example, illiteracy and overpopulation). By institutionalizing a cadre of "experts" uniquely qualified to address the "problem" of underdevelopment, these models legitimized the exercise of power over that object—here, the global south.

Despite insinuations of difference, all development practice is essentially ruled by the same "set of statements" (Sachs 1992b; Escobar 1995; Rist 1997). Underpinned by an (neo)evolutionary conceptualization of "progress" construing the West as the "advanced" stage and the rest as struggling to get there, this development discourse is marked by a preoccupation with (abnormal) poverty and its elimination via the rational, technological application of (Western) scientific knowledge. Knowledge liberates people. Moreover, urbanization and industrialization are inevitable and necessary components of development, though dependent on capital investment.

Given this view, some post-structuralists argue that development was—and largely continues to be—"a top-down, ethnocentric, and technocratic approach, which treated people and cultures as abstract concepts, statistical figures to be moved up and down in the charts of 'progress'" (Escobar 1995:44). Indeed, the development apparatus, mired in "scientific" economic theory and praxis, operates according to an invented understanding of "poverty" at the same time that it embraces a myth of modernization (Escobar 1995; Sachs 1992b). Escobar (1995:23) suggests that the development discourse is so pervasive that the global south can scarcely be thought about in any other terms than its essential trait: poverty. In short, some discourse analysts argue that development has been and continues to be only about economic growth underwritten by "faith" in modernization (Rist 1997). Growth and modernization further are linked to industrialization, accumulation, competitive advantage, technological sophistication, urbanization, high levels of consumption, and international trade (Escobar 1995; Rist 1997).

Echoing the sentiments expressed in the previous section by economists in response to the aid crisis, Wolfgang Sachs (1992b:1) declared, "Delusion and disappointment, failures and crimes have been the steady companions of development and they tell a coming story: it did not work. . . . Development has grown obsolete." These post-structuralists argue that it is time to write development's "obituary" (Sachs 1992b:1). In the introduction to *The Development Dictionary*, Sachs outlines four reasons for the death of development. First, the supposed superiority of the industrialized north has been exposed as a sham. With ecological destruction rampant and irreversible, the north no longer can be hailed as a model of advancement. Second, with the end of the cold war, the ideological justification for development no longer exists—as we noted earlier in discussing the current crisis in aid. Third, the gap between the rich and poor—both within and between countries—has risen dramatically since the dawn of the development age, and it continues to rise. Fourth, development's "hidden agenda"—that is, westernization of the globe—has been exposed as contributing to the loss of diversity and the disappearance of the "other" (Sachs 1992b:1–4). As Sachs makes clear, some post-structural development scholars are not interested in resuscitating development; they are interested in burying it, for good.

Responding to post-structural discourse analysts such as Escobar (1995), Rist (1997), and Sachs (1992b) who suggested that *a* development discourse directs all development knowledge and practice, other post-structural scholars (for example, see Arce and Long 2000b; Gardner and Lewis 1997; Grillo and Stirrat 1997)—for the purposes of this debate I will describe them as "anthropology of development" post-structuralists —have questioned the notion that a single discourse generates all development theory and practice. Anthropology of development embraces discourse as vital to understanding the creation and transmission of development knowledge and power, but it also suggests that some discourse analysis—like that outlined above—has gone to extremes by ignoring or telescoping great diversity in development theory and practice in order to construct a coherent metanarrative of development's failures. In reality, even though a single discourse may be hegemonic, it is always subject to multiple challenges and open to multifarious interpretations.

For example, Grillo (1997:21) suggests that development knowledge is not usually a single set of ideas and assumptions. "While it may function hegemonically, it is also created and recreated by multiple agents, who often have very different understandings of their work" (Grillo 1997:21). He labels the assumption that development is a monolithic enterprise the "myth of development," and he claims that this myth pervades much critical writing in the field. Citing Escobar as an example, Grillo (1997:21) says that the myth is based on poor or partial history, is impaired by lack of knowledge of colonization and decolonization, and is ethnocentric, a view from North America grounded in "victim culture."

Similarly, Gardner argues that ideological positions and meanings given to development are fluid, mixed, and continually shifting and that they will "vary internally according to what [people] are doing, when and where they are doing it, and to whom they are talking" (Gardner 1997:145). Rather than just one discrete definition of development, the majority of people hold several. Accordingly, development is better understood as ever-changing discourses, as knowledges and practices endlessly interlinked, negotiated, and dynamic (Gardner 1997). Gardner argues that in order to see how discourse is produced through everyday conditions and activities—and therefore is subject to change and to the agency of individuals—scholars have to look at discourse as practice, rather than as a systematized body of knowledge (Gardner 1997:154).

Others argue similarly: "Discourse cannot be viewed as distinct from specific, situated practices. . . . Discourse is itself a form of practice, entailing the active production of interpretations of specific problematics by making specific connections between concepts and empirical reality" (Nuijten 1992). Like Grillo and Gardner, Nuijten suggests that while dominant discourses are at play, they also are changed, diverted, and neutralized in interpretation and practice. Thus Nuijten agrees that belief in growth and modernization continue to guide much development theory and practice, but she also suggests that development is subject to multiple, divergent, and sometimes conflicting interpretations and constructions. Moreover, the hegemony of modernization does not and cannot exclude the many other paradigms, theories, and models that also guide development.

Agreeing that new practices and knowledges can be and are introduced into the hegemonic discourse, and therefore have potential to alter development, Gardner and Lewis (1996) add that development is not monolithic. "Although structured by relations of power in which particular countries, institutions and groups dominate, development practice and policy are increasingly heterogeneous, and are constantly challenged from more 'radical' positions by people working both within and outside mainstream development institutions" (Gardner and Lewis 1996:103). Development, then, comprises a variety of countervailing perspectives and practices, as well as a multiplicity of voices.

Norman Long (1992:165) says that discourse is a useful concept because it provides an understanding of the modes of action and cognition that actors construct over time and in particular contexts. To understand these constructions requires taking account of the negotiations, manipulations, and accommodations made between actors. For Long, all discourse is realized as event, so discourse involves a continuous practical engagement with the material and social world (1992:166).

Discourse, he argues, is not a tangible or objective substance that can be measured; rather, it can be described only in relation to what people say about their motivations, actions, and statements and to how we observe the negotiations taking place. "Interpreting discourse in this way enables us to examine how local actors use and assign meaning to their material and social world" (1992:167).

In later critiques, Long teams with Arce (Arce and Long 2000) to argue that many post-structural development scholars fail to grasp "diverse and discontinuous configurations of knowledge" (Arce and Long 2000:24). That is, despite the horizons of understanding opened to us through discourse analysis, ultimately Escobar (and others like him) falsely reduce development to a monolithic knowledge and practice, while emphasizing how individuals are constituted as subjects—how power and knowledge combine to create discourses that shape people, setting limits to what they can think and feel, defining what is rational, and what is possible. Post-structuralism is not about agency but rather about how external forces mold and shape people (and institutions), forcing them in line with particular relationships of power and social control. In contrast, Arce and Long (2000) insist that development is really a complex site of contestation, where actors battle to create meaning. Actors necessarily will understand development in diverse terms and will interact with it in ways that may not precisely reflect the original hopes and goals of development implementers and practitioners. Little's (2000) attempt, discussed above, to distinguish between development approaches and theory is important to mention again here. Little wants to draw a distinction between anthropologists "doing" development within institutions such as the World Bank and those purely theorizing about it, such as Wolf and Sidney Mintz (1985). Like Gardner (1996) and others, Little ultimately rejects the divide between applied and theoretical development anthropology as untenable, but he wants to highlight the contributions that anthropologists have made in theorizing about development, outside the reach of the "development machine." For example, he discusses in detail how ethnographic studies of intra-household relations, common property systems, and informal economies have generated important theoretical insights apart from "practical involvement in projects and programs" (Little 2000:122). This idea is important, for at the very least, it suggests that even if a hegemonic discourse has guided development *practice*, anthropological development *theory* perhaps has stood apart from that discourse, to some degree. Moreover, it allows for the possibility that specific practices, or approaches, might have been deployed to oppose or undermine the problematic growth-oriented discourses that post-structuralists have identified.

For example, one approach sometimes used to contest the assertion that all development is ruled by a focus on growth and the notion of poverty is participatory development (for example, Ferguson and Derman 2000). Though diverse in content and scope, participatory development usually includes a focus on "empowering" local-level beneficiaries (as opposed to formulating macro policy) to be active agents in their own development (Chambers 1997). As Peters (2000:6) notes, "participation ideally connotes the ability of people to share, influence, or control design, decision making, and authority in development projects and programs that affect their lives and resources." And, as Hickey and Mohan (2004:4) note, "participation essentially concerns the exercise of popular agency in relation to development . . . and recognizing existing capacities of people as claims-making agents." In practical terms, participatory development is supposed to be "bottom-up, people-centered, process-oriented, and 'alternative'" compared to the "top-down, technocratic, blueprint planning of state-led modernization" (Hickey and Mohan 2004:4). That is, it should allow for alternatives to the dominant discourses identified by post-structuralists scholars.

Participatory development has been fashionable to varying degrees in the current post–World War II development era: popular in the 1950s and 1960s "community development schemes" and in the 1970s, with its focus on basic needs and bottom-up approaches (Peters 2000). In the 1990s and early 2000s, participation has become particularly fashionable, especially in relation to "human rights, democratization, civil society, and popular social movements" (Peters 2000:6). Participatory methods and techniques, like NGOs, have become the "darlings" of the development world—highly visible and potentially "revolutionary." One explanation for this involves the supposedly greater efficiency of participatory techniques and, as a consequence, their greater success than top-down approaches. When local communities "own" particular projects, conceiving of and administering these themselves, the projects are less likely to be resisted and more likely to be culturally appropriate. Moreover, projects can be implemented more cheaply, because people are donating their own time, labor, and talents in pursuit of self-identified goals.

Participatory development, however, is not without its critics. For example, Bill Cooke and Uma Kothari (2001) argue that participatory development approaches often fail to address issues of power and politics and that such approaches are themselves often reduced to techniques and technical approaches that ultimately depoliticize poverty. Majid Rahnema (1992) contends that participatory action research, with its focus on Freirean "consciousness raising," rests on problematic divisions between intellectuals and activists who are promoting the "raising" and the locals who are being conscientized; the developmentalist perspectives of the "experts" remain unexamined, while those of the poor and powerless are targeted for transformation. In simple terms, Chambers (2005:102) characterizes some of the other concerns raised by critiques of participation as "who participates, where, when, with whom, and with what equality." That is, participatory strategies might be subject to the conflicting agendas of multiple participants; might be applied in areas where not everyone has equal access, with only a subset of "intended beneficiaries"; and perhaps could fuel great inequality in communities by targeting some for inclusion and denying it to others. These ideas about participation, its problems, and its promise are intimately tied to notions of twinning and its potential as a transformative project. They will be discussed in more detail later.

"Faith-based" development provides a second example to counter the assertion that all development is guided by hegemonic discourses of economic growth. Particularly since the 1960s, religion has become a powerful force in the design, implementation, and administration of international development. *Faith-based development* is a catch-all label describing institutions that link religion (whether Christianity, Judaism, Islam, Hinduism, or others) with development. For the purposes of this book, I am particularly interested in the growth of "Christian development" as an alternative to conventional development discourses and practices, which are sometimes referred to as "secular" (for example, Bornstein 2005; Occhipinti 2005).

Is there a distinctly Christian approach to development? For Erica Bornstein, who studied two Protestant NGOs, World Vision and Christian Care, in Zimbabwe, "Christian development" as practiced by these two NGOs encompassed two elements: "lifestyle evangelism" and "holism." Holism, or "evangelical holism" as Bornstein calls it (2005:49), in this sense refers to the rejection of economic development as a goal in of itself and to the substitution of a focus on linking economics with spirituality to promote their mutual well-being and growth. For Christian organizations such as World Vision and Christian Care, "economic development [is] a primary objective, yet development [applies] to the whole person: the full human, material and spiritual" (Bornstein 2005:49).

This idea of holism emerges in the works of others concerned with Christian development (Getu 2001; Occhipinti 2005; Tsele 2001). In talking about her work with World Vision and the Canadian International Development Agency (CIDA), Linda Tripp (1999:63) discusses her refusal to adopt CIDA's secular development approach, which she sees as focused only on

> the physical aspects of development—food, water, health-care, agriculture, and so on. Yet the vast majority of people with whom we work in development regard the spiritual realm as equally relevant to daily life. . . . To promote a secular approach would be an insult to them, and inconsistent with our commitment to holistic development.

Although it is perhaps an alternative to secular development approaches, holism is not distinctly Christian. In writing about the ways in which Hinduism could promote a more integrated form of development, Promilla Kapur (2000:5) writes, "Hinduism brings a holistic approach to development, because it does not concentrate simply on the question of economic well-being but also incorporates ideals of spiritual and sociopsychological satisfaction."

Lifestyle evangelism is the second feature that Bornstein identifies in the Christian development approach of World Vision and Christian Care. Lifestyle evangelism entails "living a life in the manner of Christ and providing examples for non-believers" (Bornstein 2005:50). This requires living a virtuous Christian life characterized by love and caring within and for the community. In the process of living "good lives," development workers become witnesses to and embodiments of Christ's love.

Similar, though not identical, ideas are also to be found in Catholic social teaching, which emphasizes charity, justice, and solidarity as pathways to community and love. For example, drawing on metaphor, Pope Pius XI said, "The whole body (being closely joined and knit together through every joint of the system according to the functioning in due measure of each single part) derives its increase to the building up of itself in love" (in Cima and Schubeck 2001:219). Commenting on this, Lawrence Cima and Thomas L. Schubeck (2001:219) write, "Love relates to justice by motivating and empowering the individual members to work together for the good of the whole." Unlike in Bornstein's remark, individual conversion is not the principal aim here; indeed, there is the subsuming of the individual in favor of the collective. But the link I emphasize is in ideas about responsibility, both to the community and to God. In the case of World Vision and Christian Care, believers are compelled to be "good," a responsibility that allows them to be models for neighbors and to better the world—both in the communal and the supernatural sense. For Catholics, the responsibility is to recognize their connection to one another, to work together so that the world can be "good."

Is there such a thing, then, as "Christian development?" To argue that *a* Christian development discourse or practice exists would be problematic for the same reasons that asserting that there is *a* monolithic development discourse would be. Christianity is not monolithic but, rather, is diverse. As Clarke notes, faith-based development organizations tend to adopt their "ethos" from the "sub-faith" to which they are attached: Catholic, Protestant, Orthodox/Coptic. Within each of these three main forms, further divisions can be made: mainline versus evangelical Protestants, for example. To assert that there is a Christian approach to development belies great diversity in practice and philosophy, particularly as they stem from different religious traditions, organizational structures, and local understandings. To take an obvious example, the extent to which Christians subscribe to or reject the capitalist global order varies considerably. Many in the tradition of liberation theology, for example, reject capitalism as a fundamentally dehumanizing and exploitive system (Occhipinti 2005). By contrast, some evangelical Protestants believe that capitalism is essentially a libratory system that can lift the poor out of poverty. For these believers, the injustice is not capitalism itself but the fact that the poor have been denied access to the benefits and opportunities it promises (Sherman 1997).

Nonetheless, Christian development specifically, and faith-based development more broadly, often do stand as counter examples to notions about the existence of a singular development discourse or practice. For example, Christian development often rejects the division between religious and economic realms, an assumed but largely unacknowledged dichotomy in conventional development discourse and practice. Remember the dearth of scholarly articles examining spirituality or religion, according to Ver Beek's survey of three leading development journals between 1982 to 1998. The divide often is taken for granted by conventional developers, who—in "typical" modernist fashion—assume that the more "advanced" a people becomes, the less "superstitious/religious" it will be.

■ Conclusion

Currently, states seeking U.S. foreign aid are encouraged to adopt practices of "good governance" that include an emphasis on trade, privatization, and reduced government spending. Moreover, states that fail to meet these good-governance criteria are excluded from formal aid regimes. The present moment is also, some suggest, an era of crisis. Aid's purpose is being questioned and its efficacy scrutinized, and overall official development aid flows, especially to the Caribbean, are in decline. Yet, according to official measures—which, it must be noted, are critiqued by anti-development scholars—worldwide poverty continues to grow and vast numbers of the world's population live without basic human rights. Some (for example, see Farmer et al. 2003)—including many twinning participants—perceive a gap between the global south's "need" for development aid and the ability or willingness of official aid regimes to deliver that aid effectively. This is the niche that lay developers are filling.

Lay developers, like those of the twinning program, have "space" at this historical juncture to become crafters and implementers of development. Not only are they stepping in to fill the roles that states once were encouraged to play, but lay developers are focusing on countries—such as Haiti—that are increasingly marginalized from official development aid regimes. Post-structural and anthropology of development scholars agree that conventional development initiatives often have been problematic—serving to depoliticize poverty while maintaining a sort of administrative control of the global south by the north—and that they have functioned hegemonically. But hegemony does not preclude the possibility of alternative manifestations, as the examples of participatory development and Christian development reveal. Rather, hegemonic discourses attempt to make other initiatives less likely and try to absorb and reconfigure them when they do occur.

A question guiding this book is: What is the relationship between these entrenched, hegemonic discourses—discourses that are institutionalized and implemented by development "experts"—and the discourses and practices of those who stand outside the "development machine"? That is, if we accept that dominant development discourses and practices have been fueled by belief in growth and development among the experts, do those who are unschooled in conventional development repeat or challenge conventional understandings? Do their discourses mask relations of power and domination, while simultaneously depoliticizing poverty, as do hegemonic constructions? If "professionalization" of knowledge is the means by which power is exercised and replicated, how do we understand what I call development's "deprofessionalization," or its increasing openness to lay practitioners seemingly able to sidestep development's structures and maybe even its guiding emphasis on growth? These are questions that I address in Chapter Six. To lay the foundation for the discussion of these questions, Chapter Four introduces twinning at St. Robert, and Chapter Five considers how those active on St. Robert's Haiti Committee conceptualize development and attempt to put it into practice in Haiti.

■ Notes

1. A survey in the 1980s located 72 different meanings of the term *development*, and there would certainly be more now because development studies has become a prominent field of study (Riggs 1984 in Martinussen 1999:35)

2. OECD, the Organisation for Economic Co-operation and Development, is made up of thirty member countries, including the United States. OECD promotes the "rules of the game" regarding development, "good governance," and market economies. See the OECD website for more information.

3. Modernity has been conceptualized as "the conquest of nature by the techniques of science, capital accumulation and investment, the users of these techniques being imbued with the values of rationality, work and thrift. The employment of medicine, public health and improved nutrition to eliminate premature death as the normal human lot is central to the modernity project, just as conquering disease and death is an essential part of humankind increasing its control over nature" (Walter and Davis 1998:653).

4. ODA is aid given by a country for development purposes, including both direct gifts and low-rate loans. In 2001, five countries—the United States, Japan, France, Germany, and the United Kingdom—provided 67 percent of the world's ODA.

5. Aid directed to refugee and emergency relief is growing. The World Bank (1997) estimates that 12 percent of all official development assistance was devoted to emergency aid in 1996, compared with 2 percent in 1990.

6. The United Nations Development Report (see UNDP 2005) is an annual publication that "measures" and compares development globally. Using the "human development index" rather than conventional measures—such as GNP and income levels—this report attempts to assess how people are faring both within their own countries and vis-à-vis others. Countries are then ranked according to their success in achieving human development.

7. Escobar defines discourse as "the process through which social reality comes into being. . . . It is the articulation of knowledge and power, of the visible and the expressible" (1995:39).

CHAPTER FOUR

Twinning at St. Robert

This chapter takes an in-depth look at St. Robert, as well as at individual twinning participants. Beginning with an overview of recent trends in U.S. Catholicism in order to place twinning in its religious context, Chapter Four then moves to answer the following questions: Who are the people who engage in twinning? How do they participate? What motivates them? What do they get out of it? In what ways do they think about Haiti and twinning?

■ Catholicism in the United States

Catholics in the United States have a long history of charitable service, dating back to the early nineteenth century. For much of this history, the American Church focused its attention on mitigating the effects of poverty on the U.S. urban poor (Oates 1992). The linking of churches in the global north with those in the south is more recent and parallels the timeline of development more broadly; that is, it occurred only over the past 50 years or so. Slightly more than a decade after President Truman's Four Point address calling for international development, Pope John XXIII issued a call in 1961 for increasing missionary work in the global south. As reported in McGlone 1997, within 2 years, the number of U.S. missionaries—mainly sisters and priests—to Latin America doubled. By

1968, the number had tripled. This missionary zeal for Latin America swept through the U.S. Church during a time of radical change for the Church more broadly.

From 1962 to 1965, the Second Vatican Council convened an international council of bishops to "open the windows" of the Church in order to let "a little fresh air in," as Pope John XXIII said (in Walch 1989:90). Although they were ostensibly about "updating" the church and making it more relevant to "the times," the changes stemming from Vatican II revolutionized the church in many ways. The bishops revised and changed Church policy and law in a variety of areas: Mass was to be said in local languages, with priests facing parishioners rather than the altar. The laity was to participate in singing, praying aloud, extending the sign of peace to one another via handshakes, reading to the congregation, and distributing communion. Lay Catholics were to play a larger role in the lives of their churches. And an important religious decree recognizing the religious rights of non-Catholics was passed (Walch 1989; Dolan 1992).

The changes associated with Vatican II were contentious, and a steady stream of priests and sisters began to leave their vocations—some estimate that 10,000 priests left in the 12 years following Vatican II (Dolan 1992; Walch 1989). During this same period, few men and women entered these vocations, so there were rapid declines in the numbers of new priests and nuns (Morris 1997). To fill this partial vacuum, the laity has become increasingly involved in ministry (Dolan 1992).

This decline in clergy also affected missionary activity. U.S. missionary activity levels began to wane after reaching their peak in 1968, and by 1992, the number of pastoral workers in Latin America had dropped to below 1962 levels. Yet despite this decline in the numbers of priests and nuns engaged in missionary activity in Latin America, there has been growing support for Latin America on the part of U.S. church communities. In a survey administered by the National Conference of Catholic Bishops in 1995, all respondents indicated that their support for Latin America had grown since the 1960s. Parishes and dioceses reported an 18 percent growth, Catholic institutions of higher learning an 8 percent growth, and religious communities a 5 percent growth (McGlone 1997). At the same time, the vast majority of these same institutions expected that their level of involvement with Latin America would stay the same or increase over the next 5 years. As McGlone (1997) notes, "in spite of the diminishing numbers of traditional missionaries, there is clearly more to the relationship than the sending of priests and sisters to work in Latin America." That wider relationship consists, in part, of expanding linkages between church communities in the hemisphere.

According to McGlone (1997), there are three dimensions to these "new" church-to-church relationships: a high degree of laity involvement, short pastoral service or an "altogether new type of relationship," and renewed mission theology. Twinning, as reported herein, reflects all three of these changes. Twinning is laity-led and predicated upon the centrality of a Haiti Committee in the United States and a priest in Haiti to facilitate sharing and exchange across the two cultures. Thus, a high degree of laity involvement and a "new type" of missionary relationship focusing on parish-to-parish relationships clearly align with McGlone's analysis. The third feature—a renewed missionary theology—is also central to twinning.

Stemming from the National Conference of Catholic Bishops' 1986 document *To the Ends of the Earth*, the renewed mission theology has reconstructed the notion of mission, calling for all local churches to be in communion with one another. The document also considers how notions surrounding "mission" have changed over time. As McGlone notes, in the past, countries were conceived to be either "mission sending" or "mission receiving." Moreover, "mission sending" countries were thought not to be in need of missionizing themselves. But such distinctions no longer hold.

> Every local church is both mission-sending and mission-receiving. . . . Together we are coming to see that any local church has no choice but to reach out to others with the gospel of Christ's love for all peoples. To say "Church" is to say "mission." (in McGlone 1997:208)

Unquestionably, twinning's emphasis on the "reverse mission" is firmly linked to the ideas raised by the National Conference of Catholic Bishops. Reverse missions are intended to be moments of spiritual growth and renewal for those traveling to the global south, rather than trips to evangelize the locals there. Twinning suggests that those elsewhere have something to offer—something to teach Americans about spirituality and faith.

The National Conference of Catholic Bishops document also called upon local churches to enter into dialogue with one another. Dialogue was defined as "a manner of acting, an attitude, and a spirit which guides one's conduct." In this way, dialogue "implies concern, respect, and hospitality towards the other. It leaves room for the other person's identity, his modes of expression, and his values. Dialogue is thus the norm and necessary manner of every form of Christian mission." More than that, "Any mission not permeated by such a dialogical spirit would go against the demands of true humanity and against the teachings of the gospel" (in McGlone 1997:209).

Central to the idea of the reverse mission and of twinning itself is the notion of "mutuality," of a coming together of U.S. and parishes abroad to share their respective gifts. Twinning calls on participants to have "concern, respect, and hospitality" toward one another, to have a "non-controlling mutuality" as the promotional literature suggests (PTPA n.d.). Twinning is not simply about giving, but about receiving, as well.

Moreover, twinning explicitly calls upon the "universality" of the Catholic Church, another theme raised by the National Conference of Catholic Bishops. In talking about a Kansas City, Missouri, parish's church-to-church relationship with a parish in El Salvador, McGlone (1997:220) remarks,

> When delegates from the United State and El Salvador visit one another's parishes they break down boundaries of provincialism so that people once considered "foreigners" become "friends." As the people of both parishes share their faith and their gifts with one another they are effectively building up their awareness and their appreciation for the universality of the faith.

These sentiments might have been taken directly from PTPA's promotional materials or from many of the narratives that I collected. Indeed, twinning intends to answer the calls of the Church to engage in missionary activity and to do so in "new ways" that affirm the uniqueness of each parish involved but that, at the same time, proclaim and strengthen the universality of the Church.

And yet, as I discuss in later chapters, this is no easy feat; these relationships can be—and often are—fraught with tensions. The rhetoric and the practice of twinning are sometimes at odds, as the difficulties and constraints of cross-cultural church-to-church partnering emerge. U.S. and southern twins enter into their relationship with one another from very different positions deriving, in part, from their very different access to and control of resources. What can emerge then—as in the case of St. Robert—is less a story of "mutuality" and common respect, and more one of accounting for twinning funds, issues of trust, and the clashing of personalities and cultures.

In 1986 the National Conference of Catholic Bishops also published *Economic Justice for All: Catholic Social Teaching and the U.S. Economy,* wherein the U.S. bishops challenged American Catholics to "live our faith in the world" (NCCB 1997). Outlining a series of moral principles and economic policy issues, *Economic Justice for All* is both a critique of current economic systems and a call to action for Catholics.

> 87. As individuals and as a nation, therefore, we are called to make a fundamental "option for the poor." The obligation to evaluate social and economic activity from the viewpoint of the poor and the powerless arises from the radical command to love one's neighbor as one's self. (NCCB 1997:47)

And

> 88. The prime purpose of this special commitment to the poor is to enable them to become active participants in the life of a society. It is to enable all persons to share in and contribute to the common good. (NCCB 1997:47)

The document directly addresses the role of the United States in the global economy and as a donor nation by critiquing the "politicized" nature of U.S. development assistance. Rather than addressing human need, U.S. development assistance often has taken "national security interest" as its primary purpose. Moreover, U.S. official development assistance is too paltry, the United States being almost last among OECD countries in terms of percentage of GNP devoted to ODA. The document implores, "The U.S. approach to the developing countries needs urgently to be changed; a country as large, rich, and powerful as ours has a moral obligation to lead in helping reduce poverty in the Third World" (NCCB 1997:94).

The document also declares that all people have a right to participate in the economic lives of their societies. To ensure this opportunity for all, the document asserts:

> 16. All members of a society have a special obligation to the poor and vulnerable.
>
> 17. Human rights are the minimum conditions for life in community. In Catholic teaching, human rights include not only civil and political rights, but also economic rights. As Pope John XXIII declared, all people have a right to life, food, clothing, shelter, rest, medical care, education, and employment.
>
> 18. Society as a whole, acting through public and private institutions, has the moral responsibility to enhance human dignity and protect human rights. (NCCB 1997:224–225)

The Catholic Church as an institution—and particularly the National Conference of Catholic Bishops—has provided, then, important guidelines for Catholic economic social action in the United States. As we shall see, many of the themes raised by the Church are present in the discourses of twinning. However, aside from Theresa Patterson, no lay participants explicitly referenced—or cited knowledge of—the statements or documents presented above.

■ Setting the Stage: St. Robert

St. Robert is a huge parish, both in physical size and in population. Located alongside a busy two-lane suburban street, surrounded by sprawling green lawns, and nestled among expensive housing developments, St. Robert is an "upscale" parish with around 8500 parishioners. St. Robert actually comprises two churches: a new, sleek modern building covered in brick and mirrored glass on the outside, with a light-colored, "open" sanctuary; and an older, darker, much smaller sanctuary enveloped by the new construction. Mass is held in the new sanctuary, with its elaborately beamed ceilings and expansive design.

St. Robert's new sanctuary is shaped like a slice of pie. Surrounding the sanctuary—imagine the pie's crust—is a large, curved gathering space, with windows onto the sanctuary running its entire length. Along the outside wall of the gathering space are chairs, so that parishioners can watch and hear—through speakers piping in the priests' and lectors' words—the entire mass without having to enter the sanctuary. These chairs, especially on Sunday morning services, fill quickly with families of young children. A hot-tub sized stone (granite?) baptismal font, with a cascading waterfall-like feature, rests in the middle of the gathering space. For those sitting in the gathering space, mass is less formal than in the sanctuary. Kids run back and forth, play on the floor, watch through the glass, and occasionally splash in the font.

St. Robert has a kind of frenetic energy around mass times. The parking lot, lined with SUVs, mini-vans, and luxury cars, hosts a kind of wild race to find parking. Many parishioners rush through the church doors, which line the outer edge of the gathering space in three main entry areas, and hurry into the sanctuary just as the priest is preparing the processional. And a surprising number of people arrive after mass has started, late by 5, 10, or even 20 minutes. There is also a tendency to leave church quickly, with long lines of cars waiting to get out of the parking lot and a sometimes not very friendly jockeying for a position in the exit line. Thus the atmosphere at St. Robert's Sunday masses is often charged. There is lots of energy, with kids running around, parents chasing them, parishioners arriving late, and trying to leave quickly. There is a real sense that these are busy people, leading active lives, and trying to make the most of every precious minute.

Similarly, St. Robert is a very busy, very active parish. There are literally dozens of ways parishioners can become involved in the life of the church, with most initiatives laity-led. Each fall, St. Robert hosts a Know

Your Parish Weekend, where parishioners are encouraged to "pick a ministry" for the coming year as a "gift to our community" (St. Robert 2003). There are opportunities to participate in typical Catholic service roles (for example, as lectors and eucharistic ministers), to enroll in educational classes, to join retreats, and the like. There are also recreational opportunities: a bridge club, golf and softball leagues, a mother's group, the gardening club. Haiti falls under the church's "Service and Outreach" activities, which are divided into categories of "Christian service" and "pastoral service." Haiti outreach is considered Christian service and is described in the parish directory in the following way:

> Representatives from the parish go nearly every year to Our Lady's Nativity parish in Verrettes, Haiti. As ambassadors of goodwill, they take our greetings and our love and return with news of how the projects we sponsor are progressing and where our focus should be in the coming year. (St. Robert 2003)

Haiti Outreach is only one of an astounding fifteen Christian service activities open to parishioners.[1] Of these, it is noteworthy that nine include some focus on food provisioning (for example, Thanksgiving turkeys, soup kitchens, pizza parties for nursing home residents, birthday parties for youth in detention), as does the Haiti twinning.[2] In brief, both the individuals at St. Robert and St. Robert as an institution are engaged, lively, and active.

Christian Service: Haiti Outreach

The almost palpable vigor characterizing mass is less evident at the Haiti Committee meetings, probably in part because the meetings take place in the evenings and there are usually no young children present. Moreover, most people active on the committee are themselves older, are established in—or even retired from—their careers, and have teenaged or older children. Committee meetings are scheduled by Cassie and now Dennis, who jointly lead the committee. As mentioned earlier, the Haiti program at St. Robert was initiated by Cassie, who invested considerable time and energy in establishing and then maintaining the twinning. Thus the twinning is identified in many people's minds as "Cassie's project." But Cassie recently moved an hour's drive away from Ada. Her role in the St. Robert twinning is diminishing, as she increasingly shares responsibilities with Dennis, who now officially co-heads the committee.

Committee meetings are scheduled on an as-needed basis, usually about every 3 months. News of a meeting is sent through the Haiti Committee email list and published in the parish bulletin, informing members of the date, time, and location. Meetings are generally held on a weeknight around 7:00, average an hour and a half to two hours in length, and typically occur in the "lounge," in the back of the church building across from the administrative offices and classrooms. There are a coffee pot and other amenities in the lounge, but generally no food or drink is provided.

One wall of the lounge overlooks the entryway, allowing those already in the meeting to see who is coming in. The couch and lounge chairs are rarely, if ever, used by meeting participants. Instead, a large conference table near the entry serves as the meeting point, and participants enter the room, greet one another, sometimes give hugs, and then take a seat at the table. Cassie sets the meeting agenda, often sending it via email and sometimes handing out copies at the meeting. Sometimes other information is also distributed. For example, newspaper articles, correspondence, or photographs might be shared.

In contrast to mass, people generally arrive on time for the committee meetings. A "core" of committee members has been present at most, if not all, of the meetings I have attended since 2001: Sister JoAn, Cassie, Dennis, Sally (who recently moved away), Mary Ann, Rod (Cassie's husband). Others have attended many or the majority of meetings: Father Lou, Sharon, Chris, Mike, Bob (now terminally ill). Still others sometimes attend meetings but not with the regularity of those just mentioned: Val and Ashley, Bill and Char (in Haiti now for 6 months each year), Tom. Finally, the email list keeps other committee members informed about the goings-on of the twinning. In all, then, about sixteen people regularly rotate in and out of the committee meetings; Cassie identified another fifteen whom she considered important members of the committee, although I rarely—if ever—saw them at meetings.[3] For the most part, those on the committee are educated, working professionals (lawyers, small-business owners, medical specialists) who are volunteering their time and talents to the twinning program.

Although they are open to the parish, meetings rarely host many "new" people. At only three of the meetings I attended between 2001 and 2004 was a newcomer present, and none has become a regular committee member. Indeed, each attended only a single meeting. In principle the committee encourages new people to become involved, but the structure of the committee, its established programming, and its population (all people who have been to Haiti, except for Sister JoAn, who cannot travel for health reasons) now effectively exclude newcomers from participating. Said one person,

> We have a constant circling of getting new members on the committee. They often want to do things or make suggestions that they don't follow up on. Or, they'll tell about someone else who does something. . . . The problem is we could spend all our time networking. And, we do. But, we have a vision that we want to do. We don't want to reinvent the wheel every time. (Interview #1)

There is a sense, at least among some members, that taking new parishioners onto the committee is inefficient and that having to bring people up to speed not only on the projects but also on what Haiti is like, slows down the work of the committee. Indeed, the person quoted above calls those on the Haiti Committee "specialists" because they have traveled to Haiti and understand the parameters of the programming. These thirty or so "specialists" are consulted on Haiti matters—either via the listserve or at the committee meetings—and are kept abreast of happenings, primarily by Cassie. At the same time that some hesitate bringing new members onto the committee, however, there is an awareness that the twinning relationship—and specifically certain needs at Our Lady— must be kept "in front" of the wider parish in order to maintain enthusiasm and support for the twinning. And so, part of the work of the Haiti Committee is to spread news of goings-on in Haiti and to report to the parish on programming progress. Significantly, St. Robert's parishioners usually get twinning information only after it has been filtered through the Haiti Committee—primarily through Cassie or Sr. JoAn.

Although one part of the committee's work is communicating to the wider parish about Haiti and twinning, its larger focus has been to establish the mission of the twinning, get projects in place to meet that mission, and then help keep them going by monitoring progress, fundraising, and tracking finances. When I came onboard in 2001, the focus of the twinning (the "vision" mentioned above) was well established. All of the current projects mentioned in Chapter One—educational sponsorship, vocational school, micro-loans, and the like—were already under way, so I did not see first-hand how they were decided upon or put into action. Rather, I saw the committee's work to keep them going, the "successes" and "failures" they experienced, and the numerous challenges they faced. Many of these challenges—including problems of communication, accountability, and the like—will be detailed in later chapters; they resonate strongly with issues encountered more broadly in conventional development practice. Here, I want to concentrate instead on the "day-to-day" activities of the committee and its functioning, as well as on the stories of its members.

■ Inside the Haiti Committee

As we have noted, relatively few committee members regularly attend committee meetings. A typical meeting has anywhere from eight to twelve people present, with Cassie leading discussion according to the agenda she has set. After initial greetings and "catching up," meetings begin with a prayer, followed by discussion of the major items of importance, as outlined in the agenda. Because meetings are not regularly scheduled and are relatively infrequent, when they do occur they generally have a specific set of issues or problems that need addressing.

Most members of St. Robert's Haiti Committee have traveled to Haiti at least once since the twinning began in 1995. And a few have done so many times. The face-to-face communications with the priests and parishioners of Our Lady reinforce the commitment the parishes have made to each other by reminding participants at both ends that "real" people are involved. The visits highlight, particularly for St. Robert's parishioners, the humanity that they share and the way poverty is working against that humanity in Haiti. According to one woman, "Traveling makes you want to do more [to help]" (Interview #4). Another commented, "You don't know unless you go. It's imperative. How can you help someone in that situation without seeing firsthand what they need?" (Interview #3).

The motivation for helping and insight into Our Lady's needs come from traveling, from bearing witness to life in Haiti. By meeting project participants, visiting with elementary students and their teachers, and simply walking through the town, St. Robert's parishioners gain a sense of what life is like in Haiti. That said, the Haitian priests—with their limited English—remain the primary contacts for the Americans, and they ultimately have significant control over the visitors' experiences. When St. Robert's parishioners are "interviewing" local Creole speakers about their needs, the priests or their associates often provide the translation. The priests help interpret and explain to the Americans what they are seeing and what might be done to remedy certain injustices. Thus, even though traveling is generally considered an essential component of the twinning, it must be understood as a "buffered" experience.

In one instance, a committee meeting was called shortly after a delegation had returned from Haiti. This meeting was organized around members' reports from the field, although, as the following account demonstrates, conversation can flow in many directions from the initial jumping-off point. Talking about the vocational school:

Committee member #1: The women have had one graduating class, and two groups of men have graduated. I don't know about jobs. When you ask about specific numbers, things get fuzzy. [Why are there no jobs for students?] Because no jobs are available. . . .

Committee member #2: Instead of having such specific programs, maybe some of the programs should shift, like to electricity.

Committee member #3: What about incorporating general health training into the school? They think only women transmit AIDS.

Committee member #4: What about literacy training at the trade school? Do the women know how to read and write? They should teach everyone to read and write. They don't know about micro-organisms, they don't know that putting a baby on the floor where the pig just ran through is a problem. They don't know that a baby gets sick from malaria. When they watched a video about malaria, they didn't think it applied to them because the mosquito on the TV was so big. They said, We don't have to worry about it because our mosquitoes aren't that big [laughter]. There needs to be more medical outreach. Why can't we use the services already in place, like at Albert Schweitzer hospital? We could use the cinema to show health videos, then give certificates. They go nuts for certificates.

Committee member #5: How do we empower the people more? What opportunities are there?

Committee member #6: We have to be very patient. Val saw improvement from four years ago. We'll never get them to our level—ever—in our lifetime. But there's the school, the new road. We're dealing with a historical and cultural reality that takes a long time to change and empower.

This exchange demonstrates several key characteristics of Haiti Committee meetings. First, participants are active in these meetings, throwing their ideas out to the group without much hesitation. But ideas are not always picked up or commented on by others at the table. Second, the focus of the discussion can become rather diffuse, even though these are "specialists" brainstorming. Usually Cassie (though sometimes others, as in the case above) tries to refocus discussion, to rein it back toward answering the central concerns raised on the agenda. Third, despite vocal exchanges in meetings, some see the refocusing of the discussion, and the lack of acknowledgement for certain ideas, as an indication that the committee is too centralized and not participatory enough. When asked about how differences of opinion are handled on the committee, one woman involved in the above exchange said, "Well,

Cassie gets her way, and the rest of us are ignored." Another member responded to the same question at more length:

> At times, I've been frustrated. When tensions get high, meetings become less frequent. But I've never seen any hostility at the meetings. Also, there's a small core group that tends to make the decisions. Meetings are an opportunity to talk about different things, to share goals. We're not using an up or down, yay or nay vote, but we have an agenda. We tend to go from point A to B, and the committee is along for the ride. But in fairness to the committee, our long-term commitment is to a relatively few . . . projects. So, if I got the bright idea to do X, Y Z, we don't have the money, because we've already committed to different programs. We tend to do the same things over and over, so there's not a lot of room for innovation. . . . I've never seen any big disagreements or fundamental differences in what we should be doing or how we should be doing it. To the extent [that disagreements] occur, people just stop participation in the committee. But I think some may have frustration that power is too centralized. (Interview #6)

The idea that power is too centralized is linked to the essential role Cassie plays in both organizing and running the meetings, as well as to her historical position as the point person for most St. Robert and Our Lady interactions. Cassie has also been particularly active in seeking out members of the parish who have special skills that might be useful in furthering the twinning. Cassie is the founder, organizer, facilitator, and leader of St. Robert's twinning program. Said another, "There needs to be more diversity on the committee. Cassie is overworked. There are not enough other people actively involved" (Interview #2). Whether this is intentional (again, by limiting participation to "specialists" and maintaining a firm control of the twinning's operation) or simply the byproduct of trying to establish and administer such a massive project in the midst of an already socially active parish, Cassie undeniably has been at the core of facilitating St. Robert's twinning, and in all likelihood, without her firm hand guiding the project, it would not have gotten off the ground.

The central role that Cassie has played is not uniformly criticized, however. Many have commented to me that Cassie is *the* reason for the twinning at St. Robert. "The Haiti program encompasses a lot [of] energy and people. Cassie has been the stronghold and leader. . . . Without her, the program would not have survived (Interview #8). Said another,

> Cassie has always been at the heart of it. . . . The rest of us floated in and out. . . . Cassie has always been the one who takes care of wiring money, sending money for airline tickets. One person has to take the overall view, and she is certainly not just committed and dedicated but [also] a very talented person. (Interview #10)

Now that Cassie has moved from the area and is increasingly ceding control of the committee to Dennis, some worry that her absence will end in the collapse of the program. At this point, however, despite some speculation that "it's really Cassie's project," the twinning appears to be stable and to be withstanding her reduced involvement.

To return to the committee meeting introduced above, after discussion of the trade school, a new thread was picked up regarding perceived trouble with the administration of the microcredit project:

Committee member #7: We need to protect the donor's intention, which is to make the money available without a lot of red tape.

Committee member #1: We just need to reform the [microloan] committee [in Haiti.] It should be Father [Yvens], the sewing teacher, the two sisters. Gerard [current head of microloan committee] uses that committee for his own power.

Committee member #2: What are people using the microcredit for?

Committee member #1: Roadside stands, re-selling. The idea is to wean them off the program so that they can save.

Committee member #7: They need a class for microloans.

Committee member #4: They don't understand the need to save 30 cents from every dollar.

Committee member #6: It's just as much about the process as the end result.

Committee member #1: It's just a stepping stone [like the trade school]. With education as a mechanic, you can go in a bunch of different directions. The dilemma is, if we're teaching too many other things, we're going to run out of space and money. The school is giving them more than an education. . . .

Committee member #4: How do we give them a sense of ownership? A sense of pride?

Committee member #3: By requiring students to give back. After they graduate, they have to give back to others. That would mean we'd need someone there to monitor, and we don't have that purpose. . . .

Committee member #8: What is our mission? Is it paving the plaza? Fixing the bell tower? The pews? What is the focus of the twinning program?

Committee member #1: We focus on education, but it's hard to learn when the environment is so poor. We need to have some focus on the physical environment.

Committee member #7: We need to improve the worship space, but the bell tower, that's aesthetic. Pews are part of the worship space. But they can have a fruitful life without having the plaza across from the church paved.

Committee member #1: But they say that the dust from the plaza blows into the church.

Again, in the midst of discussion about how to make the microcredit project run more efficiently (the microloan committee in Haiti had set interest rates higher than St. Robert felt was appropriate), a number of issues were raised, most important among them the question of the very purpose of twinning. I posed this same question to each of the people I interviewed, and not surprisingly, I discovered that the purpose of twinning was not readily agreed upon (see Table 4.1).

TABLE 4.1 TWINNING'S GOALS

Purpose/Goals of St. Robert Twinning	Number of Responses
"Help" Haitians	7
Development/Promote self-sufficiency	6
Education	5
Spiritual growth	5
Promote a better life for Haitians	5
Provide food aid	4
Financial support	4
Not sure	3
Know one another/bring two cultures together	2
Maintain church in Haiti	1
Bring peace and dignity to Haitians	1

*The total number of responses is greater than twenty-one, because most respondents gave more than one answer.

Twinning promotional literature from the Grand Rapids Diocese states that twinning is intended to "be a physical demonstration of God's love to the people of Haiti" and to encourage "personal, prayerful solidarity with Haitian brothers and sisters. The local [Michigan] parish will find many opportunities to provide resources and support to their Haitian twin in religious, educational, medical, and economic areas, while maintaining a non-controlling mutuality in the relationship" (HOP, n.d.). And indeed, as the table above suggests, St. Robert's twinning project does find its overall purpose in forging religious, educational, and economic links to Our Lady, even though not everyone I interviewed agreed that each endeavor was central to twinning's purpose.

For example, one person emphasized education and literacy as twinning goals, a theme strongly echoed in several other narratives. But this same person downplayed the spiritual components of the relationship.

From my perspective, [the goal of the twinning] is to promote literacy and education, specifically, to give them a chance for a better life. In conjunction with that, there's the school lunch program, which, to a degree, is an adjunct to learning. It's not so much to feed the hungry as to help them have a productive education program. . . . Education is the main program, subsidizing scholarships for families who may not be able to afford school. There's the trade school, where they're trying to teach life skills. At those levels, we're still trying to reinforce reading and literacy to increase job opportunities and improve the day-to-day lives of students. It may have originally been a goal, but I don't see a lot of sharing on a theological basis, from church to church." (Interview #6)

This is not to suggest that twinning does not have a spiritual component. Indeed, five interviewees mentioned spiritual growth as an explicit goal of twinning. And, as seen in discussion below, many consider Haitians to be more spiritually aware than Americans. But in the day-to-day running of the twinning program at St. Robert, most exchanges between Our Lady and St. Robert focus on the economic dimensions of their relationship: how much money is needed, how much has been wired, how the programs are progressing, how they might be improved, and the like.

In talking about what makes a good twinning relationship, Doug, coordinator of the Grand Rapids Haiti Outreach Project, emphasized bringing "two Catholic communities . . . together, partners who have abilities that will help out with what the other partner lacks. So it's also a receiving for churches in America. It should be a give and take, with both giving." However, this idea of give and take was absent from most interviewee's assessments of St. Robert's purpose in twinning. And when it *was* mentioned, it was generally to counter the notion that a parish-level give and take was occurring. Again, responding to the question of St. Robert's goals in twinning, one man responded,

To reach out to a parish that is culturally different than our own and to provide our support, our spiritual support, and our physical support in helping that parish in ways that they need help.

> Part of this, the point of the program, is that their mission is similar. Their culture and resources help our parish. It's not charity because both parishes benefit. But in reality, we receive very little physical benefit from the parish in Verrettes. . . . Originally, we were hoping for more give and take. At this end, we've found it difficult to get people up from Haiti. So it's tended to be more of a one-way street. (Interview #12)

This raises a key question: Is twinning charity? As this member suggests, some on the Haiti Committee tend not to see twinning as a form of charity, precisely because it is supposed to be mutually beneficial and rewarding for both parties. Yet the lopsidedness of twinning's practice, whereby the flows of money and people are overwhelmingly unilateral, calls such idealism into question.

Poppendieck's (1998:231–232) discussion of charity in U.S. food banks rings eerily familiar in the context of twinning. *Charity*, she says, is a word that

> helps to identify the fault lines of a culture. For some people, its connotations are wholly positive. It signifies unselfishness, tolerance, altruism, even love. . . . For many other people, however, the word has a thoroughly negative connotation. It is the gift, offered with condescension and accepted in desperation, that is necessitated by incapacity and failure.

As will become clear in later discussions, the "fault lines" in St. Robert's twinning reflect the tensions undergirding the "beneficiary" and "benefactor" character of these relationships identified by Poppendieck. In reality, rather than talking about mutuality or exchange, most people spoke about the purpose of the program in terms of what St. Robert can and does do for Our Lady in Verrettes.

> To give a helping hand, basically. To help the parish of Verrettes, to help the people there in the parish have a chance for a better life, hopefully to have a chance to know God better by keeping their ministry going. (Interview #13)

> Self-sufficiency. To help them be able to tap independently into
> the resources they have so they don't have to depend on out-
> side resources, like they have to now. That's a dream for all
> countries. Nothing is impossible with God. The goal of twinning
> is to help foster that. (Interview #3)

As a community, Our Lady generally is thought to benefit more than St.
Robert. At the same time, committee members clearly classify their individual involvement as enriching and rewarding. They can and do articu-
late the personal rewards they derive from twinning and speculate about
how others might be benefiting as well.

> I think [the goals are], number one, to help a Third World
> country. . . . I think it's allowing the Americans to get involved,
> on a much smaller basis. You don't have to be in government to
> see this, to help a little bit. I gotta think at times it's more ben-
> eficial to Americans than it is to Haitians. Maybe we're stopping
> fifty people from a small town from starving. But I can't help
> but believe people's lives here are being touched by it.
> (Interview #15)

> [I see our goals as] helping our fellow brothers, our fellow
> human beings. One parish helping another parish, a parish in
> the States helping a parish there. And I think it's a good way to
> do it because it's not, it's not just any organization, you know,
> that you're helping. You get to know people, not like the
> United Way. How much money have we given to the United
> Way, and did it change your life? The people at St. Roberts are
> so caring and concerned. I probably shouldn't say they all are,
> but those I've met. (Interview #16)

> St. Robert's is a very affluent area. And, I think that twinning
> brings home specific examples to let us know how well off we are
> and how much we need to share what we have. (Interview #21)

As hinted at in the Haiti Committee exchange introduced above, some
people were hesitant about whether, in fact, they really knew the goals of

the twinning—(for example, "Well, isn't it, as I understand it, just to help with poorer nations, with educating and feeding young people?" or "[laughs] Don't quote me but self-sufficiency, given the different focus each project has? There's the mechanics school, the sewing school . . . just to name a couple. Certainly the goals of these things are to teach the people how to live for themselves." And three people said outright that they did not know what the purpose of twinning was. As one woman admitted,

> [The goals are] cloudy to me. I'm not sure. We want to assist in the education of the children and provide food for the children. We're also helping with church. But the goals are not clear to me, short of, we have money and want to help you. Here's the money.

Echoing these sentiments, another woman, who is no longer active in twinning, said,

> I don't know what the goals are, and that's part of my frustration. I challenged them—what are the goals? What are we trying to accomplish? No one was able to answer me. That contributed to my lack of participation. (Interview #9)

And finally, "I'm really not sure. Ask Cassie. Maybe to make an improvement in their lives?" Surprisingly, two of the three respondents who were unable to identify the goals or purpose of the twinning are among the most active participants, regularly attending Haiti Committee meetings. Why they should be unclear about the twinning's goals is not obvious, but I suspect it has to do with their active participation in the committee meetings. As the excerpts illustrate, the meetings tend to focus on managing projects already under way, often taking a micro-oriented approach. And despite the agenda, exchanges at the meetings can steer off-course, become muddled, and fall prey to competing ideas about what the goals of twinning are. Perhaps their deep involvement in twinning—and for one, the "run-ins" she sometimes has with Cassie— has enabled these participants to make a more nuanced assessment of twinning. They have directly experienced the frustrations and challenges of running the program, and they know first-hand that the issues involved are not simple.

As the above meeting descriptions and narratives suggest, the Haiti Committee is a relatively loosely knit collective, bound together by an interest in Haiti but coming to the table from a variety of positions and different understandings of twinning's purpose and goals. Because these are people who have worked together on Haiti issues for a number of years, meetings are vocal gatherings where people feel comfortable inserting their opinions. However, people feel equally comfortable ignoring suggestions and conversations that do not fit with the overall "goals" of the meeting. Cassie, until recently the only chair of the Haiti Committee since St. Robert joined the twinning program, has wielded enormous influence over the program, deciding the direction of the twinning, recruiting new committee members, spearheading fundraising, calling and facilitating meetings, maintaining correspondence, and performing many other functions. Her leadership has been a source of inspiration for some and a cause of concern for others. Without question, she has been central to St. Robert's dedication to twinning.

■ Introducing the Committee Members

A "core" group makes up the heart of St. Robert's Haiti Committee. These are folks who regularly attend the committee meetings, stay abreast of goings-on via the St. Robert email list, and offer their opinions on the direction of the twinning. Many also staff the booth at St. Robert's yearly "Know Your Parish" weekend events, attend the occasional events organized by Doug and the Haiti Outreach Project, collect and organize items for shipment to Haiti, and otherwise act as the faces of St. Robert's twinning program. Who are they? What motivates them? What do they get out of twinning? This section explores these questions by looking at some especially active members of the Haiti Committee.

Who Participates?

Most (though not all) of those on St. Robert's Haiti Committee are professionals (working and retired), most are college graduates, and several have completed postgraduate training (for example, law, medicine, business). Some are younger and some older, but participants tend to be in their forties and fifties and to be financially secure. Most are married but participate individually, although three couples were among the more active members during my time observing the committee (2001–2004). Eight people mentioned having some schooling in French (most a year or two of high school French), and one person had a bachelor's degree in French. Only a few had studied Haitian Creole, the primary language of most Haitians,[4] and the Creole classes provide only a very basic introduction to the language (for example, greetings, prayers, songs). Many folks identified language barriers as a real issue, because only Cassie and Dennis are able to read, write, and speak French adequately to communicate with the priests in Haiti,[5] and no one is proficient in Creole. Similarly, the priests in Haiti have limited proficiency in English.

> It's difficult because we can't communicate with the Haitians. No one speaks French and Creole well enough to "sit in the mud" and talk about life. Communication is a barrier. I can use my hands to get what I want . . . but that doesn't help me know where they're coming from, what they need. That's hard. (Interview #4)

For the most part, those on the Haiti Committee are lifelong Catholics; one also identifies as a "born again" Christian, whereas another is quite disenchanted with the church. But eighteen are "cradle" Catholics who, by and large, are comfortable with their faith and the direction of the Catholic Church, though many expressed their dismay about the pedophilia scandal involving priests, which has rocked the Church especially hard since the late 1990s and early 2000s. Generally seeing the changes accompanying Vatican II as positive (for example, the change from Latin-spoken masses to local languages and the increasing importance of laity), Haiti Committee members might be considered "liberal" according to some definitions. Yet few subscribe to publications such as the *National Catholic Reporter,* and they do not necessarily describe themselves as "social justice" advocates. A few indicated that their participation on the Haiti Committee responded to a Catholic call to be sensitive to the needs of the poor, what some call a "preferential option for the poor"—sentiments similar to those expressed in the NCCB documents introduced earlier. But no committee members explicitly linked participation in twinning with support for liberation ideology, perhaps owing to a broader association of liberation ideology with "communism" or perhaps simply because they are not familiar with its tenets. When asked about his Catholic faith, one man said,

> Well, I guess I'm a believer in the doctrine. I have many friends, some of whom are Christian Reformed, some who are bible-based, some non-denominational. We all see the world in slightly different ways. I believe, you know, "faith without works is dead." We need to do as it says in Matthew: feed the hungry, clothe the naked, reach out to our fellow neighbor. We are to be Good Samaritans. It's only natural to me [to be involved in twinning]—as a product of the Catholic Church, which is, you know, the original church through Jesus Christ, Peter, and Paul. (Interview #12)

This man was one of six out of twenty-one interviewees who mentioned Jesus Christ during the course of the interviews; the other five, however, were not specifically linking ideas about Jesus to the practice of twinning. For example, one woman talked about the "Jesus loves me, this I know" approach to Catholicism as the "dumbing down" of the church. Another mentioned the way the name *Jesus Christ* bombards her in Haiti, on buses and signs. And a third mentioned Jesus Christ as his "hero" and then went on to comment on his reason for participating in twinning in this way:

> I guess the satisfaction that our monies are going to be lumped with other monies to do good, to help those who don't have. I can't do enough to take care of one person or patient. But together, the church can do a lot. . . . I think it's fulfilling the reason to be a church community. To give back, to help others. (Interview #11)

Yet an explicit emphasis on religious motivation for participating in twinning was actually missing from most members' discussions about how and why they personally became involved in twinning and what they "get out of it" now. Instead, most interviewees talked about their role in twinning in broader terms, tying their participation to ideas about "helping" or bettering others' lives. And although such notions probably stem from or relate to teachings of the church—such as "faith without works is dead"—interviewees tended not to make those links explicit. One man, for example, emphasized the personal relationships he forges through twinning:

> Well, regardless of the country we're twinning with, the fact that it does put you into a personal, face-to-face relationship with people with dire needs around the world is very meaningful. And when you put in a lot of volunteer time, it is amazing how much you can actually affect their standard of living, their hopes for the future. (Interview #20)

A woman framed her participation in terms of helping those who, despite limitations of age and economic standing, were appreciative of her efforts:

> What better thing can you do than to have an opportunity to help someone who needs so much help? I can't see any other reason for living. . . . Every time we visited a classroom, children would say, "Don't stop feeding us" [referring to the school lunch program]. One child gave a speech, "Thank you for coming to visit us. You've left your home and family to come and visit us." For a child to say that, it's just incomprehendable [sic]. They were so excited because we were there visiting them. (Interview #16)

Enthusiasm and gratitude were, for this woman and many others, important motivators spurring on continued fundraising and involvement in twinning. That the thanks came from children is noteworthy as well.

In the United States, it is believed that children are innocent and should be shielded from hardship and violence (Jenkins 1998). St. Robert's twinning program reflects this idea by prioritizing the needs of children. Not only are the largest expenditures directed toward Our Lady's children (for example, food project, child sponsorship), but children also figure prominently in fundraising materials, stories published in the church bulletin, and the promotional video St. Robert produced. Moreover, when the needs of adults and children are seen to conflict, children's needs are prioritized. For example, when funds ran short (as is discussed in the following chapter) in the school lunch project, children in Haiti were fed less often than St. Robert's Haiti Committee intended. Moreover, when meals were served, some teachers and parents were eating along with the children. Because their goal was to feed children, "not people off the streets," St. Robert quickly acted to limit adults' access to the project by instructing Our Lady's priest to feed children first. It is not surprising, then, that when talking about motivations for twinning participation, or describing meaningful experiences in Haiti, many people mention children. For example, emphasizing both her obligation to share and the importance of educating children, one woman commented,

> I believe we ought to share. St. Robert shares, at the grassroots level. Many organizations are sent money for charity, and ten cents of every dollar gets to where you want it to. In Haiti, that money is effectively used, and it changes people's lives. When we feed 1400 kids a day, that encourages their parents—who don't necessarily value education—to send their kids to school. Maybe they're sending them for the wrong reason (to get the meal), but the kids are getting an education. They probably wouldn't otherwise. In a country where ten percent of the population is literate, education is an enormous need. (Interview #10)

Some members also talk about the meaning they find in the cultural dimensions of twinning:

> I've enjoyed the cultural part of it, the Catholic part of it, the French part of it. Haiti is infinitely fascinating. And the needs there are such that you can't walk away from it. (Interview #1)

I was drawn [to Haiti because] I have such an appreciation and love of other cultures. I was very drawn to . . . the country. (Interview #3)

As Abu-Lughod (1991; 1993) has noted, however, the idea of "culture" has been central to the ways in which people "other" one another. That is, by thinking about differences in terms of culture—packaged generalizations that minimize *internal* differences (whether of class, ethnicity, gender, age, ability, or sexual orientation) while emphasizing differences *between* groups—people are able to imagine themselves as being very different from others. Certainly this is true of twinning, where the idea that Haitians are very different from Americans is central to how twinning is imagined, as well as to how it plays out.

Thinking About Haitians

As a busy, affluent parish in suburban Michigan, St. Robert in many ways captures an ethos dominant in white, middle-class America: the importance of "success" attained through hard work and education and evidenced through the accumulation and display of material objects. Well-educated and successful, many members of St. Robert's Haiti Committee contrast themselves, their lives, and their communities, with those of Haitians, whose defining characteristic for them is poverty. When committee members talk about Haitians, they are referring to the peasantry, to farmers, to marketers. The term *Haitian* is used generally to refer to Haiti's poor and marginalized, even though Haiti has a diverse population that spans the spectrum from rich to poor. Such differences are largely ignored, and committee members tend to speak in broad terms about who Haitians are, what they are like, and what they do by collapsing differences and instead calling forth the imagined traits of Haiti's poorest. In some ways, this is unavoidable. As Comaroff and Comaroff (1997:406) put it, "all representations of social life must limit its infinite variety and fix its flux; . . . all depend in some measure . . . on 'working' essentialisms, on 'as if' constructions." What is important to consider, the Comaroffs note, is "what degree and effect" and "whose interests served and whose subverted" in employing such essentialisms (1997:406).

In this case, the premise of St. Robert's twinning program is that Our Lady in Verrettes is a parish with significant material needs, reflecting the poverty of its parishioners. St. Robert focuses on providing resources (education, access to credit, food) to meet those needs, while also trying to equip Haitians with tools to one day meet those needs on their own. The orientation of the twinning, in other words, might be understood by scholars like Escobar, Rist, and others as centered on correcting "deficiencies" present in Haiti and/or Haitians. At the same time, however, there is an explicit focus on finding and appreciating the "mutual gifts" that each parish has to offer the other. That is, on the one hand, committee members are encouraged to address the problems plaguing their twin; on the other, they are implored to look for and appreciate their twin's unique gifts. It is not surprising, then, that Haiti Committee members often present contradictory opinions about Haiti (both as a group and within individual narratives) or that many people seemed almost surprised by the "positive" qualities or experiences they discovered while traveling there.

The comparisons that committee members draw between themselves and Haitians are, in some instances, romanticizations of what is imagined to be lacking in the lives of St. Robert's parishioners: time for family, an emphasis on spirituality, freedom from materialism. At other times, Haitians are held up as examples of what is best avoided: "welfare" dependency, laziness, illiteracy. Whether framed as examples to emulate or to repudiate, Haitians often are thought to be very different from Americans.

One word that appears throughout the narratives describing Haitians is *dignified*. In a context where poverty, hunger, and disenfranchisement are rampant, Haitians often are perceived to be overcoming or escaping what might be expected to afflict them: hopelessness, despair, and self-pity. Rather than acting like or presenting themselves as "second-class citizens," Haitians are seen to be dignified despite (and yet, because of) their poverty. "They're very clean, bathed, they stand-up tall, their clothes are cleaned, there's lots of formality in the way they greet each other. That shows dignity" (Interview #1). Coming from an environment where a "good" appearance is so central to affirming a person's worth, Haiti Committee members see the care with which

Haitians present themselves as somehow indicative of their value as human beings, as well as a sort of "pulling themselves up from the mud" spirit that perhaps is missing among America's poor. Haitians are seen to be overcoming barriers when they show up for mass so "well-dressed" (Interview #6). Said one woman,

> They are clean. Well, their feet are all dirty because they have no shoes and are walking around the streets. But in church, they are all clean and dressed nicely. Not expensively, but nicely. The clothes they wore were pressed. We don't even do that here! And to do that, they have to have a fire for the iron. That blew me away. We saw women bathing and doing laundry in the river. They take it down to the river, in baskets on their heads. Then, 100 yards up or down stream, there would be others nude bathing [laughs]. (Interview #7)

The idea that Haitians, despite facing what Haiti Committee members consider almost insurmountable adversity, continue to affirm their own self-worth via concern for appearance is inspiring and surprising to some. And it is seen as a commendable quality that Haitians possess.

Haitians are also admired for what is perceived to be a focus on family. In the United States, building a successful career is often thought to be achieved at the expense of building a close-knit family. Haitians are viewed as not "so stressed over work, work isn't their first priority. . . . I wish in the U.S. people had more time for family and friends, and had that as a priority, rather than work or 'getting ahead'" (Interview #2).[6]

This idea of family, and even of "family values" as one interviewee stated, is important to twinning participants:

> I think that we in America, as Americans, from the perspective of an American, we miss a lot. Life goes by so fast, things just happen. When we go to bed, we think, "What happened?" The kids have grown up so fast. Your wife has been worrying about the 401Ks, about the stock market, and so on and so on. Haiti is a Third World country, but if we can separate that "Third World poverty" concept from just the simplicity of living in a

Third World culture. What I mean by that is, the family structure, the unity that's involved, the simplicity of faith that's
involved. (Interview #5)

What is seen as the superior capability of Haitians to make time for
family, to "focus on what's important" is linked also to the lack of
"clutter" in their lives, highlighting the contrast between the U.S. com-
pulsion to consume and accumulate and the comparatively Spartan existence of Haitians. Their lack of materialism is heralded as a pattern to
model.

When you have fewer material things, it's always a good
example to us, who have so much and just want more.
(Interview #1)

Here, [life] is money-driven. There, their joy is in spite of not
having money. It's 'simpler living' with less stuff. (Interview #2)

Like Haiti, I would like the U.S. to be less consumer-oriented, to
be humble, and happy—even though all of our needs and
wants might not be met. (Interview #8)

In drawing parallels between the simplicity of life and the sort of
"freedom from stuff" that exist in Haiti, committee members are making
powerful critiques about what they see as the failings of American culture. The "culture" that committee members are critiquing must be
understood as that of the financially secure, white, suburban middle
class. While perhaps paying lip service to the importance of family, "successful" Americans (some committee members feel) lose sight of what is
really important in life. Success becomes, in a sense, an iron cage that
limits people's ability to live fully, making them unaware of the superfi-
ciality of their daily concerns vis-à-vis the reality of poverty in the lives
of Haitians. Twinning is thought to unlock that cage.

We're spoiled. Until you visit a place like Haiti, you don't have
a clue about people's struggles, the different ways of looking at
and living life. . . . [I'd like Americans] to be truly appreciative

for what we have. . . . Many people don't appreciate what they have, and people can do without a lot of what they do have. (Interview #3)

For many committee members, then, involvement in Haiti twinning allows them to see alternative realities, and it provides a platform for critiquing the forces at work in their own daily lives. By learning about and interacting with "others," committee members are able to question assumptions formerly taken for granted about what constitutes success, happiness, and desirability in suburban, white, middle-class Ada. The "others" in this case are not poor Americans, however. Committee members do not talk about their privilege with reference to the poor and marginalized in the United States, although they do acknowledge the relative "gifts" that their financially prosperous parish possesses. Recognition of their relative wealth, however, is linked to parishioners' professional successes. That is, St. Robert and its parishioners are affluent compared to others in the area because parishioners hold good jobs, which they have attained through hard work and education. This parallels a finding by Chris McCollum (2002:114), who, in analyzing the life histories of middle-class Americans, found that they portrayed "their professional development as an active process of cultivating and expressing inner aims and abilities." My interview protocol did not specifically probe this facet of committee members' lives, but in general discussions I got the sense that St. Robert's committee members attribute their affluence and professional success to personal initiative and ambition. In other words, they attribute their relative privilege to merit—they have earned their positions by working hard and playing by the rules.

From their very specific class and race positions, some committee members tended to generalize their view of the world as in many ways typical of the American experience, writ large. For example,

I think one of the big problems in the U.S. is that people think their self-value is based on how much they have, how much money they make, how much they own. They'd rather have a $400,000 house, with both mom and dad working and the kids running wild. In Haiti, there's more value on the family and less on the dollar. (Interview #16)

Analysis of their positions of privilege vis-à-vis other Americans is infrequent in committee meetings and in the interviews. But committee members clearly recognize their privilege vis-à-vis Haitians. Yet while Haiti Committee members do think of poverty as dire or problematic for Haitians, there is at the same time a notion that poverty is somehow freeing and that it allows for an unfettered vision of what is important in life:

What really struck me was how happy they are. They don't know [that they're living in poverty]—they have nothing to compare it to. (Interview #7)

[They have] more of a joy for life, especially the religious aspects. The gusto they put into mass, that would be wonderful [for the U.S.]. People in the U.S., they take communion, but anything they take in from the homily is lost as they try to get out of the parking lot in front of someone else. Haitians have a fundamental pride, even though they were people who had very little monetarily. The way they'd get cleaned up to go to mass, to go out. Their personal dignity is phenomenal. (Interview #6)

There are parallels in the academic literature to this kind of thinking. For example, Sandra Harding (1986) and Emily Martin (2001) both discuss the ways in which the "standpoint of the oppressed" (Martin 2001:190) can be more complete, more comprehensive than that of the privileged. Because the poor and powerless are at the bottom of the social hierarchy, they experience pain and humiliation, and in investigating the sources of that suffering, the oppressed come to recognize the social structures working against them. By contrast, the privileged find little conflict between the dominant ideology and their experiences and so have little impetus to question current social orders. Moreover, because the poor and powerless inhabit two "worlds"— as members of their own communities and as servants and subjects in the world of the powerful—they necessarily understand how both worlds operate. In order to survive, they need to know the rules governing life in each milieu. By contrast, the powerful rarely venture into the world of the powerless, so they have no compelling reason to understand the rules governing life there.

This analysis may apply to some committee members, who on the one hand recognize their privilege vis-à-vis Haitians but on the other hand rarely acknowledge it with reference to their position in the U.S. socioeconomic hierarchy. Moreover, this recognition can be coupled with a romanticized view of what it means to be poor—that it is liberating rather than constraining, hopeful rather than cynical, spiritually rich rather than materially deprived.

The romanticization of poverty is not uniform among committee members, however. Indeed, when asked in what ways they would like the United States to be more like Haiti, one woman bluntly answered, "None" (Interview #4). Said another,

> Not very many, actually. Many people could be more appreciative of what they have. The people in Haiti appreciate what they have. But when they're infested with worms, unable to be taken care of medically, when one in how many kids is dying of malnutrition, there's no need to emulate that. (Interview #10)

In total, six of the twenty-one interviewees said there really was not anything about Haiti that the United States should emulate.

Indeed, even among those who felt that Haitians offered good examples of how to live better and simpler lives, there was at the same time a sense that Haitians themselves were in other ways lacking. One woman, for example, viewed Haitians as naïve and unable to cope with the different material realities in Haiti and the United States. Responding to the question of whether travel to the United States by Haitians was an important feature of twinning, she replied,

> No, it's a very bad idea. You give them hope for something they can never attain in Haiti. There, there's no hardwood floors, plaster walls, padded furniture. Bringing them here gives them hope for something they could never achieve in their own

country. It's like a glimpse of heaven. It's cruel. Plus, it gives
them an impression they can ask for whatever they want.

From her perspective, Haitians should not be "teased" with hope for a
U.S. standard of living. Comparing Americans to Haitians, another said,

I find Americans in general to be honest and forthright. It might
make it sound like Haitians are dishonest. But in the U.S., we
have institutional transparency. If we ask certain questions, we'll
get truthful answers versus what someone thinks we want to
hear. In the U.S., there's personal accountability in that people
strive to attain their goals. There isn't the sense that we'll
depend on the government to provide for us. (Interview #6)

These assertions are certainly debatable, but across the narratives, the
idea that Haitians are somehow less ambitious, lazier, or more dependent
or dishonest than Americans was commonly expressed. I will have more
to say about this in Chapter Six, inasmuch as these stereotypes of
"underdeveloped" populations exemplify development thinking more
broadly. Here, it is important to note the dual "othering" that often
characterizes relations between St. Robert and Our Lady, which rest on
this idea that Haitians are very different from Americans. These imagined differences allow twinning participants both to see in Haitians certain ideals that seem to be lacking in their own lives and also to affirm
certain of their own characteristics as superior. Moreover, this attrac-
tion–repulsion toward Haitians is often contradictory in nature. For
example, many committee members romanticize the lack of materialism
and perceived refusal to value work over family in Haiti. At the same
time, however, Haitians are criticized for "lack of entrepreneurial spirit"
(Interview #6) or because they "don't have the same initiative"
(Interview #4) as Americans.

While committee members focus on Haitians as "others," they
simultaneously focus on their shared identity as Catholics. Despite differences in language, skin color, social location, and culture, there is a
sense among committee members that everyone is also "the same" in
their Catholicism. This shared identity creates "social bridges," allowing

participants to transcend their differences, to a degree, through perceived similarities in belief, religious doctrine, and religious practice. Indeed, a complex mixture of "othering" and what I call "saming"—obfuscating obvious differences in the search for commonality—characterizes committee members' views of Haitians. And this is most evident in the similarities that U.S. twinning participants see between U.S. and Haitian religious orientation. When asked about the differences between U.S. and Haitian Catholics, I was told that Catholics are Catholics wherever they are in the world; a Catholic can walk into mass anywhere and have an immediate understanding of what is going on. Commenting on the power of Catholicism, one man said,

> Universality, that's one of the neat things about being Catholic. . . . What we're singing, saying, and praying is the same in Verrettes, here in the U.S., in New Zealand. It's the universality, we're all one family. (Interview #5)

But it is through this imagined shared identity that the "othering" occurs, as well. By locating themselves within the Catholic Church, committee members often feel they compare unfavorably to Haitian parishioners. As suggested above, many believe that Haitians are more spiritual than Americans, closer to God because of their poverty, and less distracted by materialism.

> Haitians are more respectful about mass. They wouldn't ever think to go to mass in jeans. They wear the best they have. Here, people go to church because they "have to go." It seems like there's more spirituality there than with people here, at least that's the impression I got. I didn't know what they were saying [during mass]. Maybe it's because they lacked hope. Like, "If God doesn't help us who will?" Here, it's more about obligation, "I have to go to church." (Interview #4)

This notion of a special, perhaps more authentic, spirituality in Haiti is reinforced in St. Robert's church documents, such as the weekly parish bulletin, which sometimes features the writings of committee members. One column, written by a St. Robert parishioner who had recently returned from Haiti, read,

> Many of the people I met wear their faith "on their sleeve," so to speak. They actively seek out the parish priests or each other on a daily basis, and openly welcome and display the presence of God as they proceed through their day. Earlier in my life, I read somewhere that faith is believing when all good sense tells you not to; I reflected upon this many times during the trip. Given the living conditions, economy, and political instability in Haiti, good sense alone might tell you that God could not be present. However, the people we met, while not having an abundance of "things," have boundless faith and believe God is present in their everyday lives, and this sustains them. (April 18, 1999)

Constructing Haitians as virtuous also makes them "worthy" of help. Another column in the parish bulletin, reflecting on a mass where "roosters strutted through the yard and a pig snorted" during the service, says, "while the mass progressed, it occurred to me how simple and beautiful our faith really is. Unfortunately, in America we tend to clutter it up with wasteful trappings."

To an individual from a wealthy suburban U.S. parish, where SUVs jockey for parking spaces in a ferocious race to make it into church as close to the start time of mass as possible, and where the busy professionals at mass sport manicures, facials, expensive haircuts, and the latest fashions, the material conditions in Haiti are stunning. And, it is traveling to Haiti—what one parishioner called the Haiti experience—that allows St. Robert's parishioners to juxtapose their daily reality with that of their Haitian "brothers and sisters." What they find often causes them to question the assumptions they have about conspicuous consumption and materialism. Reflecting on her trip to Haiti, one woman wrote in the parish bulletin,

> As we watched the baptism service, I whispered to Doug that they probably won't use water because it's so scarce. To our surprise a porcelain washtub with water and a plastic cup were

brought up to the altar. As I saw this I wept. But my tears were
not for them. They were for us—because we think we have to
have a marble Christening bowl. (July 18, 1996)

In reality, then, despite some focus on "sameness" through Catholicism,
Haiti Committee members tend to invest more heavily in notions of difference.

To return to the idea that Haitians are, at once, models to emulate
and repudiate, it must be noted that some of the "negative" characteristics attributed to Haitians echo dominant racist U.S. stereotypes of
African Americans. In fact, some committee members made
unprompted explicit comparisons between African Americans and
Haitians, as described below.[7] Perhaps not surprisingly, most members
of the Haiti Committee were raised in racially and culturally homogeneous environments and thus had very little interaction with people of
color when they were growing up. Responding to a question about the
types of interactions he had with other "races" or cultures while growing
up, one man said, "Very limited. We lived in a white Catholic community. And, the most ethnic person I ever saw was an Italian, who was also
Catholic" (Interview #12). Said another, "Almost none. Catholic schools
were, uh, predominantly white. As matter of fact, I didn't go to school
with any black kids until high school. And they weren't even in my
grade. One was ahead of me, and a couple were behind" (Interview #13).
In sum, many of those most active on the Haiti Committee had few
direct or personal experiences with racial "others" during their formative
early years.

This is hardly surprising, given that the United States itself continues to be a highly racially stratified society. This "racial social geography"—the constitution and mapping of environments in racial and
ethnic terms (Frankenberg 1993:44)—is likewise a feature in Grand
Rapids, Michigan. Suburban communities, including Ada, continue to be
predominantly white,[8] a fact mirrored at St. Robert. And yet, a larger
public discourse on the importance of racial diversity, inclusion, and tol-
erance—particularly among white, middle-class Americans—often
clashes with the experiences and understandings of committee members
and with their own (latent) racisms.

I can say that the . . . Haitians are very respectful and dignified. Blacks in America are very snotty. And I have some black friends. But Haitians are more timid than American black people. (Interview #4)

My first visit and the second part of my second [were] frightening, never having been involved in that level of poverty and never having been around black people. (Interview #15)

I own several pieces of rental property, and I rent to a lot of African Americans, probably 30–40 percent are African Americans. With very few exceptions, the biggest thing I see in regards to them is their lack of education. You don't see any real need for an education. An education isn't a priority for them. I think it's just been passed down from father to son, mother to daughter for a hundred, two hundred years. Education is not a big thing in their families. That's not necessarily true of all African Americans, but with the people I deal with it is. They're poorly educated, and they have low-paying jobs as a result. A lot of them want more but aren't willing to do what it takes to get more. They feel it's the government's job to give handouts. Sometimes we do too much of that, other times not enough.

Significantly, this emphasis on education characterizes St. Robert's overall mission in Haiti. Emphasizing schooling, literacy, and development, nearly every interviewee mentioned the importance of educating Haiti's citizenry, as I have said elsewhere. But here I want to suggest that the twinning program provides some committee members a relatively "safe" platform through which to "work out" issues of identity, race, and racism. As Frankenberg (1993:44) discusses in her exploration of racial identity and racism among white women in the United States, daily environments help shape racism and ground it materially in particular social, historical, and political environments. For twinning participants who travel to Haiti—again, a pivotal and life-altering experience for many—the racial geography becomes unanchored and detached. Haiti Committee members become "defamiliarized" from their usual surroundings (Frankenberg 1993:44). Their privilege vis-à-vis Haitians —in terms of race, class, and nationality—becomes visible through twinning. They become aware of their own ability to access clean drinking water with ease, to enjoy convenient transportation, to interact with people who are like themselves, to travel freely across borders, and to choose a career.

This type of "othering" complicates ideas raised by Escobar (1995:30), who suggests that development has proceeded by "medicalization of the political gaze" whereby popular classes are perceived not in racial terms but as "diseased, underfed, uneducated, and physiologically weak masses." This is only partially the case among St. Robert's twinning committee, where Haitians *are* racialized *and* constructed as physiologically compromised, but are also held up as models to emulate, in many regards.

How can this dichotomous understanding of Haitians be explained? Typically, the construction of "difference" is theorized to include stigmatization and hierarchizing. As Abu-Lughod (1993:13) suggests, "A difference between self and other will always be hierarchical because the self is sensed as primary, self-formed, active, and complex, if not positive. At the very least, the self is always the interpreter and the other the interpreted." And yet, members of the Haiti Committee confound this stylized understanding, because they in some ways hierarchize Haitians above themselves, in terms of "goodness," religiosity, and commitment to family.

I think parallels might be drawn between the "categories of analysis" that twinning participants employ to understand who they are in relation to Haitians and Chandra Talpade Mohanty's (1997:81) work on Western feminism, which takes "women" as a "category of analysis." Mohanty explains this as "the crucial assumption that all of us are the same gender, across classes and cultures, [that we] are somehow socially constituted as a homogeneous group." This *a priori* definition of sameness is present in twinning, as well—where the commonality is Catholicism. I will not go so far as to assert that St. Robert's parishioners imagine themselves and Haitians to be a "homogeneous group" of Catholics; clearly, they do not. But this shared identity provides the entry point for imaging Haitians as "other" and for ultimately construing

Haitians themselves as a homogeneous group. This encourages a reading of Haitians whereby they all "have similar problems and needs . . . similar interests and goals" (Mohanty 1997:83). And it disallows, to a large extent, differences among Haitians in identity, wealth, power, and the like.

Thinking About Haiti

To each of the interviewees, all but two of whom have traveled to Haiti, I posed the question "When you think of Haiti, what are the first five words that come to mind?" Interviewees tended to quickly list the first few words that popped into their heads, although some gave more elaborate answers using phrases or full sentences. To gauge how people generally thought about Haiti, and whether their perceptions mirrored the problematic negative constructions dominant in U.S. culture (for example, see Farmer 1992), I sorted answers into what might be considered positive, negative, and neutral categories.

Somewhat surprisingly, the responses did not reflect broader stereotypes often cited as typically held by Americans—for example, AIDS, Vodou, boat people. Of the eight-seven answers I collected, thirty-three would generally be considered positive, forty-six negative, and eight neutral. Thus, although slightly more than half of the answers might be classified as representing a negative image of Haiti, overall, the interviewees gave a fairly diverse range of answers. Perhaps this reflects the contradictions inherent in identifying a people and place as both deficient and inspiring at the same time—that is, as illiterate, diseased, and hungry on the one hand, and family-oriented, spiritual, and non-materialistic on the other.

Given the focus of St. Robert's twinning on mitigating poverty at Our Lady, as well as the strong reactions that committee members have to the material reality in Haiti, it is not surprising that poverty was the response cited most often, by thirteen of twenty-one interviewees. In fact, it is remarkable that more people did not mention it. Moreover, given current rates of AIDS in Haiti—HIV prevalence is around 5.6 percent (UNDP 2004)—as well as the stigmatizing of Haitians as a "risk group" for AIDS in the 1980s United States (see Farmer 1992), it is also noteworthy that only one person responded to this question by mentioning AIDS. And this person was not simply reciting the U.S. stereotype; he had been personally affected by AIDS, having recently lost a dear Haitian friend to the disease.

Overall, the negative conceptualizations of Haiti focused more on its suppression or oppression (for example, government failure, injustice, isolation) than on sensational stereotypes, as can be seen in Table 4.2. At the same time, there was again a clear pattern in perceptions of Haiti as deficient, as lacking, for example, adequate food, environmental quality, and education—all problems that St. Robert sees itself as capable of addressing, if not on a national scale, then at least locally. Responding to a question about his hopes for Haiti, one man said,

> [My wish is] that the people will develop their own visions for their country and have the ability to implement them. [TH: Do you think this will ever happen?] Hmm, probably not. At the national level, probably not. But I can work at the local level." (Interview #2)

But in response to other questions (for example, "How did you get involved in twinning?") Haitians were criticized for other perceived problems. For example, four people declared "sharing" among Haitians to be problematic. Ironically, Haitians were critiqued from both angles: for sharing too much with others and for not sharing enough. For example, one woman, in talking about the "ingrained attitudes" that Haitians need to "overcome," said,

> Well, I think there's a kind of a bullying—I can't think of the word—when someone has something, and they try to share it (a nice word for it). But, it's really not so nice; they're extorting things. Whenever we have someone we want to give things to, they'll be asked by everyone they know for a piece of it. You'll be told it's the "Haitian way," but it's discouraging. (Interview #1)

Indeed, Haitian peasants—like poor people in many places—are well known for sharing as a way to mitigate risk and help level disparities in wealth (for example, see Smith 2001). Sharing is a strategy that allows

TABLE 4.2   FIVE WORDS THAT COME TO MIND REGARDING HAITI

Positive (33)	Negative (46)	Neutral (8)
Beauty (3)	Poverty/Poor (13)	Hot (3)
Children (3)	Hopeless (3)	Different world
Dignity (3)	Heavily populated (2)	Education
Friends (3)	Hungry (2)	Life-altering
Joy (3)	Sad (2)	Political
Happy (2)	AIDS	Trade school
Love (2)	Corrupt government	
Acceptance	Deplorable	
Art	Depressed	
Awareness	Exploited	
Determination	How they can produce enough	
Energy, energetic	food just to feed the population	
Family	Incomprehendible [sic]	
Friendly	Injustice	
Grateful	Isolation	
Incredible	Lack of foliage	
Loveable	Lack of life quality	
Opportunity	Lack of quality	
Patience	Need	
Pride	Need a dramatic shift in focus	
Smiles	Neglected	
	Oppression	
	People that want more but probably	
	will never have more because of the	
	political situation	
	Primitive	
	Smells	
	Starvation	
	Struggling	
	Undeveloped	
	Uneducated	
	Unrest	

families or groups to minimize their economic vulnerability. "If I share with you today, then when I need help, I can call on you tomorrow." But sharing is "discouraging" to those in Michigan, who intend to help certain individuals, only to find their intended beneficiary has willingly (or unwillingly) shared his or her newfound resources across a social network. In fact, sharing is not only discouraging, it is also discouraged, as in the case of the school food project mentioned earlier. Those outside the targeted population for food aid were to be cut off from the school lunch project. "We are trying to actively dissuade parishioners from sharing meals," as one man put it (Interview #6).

At the same time, however, Haitians are perceived to be stingy for not sharing enough: "I think that mentality of not sharing, that mentality of taking what they can get for themselves and not sharing it around to help our brothers and sisters [is a problem]" (Interview #11). This idea of sharing (or not) did not come out in the free-listing exercise but was mentioned in other sections of the interview.

I think these contradictory ideas might stem from some committee members' unclear sense of who Haitian peasants are and their general unfamiliarity with the coping mechanisms of the poor. As discussed elsewhere in the book, committee members often interact with Haitian twinning participants in moderated and buffered ways. The inability to "sit in the mud" with Haitian participants prevents most St. Robert's twinning participants from gaining a grounded understanding of what might characterize "typical Haitian culture," if such a thing were to exist. Instead, perceptions of sharing, whether it is practiced, and whether it is a problem are based largely on the views of the Haitian priests, Tom, and others in Haiti as they intersect with the committee's ideas about who should benefit from twinning.

In terms of the positive traits imagined, those most frequently cited focused on the qualities of Haiti's people. That is, whereas most of the negative responses were more broadly focused on what's wrong with Haiti—as a country or as a socioeconomic/sociopolitical system—interviewees, when responding positively to the question, tended to describe traits they imagined Haiti's people to possess. Again, reflecting the narratives introduced above, answers included "dignity," "joy," "happy." Haitians, despite limitations of poverty, are thought to evince a certain *joi de vivre* and self-respect that translates into "smiles," "pride," and "lovability." Haitians are thought to be extraordinary examples of how the human spirit persists in spite of—or perhaps because of?—economic and political limitations. The traits that were seen to be more destructive or harmful to Haiti's people—for example, laziness, lack of ingenuity, or evasiveness—and were mentioned elsewhere in interviewees' narratives were missing in responses to this question. This suggests that even though Haitians can be—and often are—conceptualized in negative terms, perhaps these are not foremost in most committee members' minds. Rather, they are evoked as a way to explain why Haiti is so poor and to legitimize the need for St. Robert's intervention, as will be discussed in Chapters Five and Six.

■ Conclusion

St. Robert is a large, active, affluent parish, with an array of programs and projects led by and peopled by its laity. The Haiti program, St. Robert's largest in terms of budget, is guided by a core of committed parishioners who give their time, their talent, and often money to facilitating and maintaining links to Our Lady parish in Verrettes. The committee is a loose collective that includes about twenty-five central members who are important to shaping St. Robert's twinning program. They are charged with implementing St. Robert's vision for its relationship to Our Lady—even when that vision is not always readily apparent to them.

St. Robert's Haiti Committee does not meet often—usually once every 3 or 4 months, when something pressing requires discussion. A "core" of eight to twelve people is likely to attend any given meeting, which means that the overall direction of St. Robert's Haiti program tends to be determined by relatively few people. Larger discussions involving more people are sometimes held via the committee email list, but the list—like the parish bulletin—is more a conduit for disseminating information than a forum for dialogue.

From the beginning of St. Robert's ties to Our Lady, Haiti Committee meetings have been led by Cassie, a strong and sometimes controversial leader who initiated and built the twinning program.

Cassie's vision for twinning has guided both the development of projects in Haiti and the structuring of the Haiti Committee at St. Robert. The result is a rather centralized program and one that, during my time observing the committee (2001–2004), few newcomers joined. But, with Cassie's departure from St. Robert, and her gradual withdrawal from the Haiti Committee, the nature and formation of the committee may change. Some speculate that the twinning program itself may not survive. But with the "passing of the torch" under way, the clear commitment of new co-chair Dennis, and the crucial support of Sr. JoAn to maintaining the twinning, it certainly appears that the program will survive Cassie's exit.

The goals or purpose of St. Robert's Haiti program are not always clear to committee members. Although many members emphasize the importance of supporting education and literacy in Haiti, others highlight broader goals of "helping" Haitians or promoting development. A few members, including two especially active in twinning, said they did not know what the goals of twinning were. Their uncertainty might reflect the contradictions and challenges inherent in forging these types of transnational, cross-cultural relationships.

Committee members tend to conceive of Haitians in simple terms; there is a consistent homogenizing of Haitians, with the poor and marginalized taken to be typical Haitians and others (elites, the middle-class, and immigrants) ignored or vilified, as will be discussed in later chapters. Committee members, then, are disposed to speak in generalizations about Haitians, who they are, and the traits they possess. These generalizations are often constructed in two opposing ways. On the one hand, Haitians are admired for their dignity, their fortitude, and their focus on family. There is a sense that because they have few material possessions, Haitians are somehow able to live more meaningful, joyful lives than Americans. On the other hand, Haitians are also ridiculed for their unworldliness, perceived laziness, and dependency on outsiders. They are criticized for not being industrious enough to escape the poverty that binds them and thus to be so in need of outside help—which, in this case, is delivered predominantly via education.

These twin conceptualizations—Haitians as models both to emulate and to repudiate—reveal a central feature of twinning: It rests on perceived inherent "differences" between Haitians and Americans, despite the "saming" that occurs under the banner of Catholicism. Moreover, twinning is predicated on the need to correct the seeming deficiencies of Haiti and of Haitians, as well as their "otherness." Yet committee members tend not to adopt or verbalize the negative stereotypes of Haitians that predominate in the United States—for example, associations with AIDS, Vodou, and boat people. Instead, as we will see in later chapters, their negative assessments of Haitians tend to reflect dominant development discourses about "underdeveloped populations."

▪ Notes

1. Wuthnow (2004:62) suggests that "the presence of special-purpose groups accounts for the fact that many congregations adopt a portfolio of causes and ministries, rather than devoting their energies fully to one cause or ministry. Contributing in small ways to many programs means being able to respond positively to particular interest groups."

2. Perhaps this is for the same reasons noted by Poppendieck (1999:39–40): "Hunger is probably the most common evocation of poverty and injustice found in either testament. . . . The filled stomach and the shared table dwell close to the heart and hearth of religious imagery, liturgy, and practice" (39). Wuthnow (2004:62) suggests that food programs are so popular among congregations because they are "familiar" projects with long histories and well-publicized levels of need.

3. In all, Cassie identified thirty-one committee members as important to interview for this project. Of these, I interviewed twenty-one. Three people explicitly declined to be interviewed, saying they did not consider themselves active and "didn't really have anything to offer" about the program. Two had moved from the parish. One I was unable to locate. One was dying of cancer, and I did not want to burden him with an interview. The remaining participants implicitly declined to be interviewed by not responding to my requests.

4. Haitian Creole classes have been periodically organized by Doug on behalf of the Haiti Outreach Project. Classes run 6 to 8 weeks, are open to anyone who would like to participate, and are taught by local Haitians whom Doug recruits.

5. Cassie and Dennis are the only two French speakers among the most active committee members. As a parish, St. Robert has a number of French speakers, who are called upon to act as interpreters when priests visit from Haiti.

6. While generalizing about Haitians and work-related stress, these committee members tended not explicitly to link this to lack of job opportunities. With formal sector unemployment at around 70 percent (CIA World Factbook 2005), it's true that the majority of Haitians often do not have "fast track" career paths to forge. Yet to characterize them as somehow stress-free seems problematic. Many Haitians "stress" about insecurity, joblessness, and the daily reality of grinding poverty in their lives (for example, see Bell 2001).

7. Given this, I later added to the interview protocol a question to probe interviewees' explanations for African American poverty, thereby making Haitian and African American comparisons overt. See Appendix.

8. Ada Township's total population is 9882, of whom 9444—or about 96 percent of the population—self-classify as "white" (U.S. Census Bureau 2000).

CHAPTER FIVE

Crafting Development
at St. Robert

Even though parishioners at St. Robert do not explicitly situate their Haiti program within a larger paradigm of globalization and NGO-ization, most on the Haiti Committee are clear that their program intends to promote development in Haiti. This begs the question of what St. Robert's committee members mean by development. How do they define it? How do they attempt to translate these conceptualizations into actual programs and policies? Moreover, in what—if any— ways do they see their program as missionary work?

■ Theorizing Development

At the close of a committee meeting held in March 2004, I did a short free-listing exercise with the seven members present (an eighth had to leave early.) To the two men and five women, I gave a sheet of paper, divided into three columns. I first asked, "When you think about development, about what it means to be developed, what sorts of things come to mind?" I requested that they list their replies, as quickly as they could, in the left column. After a few minutes, I asked them to "rank" their answers in order of importance in the middle column, placing those features they thought most central to development at the top. In the right column, they then commented on why they had ordered their lists as they did.

Of course, the results cannot be generalized to the wider population at St. Robert, or even to the remainder of the committee, but they do point to important themes running both through committee meetings and through the narratives, as discussed below.

As the material in Table 5.1 shows, respondents used diverse terminology in their free-listing of development's features. Only a few features were listed by two or more people: agriculture, food, infrastructure, roads, health care, and business help. Education, not surprisingly, was mentioned by six of the seven members and was ranked as most important by two. But the majority of responses, forty items, were listed only once—that is, by one person.[1]

This might be taken to suggest that development is conceptualized in broad terms, which may or may not be shared among committee members. However, taken together, the narratives, committee meetings, and free-listing exercise indicate that, in fact, development among St. Robert's Haiti Committee does have a fairly rigid framework, and it is within this framework that diverse conceptualizations are debated and considered.

Developing People

As we saw in Chapter Four, twinning rests on dual conceptualizations of Haitians as models to admire and cases to "fix" through outside intervention. Haitians are at once esteemed and ridiculed for their seeming "difference," and nowhere is this clearer than in discussions about development and its purpose in Haiti.

Complementing the free-listing exercise just introduced, I asked all interviewees, "How do you define development? Progress? The 'good life'?" The answers I received ranged from idealistic, such as "encouraging [Haitians] to use their gifts, their intelligence, their generosity, and their talents" to the concrete, "good health, good food, and water." (See Figure 5.1.) But an overriding theme in most of the narratives was this idea of developing people, of equipping Haitians with the skills necessary to become self-sufficient. There's a real sense that St. Robert is providing Haitians with the skills needed to "take care of themselves" (Interview #21). St. Robert's emphasis on education demonstrates this. As one man said, through twinning, you're developing the human spirit. More children are getting an education. Education precedes quality of life. If you can't innovate, open your own business, then you're destined to work for someone else or to be unemployed. You build a workforce by educating it. (Interview #12)

TABLE 5.1 FREE-LISTING EXERCISE ON DEVELOPMENT

Agricultural/Sustainable agriculture (3 respondents)	Hope
Aid/Financial Aid (2 respondents)	Hotels/Resorts (2 respondents)
Assistance	Housing
Basic needs	Implements for work/tools to farm (2 respondents)
Carpentry/Masonry (2 respondents)	Independence
Clothing	Infrastructure (2 respondents)
Communication	Loan programs/Microbusiness help/aid (3 respondents)
Cottage industry	
Credit	Manufacturing
Cultural	Markets (free)
Democracy	Military
Dialogue	Mobility
Economic	Partnerships
Economic stability + base	Political
Education (6 respondents)	Possibilities
Electricity	Prosperity
Employment/Job security (2 respondents)	Restaurants
	Roads (2 respondents)
End of poverty	Schools
Equality	Small business
Farms, agriculture, trees, animals	Stores for people to purchase needed items in
Food (3 respondents)	
Freedom of religion	Transportation
Freedom of speech	Water
Government cooperation	Women
Health care/Clinics/Hospitals (3 respondents)	

Basic Needs Met

Baby shots	Basic needs	Clothing
Food (6)	Good health	Health clinics
Health care (2)	Hospitals	Housing
Medical progress	Necessities of life	Poverty, not so much
Shelter	Water (9)	

Government

Democracy (2)	Basic human rights and freedoms
Government	Government-sponsored, not church
"Voice" and political representation	

Law and Order

Courts	Judicial system	Law and order
Police		

Infrastructure

Electricity (2)	Gas	Infrastructure (3)
Roads (2)	Sanitary	Sanitation
Septic systems	Sewer	

Education

Community things: schools, not only for the children but the adults who have missed it		
Education (9)	French vs. Creole	Schools

Self-Sufficiency

Self-sufficient (2)

FIGURE 5.1 DEFINING DEVELOPMENT, PROGRESS, THE "GOOD LIFE"

Agriculture

Agriculture (2)	Farming (2)	Land productivity

Work

Jobs (3)	Income	Make a living (4)
Occupations	Incentives to motivate people to work	

More Opportunities

Opportunities (4)	Improving people's chances

Outlook

Hope for future	Using gifts, intelligence, generosity
Respect	Dependability

Progress

Improvement	More modern	Progressing
Self-Improvements	Moving about doing their daily business	
Doesn't look like a developed community in Michigan		

Economy

House Construction	Markets (2)	Marketing products
Manufacturing Factories	Monetary systems in order	

Collaborations

Grassroots, hands-on people-oriented action plan
Partnerships, ongoing relationship with goals and understanding

Miscellaneous

Occupied meaningfully	Sustainability
Systems to care for those needing help	

FIGURE 5.1 CONTINUED

Overall, for St. Robert's Haiti program, development tends to focus on "bettering" individuals and the community more than on reforming the larger system that keeps Haitians impoverished—for example, structural debt, political economy, predatory states (for example, see DeWind and Kinley 1998; Dupuy 1989, 1997; Farmer 2004, 1994, 1992). The problems Haitians face can be overcome through education, by giving people the opportunity to "better" themselves (Cruikshank 1999). Considering that very few people had much knowledge of Haiti before the twinning began (for example, TH: What did you know about Haitian history and culture before joining the twinning? Interviewee #11: Nothing. I didn't even know where Haiti was.), it is not surprising that committee members tend not to analyze Haiti's woes within a more "macro" frame. Indeed, to do so might result in a "paralysis of scale" whereby participants take no action because the task before them seems too large, too deeply rooted to affect (Poppendieck 1998).

That said, those active in twinning do face questions about its purpose and about how much "good" can really be accomplished in Haiti.

> I have friends who ask me, "How much good are you doing in Haiti? What kind of impact can you really have?" In the past 25 years, there are probably 2000 churches working in Haiti.... It's like taking a cup of water out of a big lake. Nobody notices. But we're doing good. They're dependent upon us to help them. And we're probably making it so some kids don't die. (Interview #19)

In fact, there are several "refrains" repeated within twinning circles to address this critique. One, which I first heard from Doug, Grand Rapids' Haiti Outreach Program coordinator, tells the story of a young man walking along a beach, throwing stranded starfish back into the ocean. Noting that the beach is covered with starfish for miles on both sides, a skeptic confronts the man: "Don't you see that you can't even begin to save all these dying starfish? What possible difference can what you are doing make?" To which the young man replies, as he stoops and tosses yet another starfish back into the water, "I'm making a difference to this one." Poppendieck (1998:307) refers to this as "partialization": When a problem just seems too large or overwhelming, it is broken into manageable pieces.

There is certainly some sense among those on the committee that Haiti's problems far exceed St. Robert's ability to remedy them. In responding to the question of whether twinning attempts to "develop" Verrettes, one man commented,

> Well, yeah, I think so. They're providing education for kids within the parish. They're sponsoring kids to go on to high school and the university. Unfortunately, it's a small impact on numbers. . . . I think they're doing a good job as far as taking a small part of the population and improving them. Unfortunately, we're dealing with at most a couple hundred people, and only some of those are being helped by the trade school. (Interview #13)

But most committee members, rather than dwelling on problems outside their sphere of influence, focus on saving the starfish within their reach: those at Our Lady. "I'm not there to help the nation, Haiti. I'm here to help Verrettes" (Interview #19).

Rather than tracing Haiti's poverty to its historical position on the "periphery" of the world economic system, to its "pariah" status following independence, or to the debt with which it has been saddled for nearly its entire history, St. Robert's committee members look to address more micro-level features that they are personally able to witness and draw meaning from: hunger, illiteracy, unemployment, and lack of education. It might logically follow that their efforts are concentrated on "developing people" as a necessary first step to developing Haiti.

And yet, these goals sometimes can come across as overly simplistic and sometimes as blatantly paternalistic. There is a persistent assumption that because Haiti's peasantry is largely illiterate and unschooled, they cannot fully undertake—or even envision—their own development. For example, responding to a question about her wishes for Haiti, one woman stated,

Interview #1: That they will develop their own visions for their country and have the ability to implement them.

TH: Do you think this will ever happen?

Interview #1: Hmmm, probably not. At the national level, probably not. But I can work at the local level.

Talking about what it means for a community to be developed, another said,

> Buildings [are important], but not as much as the people themselves having some goals, some direction. . . . I think [twinning] attempts to provide an avenue for people to do their own self-improvements. I sincerely believe the educational aspects alone would be enough to help the people move on. (Interview #11)

There is a sense that once Haiti's poor are equipped with certain "tools"—for example, the ability to think critically, problem-solve, and the like, achieved via education—they will be able to apply their own initiative and do better for themselves. Clearly, this is an idea that reverberates strongly in the consciousness of these white, middle-class developers, who themselves were raised in a milieu where education and hard work—"responsibilization" (Lacey and Ilkan 2006)—were touted as the way to attain the "American dream." As twinning participants often say, "give a man to fish, and he'll eat for the day; teach a man to fish, and he'll eat for life." American twinning participants in this sense are attempting to produce Haitian citizen–subjects willing to be responsible for their own well-being (Cruikshank 1999). Again, such homilies substantially ignore the larger structural features that limit people's opportunities to do this: national debt, concentration of wealth both within Haiti and in the global system, and the like. And yet, it is precisely these more structural features that seemingly must be addressed in order to create sustainable systems of justice and opportunity in Haiti.

The notion of bettering Haitians is not limited to formally educating them, however. Some go further in talking about developing a more sophisticated—more cultivated—peasantry. In explaining her conceptualizations of development, one woman addressed her perceptions about the links between language and opportunity for "advancement":

> I'd like to see better-educated people [in Haiti]. I'd love to see them abandon Creole and go with French. Creole is not an educated language, and without language, they won't be able to seize opportunities, to make informed decisions. (Interview #9)

And another lamented what she saw as a sort of environmental illiteracy:

> If they had a forest, they could be hunters and gatherers. But there is no forest, and there's nothing to gather. They don't seem to have the same respect for their environment. Here, you wouldn't open a candy bar and throw the wrapper on the ground. Well, we do [throw it on the ground]. But there everyone does. They open a can of pop and throw the can on the ground. They have no understanding of how their actions affect the environment. Or maybe they're just not concerned about that, I don't know. (Interview #4)

Quotations such as these, and others presented earlier, offer insight into a larger assumption that Haitians need to be changed—that as they are, Haitians are both deficient and inadequate. To "fix" Haiti requires "fixing" its people. And the first step in fixing Haiti's people is to educate them.

In explaining her ranking of "education" as most important in the free-listing exercise, one woman emphasized that "in order for all else to happen," Haitians must first be educated (Respondent #9). Said another, who also ranked education as most important, "Without education, the people can't make informed decisions about their lives, their jobs, government, etc." (Respondent #3). Some take these ideas even further to suggest that Haitians, in their current state, are simply incapable of leading themselves: "We actually should choose and select their government, help put in power, just as we're doing in Iraq . . . [to promote] Christian values and integrity" (Interview #12). And another said, "I did write to Bill Gates asking if he'd consider buying Haiti and fixing it [laughs]. I didn't get a reply" (Interview #10).

The role of government is actually a central feature in several of the narratives, and it will be discussed in more detail in Chapter Six. But I bring it up here to illustrate the idea that in the view of some participants, Haitians—as they stand now—are in need of reformation. Development can and will proceed only once an appropriate "subjectivity" is produced in Haiti, one whereby Haitians are able to assess their situations, forge their own visions, and act in their own best interests (for example, not be duped into thinking Creole is a real language). Such visions will emerge primarily via outside intervention or, as another man suggested, once appropriate leadership is nurtured through intervention:

> I'm really hoping that one of these kids that we're taking care of—that we're feeding, educating—goes on to be a shining star. Not that worker bees can't be. But I hope [that] at some point, we create leadership down there, so that some of those kids will go on to help lead their country. (Interview #19)

Both the interviews and the free-listing exercise, then, highlight the "need" to develop people, to encourage education. Education, it is believed, will unlock Haitians' potential, enabling them finally to assess their situations and formulate concrete plans for betterment. These are not themes unique to St. Robert's twinning. Rather, they are part of a larger lens through which Haitians are typically viewed by "outsiders" working for development, as we will discuss in more detail in Chapter Six. Moreover, they are also part of a broader history grounded in Enlightenment thinking about the value of education in "civilizing" the masses, a history examined in detail by Jean and John Comaroff (1991, 1997) in the context of southern Africa. In considering the links between Protestant missions and schooling, the Comaroffs (1997:412) suggest that "education, in its modern, secular form—as a privileged means . . . of producing bourgeois selves and national subjects—arose partly in consonance and partly in dissonance but always in dialogue with Protestant instruction." For South Africans, "missions long remained the major source of Western learning for indigenous peoples" (1997:412).

In similar fashion, Catholic-sponsored schools—and, more recently, Protestant-sponsored schools, as well—have provided the bulk of primary education in Haiti,[2] though they have had the effect of at once refashioning Haiti's peasantry in the image of Haitian bourgeoisie, while also denigrating "peasant culture." For example, although many Haitian peasants—like U.S. twinning participants—see education as desirable and necessary for interacting with state institutions, Suzy Castor (1988:12) has noted that "scholarly education and academics have an elitist quality" that has kept the majority of Haitians at the margins of society. Traditionally, one way this elitism was manifested was through exclusively French instruction, even though only 10 percent of the population is fluent in French. In the 1980s, a government-proposed revamping of the educational system to provide the first 4 years of primary schooling in Creole was "fiercely opposed" by the educated classes and some religious orders (Nicholls 1986:229). Education in Haiti, as elsewhere, is seated at the intersection of multiple and contradictory forces that provide opportunities for learning the "culture" and language of the ruling classes, while also serving to further entrench the asymmetry of the status quo. For twinning participants, however, education is seen primarily as a libratory project and a necessary precursor to development.

Such a project echoes Cruikshank's arguments surrounding the "will to empower" poor and powerless welfare recipients in the United States. Drawing on Foucault's concept of "biopower," Cruikshank (1999:38) suggests that "welfare" is a form of governmentality that is "both voluntary and coercive . . . a way of organizing interests . . . a way of organizing power, a way of acting on people's actions rather than procuring their apathy." Because self-governance and discipline depend on "the capacities of citizens to act on their own behalf," citizen-subjects need to be enrolled willingly into their own management. One way this is accomplished is through the production of knowledge; by identifying a series of "problems" that can be addressed, citizen–subjects become imbued with a "set of goals and self understandings" that encourage their "investment in participating voluntarily in programs, projects, and institutions set up to 'help' them" (Cruikshank 1999:41).

The projects that St. Robert sponsors in Haiti—including those focused on "educating" Haitians—might be thought as playing out on a

"territory of action" in Haiti organized fundamentally around ameliora-
tion of poverty (Cruikshank 1999). By transforming the problems of
poverty into a series of possible actions and interventions, twinning
offers Haitians the chance for self-improvement, training, and resources
through which they can become more actively engaged in their own
"development:" If they are motivated, if they are savvy, if they are hard
workers, if they educate themselves, Haitians will have the chance to
better their lives. Following Cruikshank, it seems plausible that twinning—by constituting citizen–subjects in ways that promote certain
kinds of action (for example, attending school, working in the formal
sector)—"wills to empower" poor Haitians in ways that echo and extend
the current global order, including the relations of power structuring the
interactions between U.S. and Haitian parishioners. If "successful," St.
Robert's twinning program would "produce modern, self-disciplined
citizens and states that can be trusted to govern themselves according to
liberal democratic norms" (Abrahamsen 2004:1454).

Grounding Development Locally

A second theme characterizes St. Robert's Haiti Committee members'
understanding of development: the notion that development must be
grounded locally. Despite characterizing Haitians as "backward" and in
need of education before development can proceed, a surprising number
of people also spoke of being sensitive to "local" Haitian conceptualizations of development, which are thought to differ from those of
Americans. That is, although empowerment might be thought to emerge
from education—creating the space and capacity of Haitians to act in
their own self-interest—there is simultaneously a sense that Haitians
themselves also have an understanding of what development should
mean.

In responding to the question of how she defines development, one
woman (who is also quoted in the previous subsection) remarked,

> Well, actually, that's sort of one of my issues. We cannot inflict
> our idea of development on the Haitians. We need to know
> where they're coming from. If they're happy with their houses,
> why do we have to come in and tell them they need flush toi-
> lets and tile? Clean, safe shelter and clean water and a way to

produce their own food, that'd be development for Haiti. To go in and build high-rise apartments for Haiti, that just wouldn't work. (Interview #4)

This woman is at once arguing for a locally grounded development and also imaging that the "local" in Haiti contrasts with what would constitute development in the United States. For her, meeting basic needs would be development in the Haitian context. Indeed, this idea of meeting basic needs was voiced by most interviewees, as well as most respondents to the free-listing exercise. Only a couple of people actually used the term *basic needs,* but almost everyone (nineteen of twenty-one interviewees) mentioned at least one feature of a basic-needs approach: food, water, shelter, the ability to make a living, health care. These are features of development suggested by their own personal experiences of what is "missing" in Haiti, as well as by the needs expressed by Father Jean and others in Haiti.

By emphasizing basic needs, committee members are implying that Haitians and Americans may have different desires, different goals—at the very least, different priorities for development. That is, development for Haiti is different from what would be considered development for the United States. Again, these perceived divergent visions of development revolve around notions of what is lacking in Haiti, but they are at the same time critiques of U.S.-style "overdevelopment." Commenting on growth in Grand Rapids, for example, one woman remarked,

Too many ways, there are too many ways of viewing development. Alpine Avenue, in this town, is developing in leaps and bounds. . . . There's overdevelopment, you know, building up too many homes, whatever, within in a size of a half acre or acre. That can destroy nature. If that happens in a particular area of open space or green hills, that can rob an entire area of wildlife. By many standards, we're overdeveloped. (Interview #3)

In a similar vein, another explained,

I guess [development] would mean a continual improvement, with excesses not the goal, but sustainability, dependability.

There may not be a great amount of income, but there would be income this week and next. Even if there was a catastrophic event, agriculture would be there. There'd be hope for the future, [hope] that things will improve. (Interview #6)

Excesses are not the goal of development; too much traffic and too many subdivisions are not, either. By holding up U.S. overconsumption and suburban sprawl as models to avoid, committee members are in part commenting on their aspirations for their own society, rather than on those for Haiti. Thus, what is taken to be "local" in Haiti is, in some ways, what is imagined to be contrary to the United States.

Nurturing a local-level orientation to Haiti is an explicit feature of twinning, as discussed in previous chapters. Twinning is touted as the largest "citizen-to-citizen network" linking the United States and Haiti, and PTPA emphasizes the people-to-people benefits of directly linking individual parishes to one another: Participants are supposed to become immersed, to a degree, in the local, lived reality of their parish twin. Moreover, the program also stresses that each parish has gifts to offer the other. Whereas the U.S. parish primarily offers gifts of money and other material support, the Haitian parish is thought to provide a spiritual richness, a different cultural reality, and a new way of understanding one's place in the world.

In short, the rhetoric of twinning sometimes closely aligns with committee members' perceptions of what Haiti and Haitians reveal to them: examples of how to be more appreciative, less consumer-oriented, more focused on family. And, this assessment of Haitians' "strengths"—again, focused on their difference from Americans—becomes translated into a notion that Haiti's development must likewise be Haiti-generated, so as to not squelch those desirable attributes. The implicit—and often explicit—critique of Americanism again comes to the fore.

We need to stop thinking about development from an American perspective. Development needs to be from a grass-roots perspective, a hands-on, people-oriented action plan that is long-term. (Interview #5)

This is somewhat contrary to what Erica Bornstein (2005:4) discovered in her study of Protestant NGOs in Zimbabwe, which promoted "lifestyles that encourage accumulation and consumption, under the guise of Christian works." Bornstein found that the "Christian lifestyle" advocated by the NGOs in many ways echoed a "capitalist lifestyle" of earlier "civilizing missions" in southern Africa. As discussed in more detail below, although a middle-class modernity certainly underpins twinning, it is both cautious and self-conscious about accumulation and consumption, which would threaten the "simplicity" and spirituality that Haitians now have.

Some committee members extend this understanding, saying that development—wherever undertaken—should be conceived of in local terms. That is, rather than suggesting that only Haitians are different from Americans and therefore will hold different notions about what development should mean to their communities, some propose a more general understanding of the need to ground development locally, wherever it occurs. In explaining his ranking of assistance, dialogue, and aid as most important to development, one man said,

> I think that development will be received differently by various cultures. So, first offer to assist them with what they would like to accomplish. Obviously, a constant dialogue would be necessary to understand what they need. Then [provide] the aid. (Respondent #8)

In fact, this is exactly what St. Robert's twinning program seeks to do, as discussed in the following section.

▪ Professional Practice: Parishioners as Developers

Thus far, I have suggested that although those active in St. Robert's Haiti twinning program often conceive of development in diverse terms, they also find common ground in notions of developing Haiti's people and situating development in (supposedly) local terms. In this section, I move beyond the imagining of development to the way it is carried out, interpreted, reworked, and challenged by the Haiti Committee.

As discussed in Chapter Three, the meanings attached to development are "fluid, mixed, and shifting, and they vary according to what people are doing, when they're doing it, whom they're talking to" (Gardner 1996). Thus it is necessary to consider both what people say about their motivations and what they actually do (Long 1992, 2000). St. Robert sponsors a number of projects in Our Lady parish: a school lunch project, student sponsorships, agricultural extension, microcredit, augmenting teachers' salaries, trade school. The parish also sends money for church repairs and necessities, catechism books, and other goods or services requested by Father Yvens. St. Robert ships medicines to Haiti regularly, and—though less so now in the 2000s than in the 1990s—sometimes other materials or goods (for example, books, sewing machines, bikes, and tool kits). All of the projects currently sponsored by St. Robert were in place by the time I joined the committee in 2001. Consequently, I have relied on what others have told me, as well as on written documentation (such as bulletins, correspondence, and meeting minutes) to trace these projects' creation. Moreover, during my stays in Verrettes, I had a chance to see many of these projects "in action." Piecing together the projects' histories with what I observed, I suggest that, overall, the many projects and activities that St. Robert funds indeed seem to reflect the broad consensus that development must focus on developing Haiti's people and must be locally oriented. But a closer look at the projects suggests some fluidity and disjuncture, as well.

The problem St. Robert faces is that it cannot effectively administer the projects, enroll and monitor the beneficiaries, or evaluate its successes from afar. Rather, because twinning is intended to be a partnership between the U.S. and Haitian parishes, and presumably because the U.S. parish is simply providing the material resources to meet the needs identified by the Haitian parish, the St. Robert program funnels its funds primarily through the priests of Our Lady parish in Haiti. Our Lady is then in charge of all phases of actual project implementation and administration. St. Robert's Haiti Committee was interested in working with me on this project primarily because they hoped that I would be able to give them a grounded and detailed assessment of their program in Haiti.

When St. Robert began twinning with Our Lady in 1995, the then priest—Father Jean—had an amicable relationship with St. Robert. He and the Haiti Committee in Michigan worked together well, and the folks at St. Robert trusted that he was generally a "good steward" of the twinning money. As noted in Chapter One, many of the programs that St. Robert first began funding—student sponsorships, the food project, teachers' salary augmentations—were initiated at the request of Father Jean.

Yet the twinning relationship between St. Robert and Our Lady has been under tremendous strain since Father Jean left Our Lady in late 2001. Promoted to a more senior position, Father Jean now is assigned to the cathedral in Gonaïves. Father Yvens, who took his place in Verrettes, has not always been welcomed by the St. Robert Haiti Committee. Indeed, some on St. Robert's Haiti Committee strenuously objected to Father Jean's transfer, even going so far as to contact Father Jean's "boss," the Bishop of Gonaïves, to ask that Father Jean be permitted to stay at Our Lady.[3] Committee members were concerned about the fate of the many projects under way in Verrettes, about whether St. Robert would have a good rapport with a new priest, about the ability of a new priest to manage the extensive projects already launched. It was with great skepticism and reservation that St. Robert's Haiti Committee accepted Father Jean's transfer from Our Lady.

This was the climate into which Father Yvens entered as new head pastor of Our Lady in January 2002. Father Yvens is perceived to be very different from Father Jean. Whereas Father Jean was gregarious, hospitable, and charming, Father Yvens is much more reserved (some even say shy), less inclined to host visitors from Michigan, and more reticent about communications. The Haiti Committee feared that the new priest of Our Lady would not be a "suitable" replacement for Father Jean, and they feel that in many ways their fears are being borne out.

For a number of reasons, real tension now characterizes the relationship between St. Robert and Father Yvens. In part, St. Robert's Haiti Committee wonders whether Father Yvens is really trustworthy. Some trace the fallout to the "problem with the church pews." From several sources, I heard that Father had requested money to build pews for the church. He then used some of that money to fund a backyard improvement project, including a gate and new walkway leading from the rectory to the church next door. These improvements were "discovered" by a couple of members of the St. Robert committee during their visit to Verrettes. Asked where he had found the money to pay for the improvements, Father Yvens replied that he had used money left over from the church pews project. But shortly thereafter, Father approached St. Robert for additional pew money, saying more pews were needed. St. Robert committee members did not respond favorably.

> We said no, they should've built more church pews with the money we gave them. Father probably felt he had a lot more discretion with that money than we felt. I understand that he even mentioned it in church. "White people come here and tell us to spend more on church pews." (Interview #1)

Some tension necessarily undergirds twinning relationships. On the one hand, twinning is supposed to be predicated on mutuality and respect and on the recognition that both parties are equal partners in the relationship. But on the other hand, having material and financial resources to bestow on one's "partner" almost necessarily ensures that a benefactor–beneficiary relationship results, especially when the money is supposed to flow for specified purposes. St. Robert Haiti Committee members feel compelled to "protect the intention of the donors," from whom they collect funds; this requires that they impose restrictions on how money can be spent in Haiti. Obviously, such restrictions reinforce the lopsidedness of St. Robert's economically more powerful position and—especially for the priest in Haiti—expose as an illusion the idea that twinning is really an equal partnering.

Several people on the Haiti Committee and in Haiti have suggested that Father Yvens is not happy with his post at Our Lady. Not only is he thought to be accustomed to city life, but he is believed to be upset about having to administer the projects funded by St. Robert. In fact, one story that has been circulating among committee members since shortly after the arrival of Father Yvens suggests that he sees his primary role as that of a priest, not that of a development worker or administrator. Some committee members believe that Father Yvens feels pulled away from his pastoral duties by the extra work that comes with running the many projects St. Robert sponsors in Haiti. Someone even suggested that perhaps Father Yvens has been unfairly burdened by the multiple obligations that come with being head pastor at Our Lady. "He had no idea all these programs were going on [when he took over Our Lady]. He just walked into it." These perceptions of the pastor's unease are called upon to explain the awkward relationship between Father Yvens and St. Robert.

This leads back to the discourse, especially advanced in the interviews, that development needs to be "locally grounded" in order to be meaningful and relevant. As mentioned earlier, the success of twinning hinges on the priests in Haiti working in concert with committees in the United States. In and of itself, this orientation raises questions about (1) how accurately priests (who are highly educated and respected compared to their parishioners) are able to gauge the needs of their communities, (2) on what basis priests make their recommendations, and (3) how best to access and assess the "local."

Haiti Committee members do travel to Haiti, but without the benefit of speaking Creole, they are beholden to translators—often the priests themselves—to make sense of what they are seeing, hearing, and experiencing. Hence, the centrality of the priest is fortified, and the "local" is (re)interpreted from his perspective. The primary way for St. Robert to do "locally grounded" development, then, is to work through the priests, which is indeed what the twinning program directs U.S. twins to do.

At the same time, however, the priest is not always fully authorized to implement his vision of what needs to be done. Exercising too much "discretion" with funding foments distrust, occasions additional scrutiny of future spending, and results in a reduction in funding. There are real penalties for failing to "toe the line." Is the discourse of "locally grounded" development, then, in sync with the way twinning is actually practiced? In this case it is not, but for two opposing reasons. First, priests are seemingly vested with too much authority; they are simply assumed to represent their community's interests. But how do we know the needs expressed by the priest are actually those that people within the community identify? Or, assuming that competing "needs" exist, as literatures critiquing participatory action approaches suggest (see, for example, Gardner and Lewis 1996), whose needs get prioritized and why? Second, because priests are virtually the only medium for accessing the "local," when they are marginalized or excluded from decision making, or are penalized for decisions they do make, then the local—even though problematic—becomes almost entirely disconnected from Haiti Committee activities.

For example, the design of the school sponsorship project was under review in 2005 because St. Robert saw that in the future, it would not be able to sustain the program as currently run. Right now, the sponsorship project supports students through high school, as well as a handful of university students. Assuming that more children than ever will soon be attending high school and college—because, presumably, more are now able to attend elementary school—the costs for educating "advanced" students could soar. Where should St. Robert prioritize its funding? Some have suggested that funding minimum levels of education—ensuring that all children have an opportunity to go to school through sixth or eighth grade—should be the highest priority. As a result, the committee was going to propose a policy whereby St. Robert would no longer sponsor students in high school or university. In many ways the decision had already been made as a result of conversations among and assessments by committee members themselves rather than with sponsored families in Verrettes or feedback from teachers or others at the affected schools.

This highlights another important feature of St. Robert's development discourse and practice alluded to earlier: Themselves recognizing development as fluid, mixed, and shifting, as well as difficult to practice from afar, St. Robert's Haiti Committee wrestles with the best way to find out what is "really" happening on the ground in Haiti and to figure out how to make the projects run more smoothly, more efficiently than they currently do. They struggle with whether the priest should be fully trusted, merely given the benefit of the doubt, or held up for scrutiny. There is a real sense among some on the committee that they do not know what is happening in these projects, whether they are "successful" or not, whether they are well run or nonexistent. In short, a question that has been hanging over the committee since I joined it in 2001 is "Where is our money going and is it making a difference?" This question is unanswerable the way the program is currently structured. As one man said at a committee meeting,

> With all the money we've spent, we're just taking a flying leap into the darkness. We never land on ground. Even you [Char] were there, and even you say, "I don't know [what's going on in Haiti]." (Committee Meeting 3/31/05)

Although Bill and Char do reside in Haiti for several months out of the year, their inability to speak Creole, their relatively distant relationship with Father Yvens, and their social isolation from the local community limit their ability to comment in-depth on the sponsored projects. Moreover, there is disagreement about what constitutes "making a difference." I asked one woman what happens when Our Lady asks for something that St. Robert does not want to provide. She replied,

> [Our Lady] usually gets what they want from us. We have told them no [to certain things] now that this church bench thing came about. . . . But it doesn't stick because Cassie is so liberal. She says, "At least somebody is benefiting." No, it doesn't stick—it doesn't help them to help themselves.

The Haiti Committee has attempted to have more people on the ground in Haiti and to integrate Bill and Char into the management of certain programs there. An American nun—fluent in Creole and stationed in Verrettes since 2001 as part of the United States Province of the Religious Sacred Heart—became an important contact for St. Robert. Sister Judy Vollbrecht was enlisted to assist in facilitating the twinning in a variety of ways. At the most basic level, she sometimes would carry letters sent via email from St. Robert to Father Yvens. She also became deeply involved in administering the school sponsorship project, along with Bill and Char.

When Father Jean was in charge of Our Lady, student sponsorship money was said to be dispersed by him directly to recipients' families. "Because he knew everyone in town," having grown up in the area, Father Jean was trusted by St. Robert to know who the needy students were and whether the dispersed money was actually being used to send those children to school. As discussed earlier, when I was in Verrettes in 2002, I attempted to "trace" St. Robert's lists of sponsored children to the actual schools in the area. I had very little luck. The lists were outdated, inaccurate, or otherwise incomplete. In the one school where I was able to compare the current roster with my list of students supposedly sponsored at that school, I found little overlap. At another school, the principal refused to let me look at the official roster until the priests gave their explicit approval, which never happened. Something clearly was amiss in the record keeping among St. Robert, Our Lady, and the local schools.

St. Robert asked Bill and Char—along with Sr. Judy—to help "formalize" the student sponsorship project. The new "committee" in Haiti was to take pictures of each of the sponsored kids, collect report cards at the semester's end, and pay the schools directly for tuition, rather than paying the families. The sponsorship project was reorganized to allow for more "surveillance" to ensure that sponsored children were actually enrolling in and actively participating in school.

This new "on the ground" awareness did bring to light many issues no one on the committee had recognized until then. For one thing, distributing school funding can be rather "dangerous." Sr. Judy, Bill, and Char were targeted for intimidation as a result of having to turn away scholarship recipients. For example, disgruntled town residents who had been denied school funding protested by throwing rocks at Bill and Char's house. Second, the time necessary to administer the project was enormous. The sheer volume of information generated (names, grades, payment history, pictures, sponsors' information) was huge and required someone to organize and manage it. Someone also needed to go to the bank to arrange money transfers from the sponsorship coffers to the individual schools. Because students change schools with some frequency, maintaining up-to-date paperwork was an ongoing challenge, as was arranging multiple payments to different schools for a student. Sometimes books and uniforms were also supplied, and this might necessitate a trip to Port-au-Prince, several hours' drive from Verrettes. In short, the volume of work skyrocketed when responsibility for the program was shifted from the priest and families to a "committee."

In fact, the workload is so great that Sr. Judy felt she could no longer continue helping with the sponsorship project. She has her own mission in Haiti, which is unrelated to the twinning between Our Lady and St. Robert. Moreover, Bill and Char may not be able to continue with the project; health issues have forced them to leave Haiti earlier than intended and may affect their ability to return. This leaves the Haiti Committee in the position again of deciding how best to run the student sponsorship project. Should Father Yvens be in charge? Should it run through the schools? Should they "hire" someone locally to coordinate the paperwork and payment? It seemed easier with Father Jean. "He knew the community. Father Yvens, he doesn't know." At this point in 2005, with the plan of scaling back assistance for upper levels of education, St. Robert is unsure how to proceed.

The members of St. Robert's Haiti Committee have multiple ideas about what development means, and they have implemented a set of projects that they feel will help put their vision into practice. But in the course of trying to "do" development from afar, they have run into a number of obstacles (most notably, the demands of working with a priest who they are not convinced is completely trustworthy) that have challenged some of their notions about development. In particular, real tension swirls around this "need" to ground development locally. Although it is an important ideal expressed in the narratives, locally grounded development is particularly difficult to achieve in the context of twinning. Not only is the hierarchy of the program such that Haitian priests are given authority to speak for their communities, but Haiti Committee members in Michigan remain unconvinced about the priest's priorities. This challenges the committee to reassess its visions for development and come up with a set of questions geared more to finding out what is happening in the projects than to finding out what the "true" needs—and visions for meeting them—are in Haiti.

■ Twinning: Missionization versus Development?

As mentioned in Chapter One, when I first began studying twinning, I was perplexed by whether participants considered twinning to be about "development" or about "missionization." What I have since discovered is that most people see twinning as a hybrid of the two. When asked directly whether they thought the St. Robert twinning attempted to develop Verrettes, only two people said no. The others felt that development was indeed a central feature of twinning. Similarly, when asked whether they saw twinning as missionary work, only one said no. Two were more ambivalent, saying that twinning was "somewhat" missionary work. This section attempts to make sense of this duality by exploring the multiple ways in which committee members give their Haiti experiences meaning, especially as related to missionary work.

Part of the challenge in categorizing twinning as missionary work is the fact that these are two Catholic parishes in partnership. Unlike other faith-based initiatives—for example, Protestant NGOs World Vision and Christian Care (Bornstein 2005)—twinning does not focus on conversion per se, because the people being targeted in Haiti are presumably already Christians. In reality, of course, most Haitian Catholics blend Catholic and Vodou traditions in syncretic practice. But this generally is not a focal point for parishioners at St. Robert. No one on the Haiti Committee mentioned subverting or weakening Vodou as a goal or purpose of twinning.

Indeed, I explicitly asked all interviewees how they felt about Haitian Vodou, and I was surprised by the number of people who spoke of it dispassionately or as rather intriguing. I expected to find more intolerance and negativity than I actually did. In conversations with Protestant missionaries in Haiti, I had heard time and again that Haiti is so poor *because* of Vodou and that Haiti's tribulations are a direct punishment from God for Haitians' blasphemy and worship of false idols. This sentiment mirrors one raised by Bornstein's (2005:31) work in Zimbabwe, where a Protestant "Gospel of Prosperity" asserted a "direct correlation between the attainment of one's wishes, belief in God, and material success." Yet among twinning participants, only a few people expressed a negative view of Vodou, and only one put his understanding of faith and prosperity in terms that explicit.

> I think it [Vodou] is what is wrong with Haiti, in every aspect. Leviticus 26 says God wants to be worshipped by his people. He does not want to share. If they don't do that, they will be punished. If they don't change, they will be punished more. If they don't change again, they will be punished even more. He has punished [Haiti] more and more. . . . I have to believe God is not happy with Haiti because of the Vodou.

This man was raised Lutheran, and his comparatively extreme view might stem from his "Protestant" background. While active in St. Robert's Haiti Committee, he has never officially converted to Catholicism; he has attended Catholic parishes (and partaken of the Eucharist) because his wife is Catholic, but he does not consider himself Catholic.

More commonly, committee members instead typically expressed a degree of ignorance about Vodou, and sometimes a desire to know more.

> I don't really have any feelings. It's there, it exists. So what? (Interview #11)

> I don't have a whole lot of knowledge of it. But, um, you know, I think it's one of their cultural items that has come through the generations. (Interview #21)

This is not to suggest that committee members warmly embrace Vodou or that they want to promote it. Rather, overall, people simply do not pay much attention to it.

> I don't know much about it. I am more or less ambivalent about it. I'm not superstitious . . . To me, it's sort of like a Haitian drycleaners. I didn't have the opportunity to go into one, and I don't care. (Interview #6)

Or, alternatively, they treat Vodou as a quaint oddity that is more intriguing than threatening.

> I don't know much about it. I wanted to go to a witch doctor's house and no one would let me. (Interview #14)

> In the middle of the night, I heard some chanting. Turns out, it was a Vodou ceremony. So, that was pretty cool. (Interview #7)

The point here is that even though most Haiti Committee members say that they see twinning as a missionary activity, they do not see conversion as its goal. Vodou, which is widely practiced in Haiti, is neither a focus for St. Robert's twinning committee nor a cause for much concern. Rather, in talking about missionization, most people emphasized the "helping hand" aspects, as discussed in Chapter Four. In responding to the question of whether she considered twinning missionary work, one woman responded,

> Yes, I suppose it is, although a lot of people when they do missionary work, it's a form of proselytizing. That's not nearly as important to me as attending to the people. I think when it comes down to it, it doesn't matter a hill of beans what religion you belong to. I don't know if that [religion] is where it's at. (Interview #10)

As one man speculated, for those most active in twinning, there is a romanticization of missionary work—not in religious terms, but through a notion that "I can do more than just give money. I can motivate people. I can take on relationships" (Interview #4). This was borne out in the interviews and committee meetings, as I discuss in Chapter Four. Some make explicit their feelings that twinning is unusual in bringing "beneficiaries" and "benefactors" together face-to-face. Participation allows for more than simply writing a check each month, although that is an option for people who want only that level of involvement. But for those interested in "doing more" than giving money, twinning provides an avenue for travel, cross-cultural exchange, and hands-on problem solving through project conception, design, implementation, and evaluation.

The quotations above raise another interesting feature: Many respondents seemed almost caught off guard by the question of twinning's relationship to missionization, as though they had not really considered it before. One woman, for example, mused,

> Oooh, I guess it would be classified as that. You just never know who you are going to touch when you're in that type of situation. The parish that's there is a Catholic parish, but, um, in terms of "converting the heathens" or whatever, in terms of that kind of missionary, you never know what those outside the parish might see, what type of impact it might have (Interview #21)

This response reminds me of Bornstein's "lifestyle evangelism" concept, which I mentioned earlier—the idea that by living a good life, one can serve as a model and inspiration for the "unconverted." Here is another response:

TH: Do you think of twinning as missionary work?
Interviewee #11: Mmmhmmm [hesitantly].
TH: How so?
Interviewee #11: Taking, giving. Time and supplies. Helping people perhaps to get on their feet.

Indeed, although most people, when directly questioned, said twinning was a missionary activity, the religious aspects are rarely mentioned in interviews or discussed in committee meetings. Every 2 years, St. Robert pays for catechism books for Our Lady, but directly promoting or supporting religious activities is a small component of the overall Haiti budget and programming. For example, Father Yvens requested money to pay for radio broadcasting of his sermons to the surrounding mountain communities, a request that St. Robert rejected as not central to their work in Verrettes. Despite proclamations, then, that twinning is "missionary" in nature, the goals, discourses, and practices of St. Robert twinning tend to focus more explicitly on development in Verrettes.

This may reflect the reality that these are two Catholic parishes working together, so the "conversion factor" is superfluous. It may be because Haitians—rooted in poverty—are construed as more spiritual than Americans. Indeed, the idea of the "reverse mission" rests on assumptions about Haitians' ability to teach Americans about spirituality. Or it may be that lay Catholics are less inclined to engage in explicit missionary activities than members of other Christian denominations (for example, Bornstein 2005), despite nudges given by the Church and spelled out in NCCB documents. Indeed, Sr. JoAn and Doug noted that there is a Catholic "obligation" to do missionary work but also acknowledged that Protestant churches tend to send more missionaries overseas. For Catholics, there is a sense that missionary activities are the domain of the clergy or of societies such as Maryknoll, who have expertise in that sort of work. Unlike the "anti-establishment Protestants" described by Bornstein (2005:17), "Catholics aren't big on that [missionary work]," as Sr. JoAn reflected. Seeming to affirm her analysis, another woman remarked,

> I don't feel [that] as a Catholic I'm an evangelist. I don't see Catholics taking on that role, so much. I don't see the twinning program with that as its goal, personally. I was never comfortable being referred to as a missionary. People visiting Haiti would be referred to as missionaries. I never felt that. (Interview #14)

Even Bill and Char—whom some on the committee *do* classify as missionaries because of their commitment to living in Haiti—were at times hesitant about adopting the label themselves. Said Char,

> We never really did [consider ourselves missionaries] because we have no real expertise in that, but people refer to us as missionaries. But, we ourselves, we didn't go to college for that. We have that vision of us as missionaries [that we'd like to be missionaries.] It's just that as missionaries, they go in and they spread the gospel, spread the word. They usually have training, they have people that are backing them. That's the norm. That's the tradition.

Thus, significantly, it is partly on the basis of lack of training that Char and Bill are reluctant to adopt the missionary label. That is, they feel they somehow cannot fully claim the title *missionary* because they do not have the proper qualifications. It would seem that the "cult of the expert"—the idea that training and credentials qualify one to engage in certain activities as an expert—is alive and well when it comes to considering oneself a missionary. Perhaps this reflects the hierarchical nature of the Catholic Church more generally, where only in recent years have significant opportunities arisen for lay men and women to take on leadership roles in their parishes, even though the priest remains at the peak of the parish pecking order. Notably, however, in the more "secular" domain of development, the cult of the expert has been thoroughly demystified, as is discussed in prior chapters and will be explored more fully in the following chapter. Development can be and is designed, carried out, and evaluated by lay men and women, who are able to draw on their experiences living in a "developed" nation to cast themselves as development experts.

As mentioned earlier, trips to Haiti by committee participants are called reverse missions because they are intended to provide opportunities for spiritual renewal, growth, and learning for Americans traveling to Haiti, rather than focusing on conversion or change among the Haitians. That is, the logic of twinning is explicitly about gaining knowledge or insight from Haitians, rather than attempting to convey those things to them. We have seen this is not always the case in practice, of course; a central feature of St. Robert's twinning is its attempts to enlighten Haitians and bring about a change in mentality, "vision," and attitude via education. Indeed, St. Robert has moved further away from the reverse mission model in other ways, too, specifically in terms of the purpose and practice of travel.

As we saw in Chapter One, travel to Haiti is typically an integral feature of twinning, particularly as newly twinned parishes are beginning to "get to know" one another. For white, middle-class Americans, travel to Haiti often challenges their ways of thinking, calls into question U.S. materialism and excess consumption, and offers alternative models for "being" in the world. PTPA actively promotes such transformation by assisting with travel plans and strongly encouraging these face-to-face experiences on Haitian soil. First-time travelers often visit orphanages, homes for the sick and dying, and other places where Haiti's most vulnerable populations—especially its children—are clustered together and cared for, chiefly by foreigners. These are moments for parishioners to "be the hands and feet" of Jesus Christ, to care for the sick and weak, to tend to the downtrodden. And they are often profoundly moving experiences for committee members, many of whom spoke at length about the time they spent in Haiti.

> We worked in an orphanage, run by sisters. Just to see these rooms of cribs—much smaller, maybe two-thirds the size of a U.S. crib, made of metal—end to end and all these babies. Some of them reach their arms out to you. We tried to hold them for a little bit. Some of them were sick, with different tubes, oxygen, really snotty noses. We wore rubber gloves when diapering them because of the huge AIDS situation going on. It was really neat helping out with these little babies. They're precious, they just cling to you. In another part of the orphanage, they have older kids, maybe 2 to 8 years old. They gather around you and cling to you. If you pick one up, the others would try pushing them away so they could get up. They were pushing, trying to get closer to human contact than others. It's not so much about the attention, but they're seeking human contact. They get it there [from the sisters at the orphanage], but there is not enough to go around. (Interview #7)

And it is from these trips that committee members relate their participation in twinning to a larger vision of how to be a good Catholic, often by referencing the work of Mother Theresa.

TH: Who are your heroes in the Catholic faith?
Interviewee #9: I guess I would say Mother Theresa; it was a strength issue. She was extremely strong, very confident in her own skin. She was a calming influence, like the Sisters of Charity we visited in Haiti, just her insight, her vision. She required that all the sisters speak English, fluently. It made it very easy to go anywhere. The orphanage [that we visited in Haiti] was rather

chaotic when we went in there, but the sisters were the picture of calm. It was really, um, you could feel the grace.

In talking about her travels to Haiti, another woman maintained,

> Unless you visit a country like that, you don't have a clue. I guess, I recently I heard a quote from Mother Theresa about how not to be overwhelmed by that kind of atmosphere. . . . That's exactly how I approached going into an orphanage. There were kids from infancy to early childhood, and they are so starved for attention and love. You only have two arms, that's all you can handle. You can't do more than that. If a child is starved for touch, that's the one I'm holding. (Interview #3)

As in the larger projects, these are personal experiences, focused on touching individual lives or the lives of those in small communities (for example, orphanages and hospitals). The focus is not on the structural features that necessitate women's giving up their babies for adoption or leaving them on hospital doorsteps so that they might receive desperately needed medical care. Rather, the idea of the "starfish"—the one individual whose life might be touched or bettered by the work of the committee member—again predominates.

To return to the point introduced earlier, the reverse mission model at St. Robert has abated in recent years. Given that few new people join the committee these days, there is less need to introduce members to the "reality" of Haiti. Many of those now traveling to Haiti have participated in these types of "reverse mission" experiences on previous trips and so are familiar with their power. But more important, the nature of the twinning between St. Robert and Our Lady has shifted to focus more on project administration and evaluation. That is, when committee members travel to Haiti now, it is more often to check up on what is happening in their sponsored projects than to learn more about Haiti and Haitians.

One reason for this change is the tense relationship St. Robert has with Father Yvens in Haiti. Father Yvens is less inclined to invite groups down to Haiti, telling the committee that he feels somewhat compromised by their visits.

> Instead of sending a group of non-specialized people [to Haiti],
> we work with people who've been there before, specialists.
> Father Yvens does not encourage us to send groups. He's afraid
> people will try to extort money from him after we leave. The
> openness of the past—the ignorance of what was going on
> [people pressuring the priest after we left]—that has changed.
> (Interview #1)

A second reason for the change in orientation stems from critiques about
the value of reverse missions. Some view them more as tours than as spiritual encounters and, given the burden such tours place on hosts in Haiti,
have suggested that St. Robert reform its travel priorities and purpose.
They argue that, rather than being cultural tours or spiritual missions,
trips to Haiti should be about quick program evaluation, "getting in and
getting out" with just a few people, over a few days.

> With a ["regular"] mission trip, all eight people are building a
> house, all eight people working. The part I didn't like [about
> the reverse mission] is that it was too much of a tour. When I
> first got involved, I didn't feel like we needed to send eight
> people over to tour Haiti. [I thought we should do shorter,
> smaller, more focused trips.] I brought it back to the Haiti
> Committee, and they said okay. I understand, not every person
> has my knowledge in construction, not everyone has Cassie's
> ability to lead. But Haiti is not a freak show. We shouldn't be
> going there just to gawk. So I brought those concerns back.
> Cassie reacted favorably, as did the rest of committee. Am I
> wrong? Maybe. But my trips with two to three people are the
> best. I don't think we need to bother them, don't need to camp
> out for a week, unless there's a reason for it. . . . Your new
> people on the committee can tag along to see what they can
> do. But it's just not good to take eight to ten people at a time.

These thoughts were echoed by others, who felt that traditional reverse
missions did not give them an opportunity to "do" anything. As
reverse missioners, travelers get the chance to learn on these trips

rather than actually proposing and enacting solutions. And for a program that is established and quite rigidly focused, as is St. Robert's, the reverse mission format can be understood as an inefficient use of time and resources. Therefore, in recent years, St. Robert has been sending smaller groups of two to three people, who travel directly to Verrettes—rather than spending a few days in Port-au-Prince's orphanages and hospitals—to check out their sponsored projects, meet with the relevant "players" in Haiti (priests, committee members), get reports, go over the accounting ledgers, assess any current requests for assistance (for example, does the church roof really need repair?), and then depart for Michigan.

The practice of St. Robert's twinning, then, diverges a bit from its discourse. Although the missionary aspects are widely agreed to be integral to the twinning, they are also sidelined in pursuit of efficiency and effectiveness. With a focus on meeting material needs in Haiti through the various projects they implemented, St. Robert's Haiti Committee ultimately prioritizes development over (reverse) missionization. This might be explained, in part, by the fact that participants do not need to convert Haitians to Catholicism; they assume they are already working with highly devoted Catholics. Thus there is no overriding impulse to evangelize, as I have seen in other (Protestant) programs.

At the same time, the "cult of the expert" remains. Lay men and women are taking on ever more prominent roles in their churches, but the Catholic parish is still very hierarchical, with the priest at the top. Perhaps parishioners do not feel it is their role to engage in direct missionization, which they assume is better left to the "experts"—to clergy and societies such as Maryknoll. Although they cannot offer Haitians religious insight, committee members do have "expertise" on living materially sufficient, economically successful lives. Perhaps they feel they can offer Haitians opportunities for material enrichment, particularly by providing educational opportunities. A question that emerges is whether Haitians are able and willing to actually implement projects according to the vision established in Michigan. Attempting to answer this question dominates St. Robert's travel agenda, more so than the "reverse mission" motivation of the past.

■ Conclusion

For St. Robert's Haiti Committee, development primarily means meeting basic needs in Haiti, being sensitive to local conditions, and offering people the opportunity to better themselves—and their chances for success—via education. Discourses of "developing people" and locally grounding development are unevenly put into practice, however. Accessing and assessing the "local" is particularly difficult for committee members, because none of them speaks Creole. Moreover, the Haitian priest's position as a mediator between his parish and that of its American twin sometimes becomes an obstacle. For example, when communications between the priest and the Haiti Committee broke down, so did the opportunity for exchange—in terms of both travel and contact. Of course, even when the Haiti Committee and priest had a good working relationship, the extent to which the priest was able to truly capture the diverse needs of his congregation remains uncertain.

The discourses and practices that characterize St. Robert's development efforts can be related, in part, to the very structure of twinning, which at once diminishes the cultural distance between two parishes and reinforces the perception of differences between them. Indeed, St. Robert committee members construct a duality wherein Haitians are admired for avoiding U.S. "over-development" but also are criticized for their inability to envision how to create a better, more materially secure future. This vision, committee members assume, will be planted and nurtured by resources from outside Haiti, from those like themselves who are able to fund educational initiatives. Thus, at the same time that committee members maintain that development must be rooted in the particulars of Haiti, they simultaneously suggest that Haitians—at present—lack the capacity to create their own visions for how to proceed. Crafting development, then, is a matter of equipping individuals with the proper tools to build their own "self-sufficiency" rather than a matter of changing the structural forces that keep most Haitians marginalized and impoverished. This echoes the "will to empower" the poor and powerless as a new form of governmentality (Cruikshank 1999; Ferguson and Gupta 2002), which produces and enrolls citizen–subjects in their own management.

Most on the committee believe that twinning is about both development and missionization in Haiti. But most also clarify that missionary work to them does not mean religious conversion of Haitians. Rather, missionary work is about giving a "helping hand" to Haitians, sharing resources with them, giving them a chance for a better life. The religious aspects of twinning tend to be overshadowed, then, by the developmental facets. Committee efficiency and project evaluation have become central features of travel to Haiti, rather than opportunities for parishioners to be the "hands and feet of Jesus Christ."

■ Notes

1. Particularly striking is the difference in numbers of responses made by women and men. Obviously, because I administered the free-listing exercise to a total of only seven people, generalizations cannot be drawn from the data. But it is worth pointing out that the five women respondents averaged 12.2 responses per person, compared to 3 person for the men.

2. Ninety percent of primary and secondary schools are privately owned (United Nations International Report 1995:8), and only one-third of children enrolled in primary school complete the cycle. Rates of education of females are the lowest in the Western Hemisphere (United Nations International Report 1995:8).

3. Cassie told me that she had consulted the bishop prior to the twinning between St. Robert and Nôtre Dame, concerned that the large infusion of cash into Verrettes would require a steady presence at the parish to manage it. Cassie said the bishop indicated that Father Jean would be that presence and that the bishop did not plan to transfer him elsewhere. With Father Jean's departure, Cassie felt the bishop had gone back on his word. In a telegram to the bishop in November 2001, Cassie wrote, "Disappointed Fr. Francique transferring. Too late to stop? Hard to maintain support without him. 25 delegates who have visited very loyal to him. Others in parish question amount going to Haiti. Have worked with other priests, not the same. Trust is a fragile thing."

CHAPTER SIX

Development
and Its "Discontents"

As international development becomes increasingly privatized, "non-professionals"—such as those active in parish twinning—have increasing space to design and deliver development projects. In Chapter Six, I consider the extent to which formal and lay development are similar to and different from one another. The analysis focuses on three related questions. First, in what ways do lay and professional initiatives overlap, converge, and/or diverge from one another? Second, what is the relationship between the entrenched, hegemonic discourses that both post-structuralists and anthropology of development scholars agree exist—discourses that are institutionalized and implemented by development "experts"—and the discourses and practices of those who stand outside the "development machine"? Third, is twinning "development as usual," alternative development, counter-development, or something else?

The previous chapter explored the various ways in which development is imagined and implemented by those active in St. Robert's Haiti Committee. Focusing on promoting education and locally grounded development in Haiti, committee members regularly encounter a host of problems and concerns at once both typical of more conventional initiatives and particular to their unique circumstances as "equal partners" in the development process. By considering the trends, missteps, and concerns of conventional initiatives, this next section attempts to place lay development within a broader framework in order to assess the extent to which lay and professional approaches are related.

■ Framing Human Development

Twinning at St. Robert, like other forms of faith-based development (for example, Bornstein 2005; Occhipinti 2005), in many ways echoes what in conventional development is considered a "human development" approach. The United Nations' Human Development Programme (UNDP) Report defines human development as a process of enlarging people's choices, especially those that enable people to lead long and healthy lives, to acquire knowledge, and to have access to resources needed for a decent standard of living. Such basic choices are deemed foundations for further opportunities.

Through its Human Development Index (HDI), UNDP measures the extent to which countries succeed or fail at giving their peoples such choices. HDI measures literacy rates, life expectancy, access to potable water, and other features in order to compare and rank "human development" among the world's countries. In the 2004 report, Haiti is ranked 153rd out of 177 countries—an indication of its comparatively "poor" human development (UNDP 2004). Those on the St. Robert Haiti Committee do not reference the HDI or UNDP, but they do frequently refer to Haiti as "the poorest country in the Western Hemisphere" throughout the twinning promotional materials.

In literature drawn and distributed by both PTPA and HOP, Haiti's current position at the bottom end of development scales is highlighted. For example, a "Facts about Haiti" sheet distributed by HOP reads,

> Haiti faces a difficult challenge of restoring a devastated economy. The island has been robbed of most of their [sic] natural resources. They are at 97 percent deforestation, and 85 percent illiteracy. There is no medical care for the masses, and only 13 percent of Haiti [sic] has a source of clean drinking water. All this has crippled Haiti, which is now the poorest country in the Western Hemisphere. (HOP n.d.)

Similarly, PTPA, in its own "Facts about Haiti" sheet, highlights Haiti's high infant mortality rate, low life expectancy, high levels of illiteracy and unemployment, and low annual incomes. As Cruikshank (1999:40) notes, "To solve the 'social problems' of poverty, delinquency, dependency, crime, self-esteem, and so on, it [is necessary to] have a certain kind of knowledge that is measurable, specific, calculable, knowledge that can be organized into governmental solution." HOP and PTPA have compiled such "facts," from which St. Robert committee members prioritize a number of concerns also raised by UNDP in its reports: education, health, water supply, and the like.

In conventional development channels, these concerns evolved out of the notion of meeting basic needs, an approach particularly popular in the 1970s. Under a "basic needs" strategy, development assistance is supposed to be targeted directly to the poor, rather than "trickling down" from above or through the state (Peet and Hartwick 1999). Although the basic needs approach is not directly linked to a set of prescriptive measures, it does suggest three primary areas of concern: (1) individuals' and families' need for food, shelter, clothes, and other necessities of daily life; (2) access to public services, such as potable water, sanitation, health, and education; (3) the ability to participate and have voice in local and national politics (Martinussen 1997:299; Moser 1993).

Both the basic needs approach and its more recent incarnation as human development emphasize the elimination of poverty as a moral imperative, as a "mission" to be undertaken by the global north on behalf of the south. The mission was most recently expressed by the UN in terms of its "Millennium Development Goals," which all UN member nations have pledged to meet by 2015 and which include such goals as eliminating hunger and poverty and achieving universal primary education (UN 2005).[1] Crucially, this mission "justifies interventions into the countries of the south, if necessary bypassing . . . local governments" through appeals based on "solidarity with the poor" (Rist 1997:164) and appeals to the supposedly more "efficient" channeling of resources directly to beneficiaries rather than through the state (see Fisher 1997). Clearly, this reverberates with the orientation of twinning at St. Robert, as well as twinning more broadly, where explicit reference is made to standing in solidarity with Haiti's poor and powerless, and where the notion of person-to-person outreach is central. In secular development, the "immorality" of poverty is explained in terms of basic human rights and the shared humanity that all people possess. In twinning, poverty's injustice takes on an additional spiritual dimension, as "our Catholic brothers and sisters" are understood to be unnecessarily suffering.

As indicated earlier, several members on the Haiti committee at St. Robert explicitly stated that their participation in twinning was more important than other types of "charity" because it puts them in direct contact with those they are helping and because both parties (in theory) benefit from the relationship. Moreover, as twinning promotional litera- ture repeatedly states, "One hundred percent of every donation goes directly to the Haitian parish or project. There is no middleman and no bureaucracy" (PTPA n.d.:4).

Indeed, both basic needs approaches and parish twinning are skep- tical of "national bourgeoisies," who, as Rist (1997:165) says, are seen "either as making off with the fruits of 'development' or as refusing to comply with funders' injunctions." Not only does twinning attempt to skirt these national interests, it simultaneously disparages them as cor- rupt and in need of reformation. Haiti's elites have, in fact, been the tar- gets of numerous scholarly and popular criticisms (Bell 2001; Farmer 1994; Maternowska 1996), critiques that are simplified and amplified in twinning networks. As striking as the poverty is to many of the white, middle-class travelers to Haiti, the visible inequality between Haiti's rich and poor can be even more shocking. And committee members firmly associate elite interests with government failure in Haiti.

■ Good Government Requires Throwing "Aristotle" Out

Lack of "good governance" in Haiti is central to most committee mem- bers' explanations for its poverty. Similarly, as discussed in Chapter Three, it is very much in vogue in current conventional development dis- course to blame the failures of development on the failure of states to properly implement it (for example, Evans 1992; Van de Walle 2001; Wade 1985; World Bank 1998a). Over the past 50 years, the "conven- tional wisdom" on what roles states should play in developing their economies has waxed and waned. In the 1950s and 1960s, states were expected to be important actors in accelerating industrialization, modernizing agriculture, and providing infrastructure for urban areas; by the late 1970s and 1980s, states were relegated to supporting roles, such as defending property rights; by the late 1980s and through the 2000s, states are again considered important players, but their role is expected to consist of maintaining "good institutions" that support open markets, free trade, and democracy (Evans 1992; Van de Walle 2001). That is, states are currently regarded as best when they assume a "hands off" posture but have "good" institutions in place that enable them to do so.

Indeed, scrutinizing development's genealogy reveals patterns that "explain" the failures of development: Development has been too focused on large-scale infrastructure building at the expense of meeting basic needs; development has ignored women and the importance of gender (Boserup 1970); development has failed to include "local participation" (Chambers 1997). As Jan Knippers Black (1999:221) maintains, "Development in theory and practice is a slave to fashion." Today's fashionable explanation eventually gives way to tomorrow's successor. At the moment, it is fashionable to blame development's past failures on funders' historical lack of concern with "government." That is, development was supposed to be an apolitical exercise remedying technical problems of development and underdevelopment. As such, it did not concern itself with promoting the "policy environments" necessary for development to actually work. That, say those currently at the forefront of conventional initiatives, is why development has failed—bad governments have been subsidized through development aid, allowing them to live beyond their means, pocket monies intended for the poor, and undermine grassroots attempts at development. In order for development to work, governments need to create "good" environments with transparency, open markets, and privatization, as discussed in Chapter Three.

This focus on "good governance" is a key factor that St. Robert's Haiti Committee twinning participants invoke to explain why Haiti is so poor:

I saw a documentary on when the Americans occupied Haiti during Duvalier's time [sic].[2] They did good things, like put in roads. But a firm government wasn't set up after they left. And since then, Haiti's been in limbo. They don't have the leadership to continue, to put in roads, to build sewers and water lines. (Interview #4)

Similarly, in response to the question "Why do you think Haiti is so poor?" several people mentioned the problems of bad government.

I would like to believe it was the government suppressing their desires to become self-sufficient. I think their leadership hasn't always been for the people, by the people. [sighs] I guess it's a mental control. . . . I think the government itself suppresses the people and doesn't allow for their advancement. Their leadership has been lousy, I think. Whatever was good for the leadership, suppressed people. (Interview #11)

I think a lot of it has to do with governments that are taking money and not giving it back to where it needs to be. (Interview #21)

They lack leadership at the government level, they lack integrity at government level, and the Haitian population doesn't have an education. (Interview #12)

As Carolyn Nordstrom (2004) notes, the power of the state stems from its ability to convince people of its necessity, of its inevitability. If citizens buy into the notion that the state is the civilizing force that keeps their barbarian, brutish tendencies in check, the state becomes legitimized and its authority is accepted. Many of those on the Haiti Committee likewise invest in myths about the "primacy of the state" to craft a society that keeps Haitians' "beast[s] as tamed as possible" (Nordstrom 2004:178). Accordingly, some extend the notion of "state failure" in Haiti to explain the "savagery" of Haiti's citizens. In other words, because the state is dysfunctional—it does not have "visionaries and the gifted" necessary to lead the country (Nordstrom 2004:178)— the state cannot properly "civilize" Haitians, who are then mob-like, violent, unpredictable, illiterate, and diseased.

TH: What wishes or aspirations or dreams do you have for Haiti?

Interviewee #1: So many things. At a minimum, to be able to feed their people and to have enough police force to protect people in jail from lynch mobs. They have police, but they don't know how to do that [protect people].

TH: In what ways would you like Haiti to be more like the U.S.?

Interviewee #16: Clean drinking water, um, better government, laws—along with that would be more police officers to enforce it, more army to enforce it, an army to ensure protection for people.

Ironically, the abuse of the peasantry by the state has risen in proportion to the Haitian state's centralization and consolidation. Historically, the state has been better able to manage—and terrorize—its population since the U.S. occupation of Haiti, 1915–1934 (Schmidt 1995), which formalized and bureaucratized the state's operations in Port-au-Prince, as well as creating what was to become the modern Haitian army (see Hefferan 1998). Haiti's peasantry has created its own institutions, procedures, and systems of justice largely outside of state channels precisely to avoid the humiliation, degradation, and vulnerability they experience in encounters with the state (for example, see Smith 2001).

There is a duality, then, in the way the Haitian state is imagined by some on St. Robert's Haiti Committee. On the one hand, the state is acknowledged as a source of corruption and repression and as perhaps the primary reason for Haiti's poverty. On the other hand, the state is seen to need strengthening in order to keep in line the otherwise untamed hordes of savages who threaten (or outright undermine) civilization in Haiti.

When asked to clarify the type of state they imagine or wish for Haiti, committee members often drew on "liberal" conceptualizations of the state, reflecting their white, middle-class American positions. Not surprisingly, their conceptualizations overlap with those currently in vogue in formal development channels, as well. In responding to the question "What does 'good government' mean to you?" interviewees focused on personal freedoms—such as those contained in the U.S. Bill of Rights—property rights, democracy, trade, even privatization. For example,

> Good government provides an environment where an economy can flourish, where an individual's rights are respected. If you don't have a good government, people can't flourish, an economy can't flourish. When you don't have personal rights, when you don't have an economy, when you do not have integrity, you have anarchy. And that's what they have in Haiti. (Interview #12)

> Opportunities for people, laws, safety, infrastructure, trade. There's nothing like that in Haiti, it seems like. (Interview #14)

> Democratic government, major privatization, and regular law and order, not vigilante—which is more disorganized. . . . You need to get, you need to have armies and police in governmental hands. No private police, no private armies. (Interview #20)

Good government in these instances parallels its usage in the development literature:

> Good governance . . . is oriented around the twin tracks of enhancing the efficiency of the state administration (i.e., combating corruption) . . . [and] the so-called "second generation reforms" to build the critical physical infrastructure and promote individual skills and collective capacities. (Kempa, Shearing, and Burris n.d.:7)

I also asked committee members what they thought the role of the U.S. government should be in promoting development in Haiti. Opinions varied, with some asserting that the government has no role in the affairs of other countries and others suggesting that the U.S. government needs not just to provide aid to Haiti but should initiate an outright overhaul of the Haitian government. Following on the heels of President Jean-Bertrand Aristide's controversial exit from Haiti in March 2004 (see Chomsky et al. 2004), one man speculated about how the United States could help steer Haiti out of poverty.

[The U.S. should] throw Aristotle [sic] out, which they've done. Then the U.S. can put in a government that will, in fact, that can be trusted to be good stewards of the money that will be given to rebuild that nation and economy. (Interview #12)

The proper role for states in promoting the development of their economies is a key issue for conventional development initiatives. It is also a preoccupation of those active in St. Robert's Haiti twinning. Yet even though both groups focus on the need for good policy environments—which include such things as secure property rights, privatization, trade, institutional transparency, and personal freedoms—only conventional initiatives are penalizing those nations failing to conform to the standards of good governance. In the case of Haiti, hundreds of millions of dollars in official development aid were withheld in response to what have been termed 2000's "fraudulent elections" (Robinson 2004; Farmer et al. 2003). In a dispute arising from the formula used to calculate the winners of seven senate seats, the United States and others—including the World Bank and the International Monetary Fund—alleged vote rigging in Haiti and, siding with anti-Aristide activists, demanded that the election be rerun. Labeled by some a "financial embargo," the response to perceived governmental corruption was to withhold official development aid and loans to the government of Haiti (Robinson 2004). In contrast, while those active in the twinning program acknowledge—indeed blame—the failures of government to promote democracy and development in Haiti, they also suggest that they are there to care for Haiti's citizens in the absence of the state's capacity or willingness to do so. Their work "fills the gap" in meeting perceived critical needs in Haiti. When asked whether they could imagine a time when the twinning program would no longer be necessary, several interviewees said they could envision the end of twinning only *after* the government was reformed.

I would guess if either the government was stable enough that the government could assist people or that the community was self-sustaining, with people not going hungry and able to go to school. (Interview #21)

I think if Haiti lost its Third World status, and the country developed a political system, gave basic human rights to people, freedoms, if the education were developed so people got an education, could do more for themselves, I guess then, twinning wouldn't be necessary. (Interview #13)

Thus, both conventional and lay initiatives draw on "good governance" discourses to explain poverty and the failure of development, but conventional initiatives respond by withdrawing from and punishing states with "bad policy" environments, whereas lay initiatives such as twinning step in and attempt to make up for the state's deficiencies. The goal in both instances, however, is to encourage "the capacity of 'weak' Southern states to attain more responsible 'citizenship' in the international community of liberal democracies" (Craig and Porter in Abrahamsen 2004:1462). That is, denying aid to "bad governments" and funneling aid directly to the "grassroots" are both maneuvers to "produce modern subjects" that will "practice their freedom responsibly" (Abrahamsen 2004:1462) in line with neoliberal principles.

■ "Troubles" with Development

Just as a variety of barriers have forestalled development, according to both conventional and lay theorists and practitioners, so too have a number of difficulties beset those attempting to implement development. In this section, I explore some of the challenges that St. Robert has faced as it works for Haitian development and consider whether these are peculiar to St. Robert or symptomatic of development more generally.

As both concept and practice, development was instituted in and by the global north on behalf of the south. Thus, much of its framework reflects Western, Enlightenment thinking, with a focus on science, rationality, and Truth. And despite rhetoric on the importance of "participation" and of generating development locally, only certain locally based practices are deemed acceptable. Corruption is not among these; rather, corruption is defined in negative terms (as the absence of impersonal bureaucracy, objectivity, and professionalism), and its presence is attributed to the failures or flaws of the systems (and people) in which it occurs.

Development professionals have long been preoccupied with understanding and explaining corruption, with the goal of eliminating it. Whether it is characterized as a "primitive" or transitional moment in the evolution of state bureaucracy (Myrdal 1968) or as rooted in a traditional culture (Egbue 2006) that allows friends, family, and others to call upon "bureaucrats" for favors, corruption generally is defined, assessed, and measured in normative Western terms. Corruption is framed as a problem to be overcome. And indeed, those working within state bureaucracies often *are* able to capture official development aid intended for the poor and powerless. Corruption is a complex phenomenon that remains foremost among the concerns of conventional development.

St. Robert also has experienced the "troubles" of corruption. In spite of their emphasis on the "no middleman" nature of twinning, many U.S. parishes, including St. Robert, have experienced the challenges of working through middlemen. For example, many parishes send "sea containers" of goods to Haiti. School supplies, bikes, sewing machines, medicines — the list of items sent from the United States to Haiti is lengthy. And most containers do not arrive at their Haitian parish twins completely intact. Usually, at least some — and occasionally most — of the goods have been "stolen" along the way. While sitting on the docks for months awaiting clearance from customs, the containers are thought to be accessible both to corrupt customs workers and to people "off the streets." I have heard of tool boxes intended for trade school graduates, sewing machines, medical equipment, and bikes disappearing from the containers, and this has been a real source of frustration for those on St. Robert's Haiti Committee.

> You'd like to do something, but it's very hard because a lot of stuff that is sent has to go through the government. There's so much graft that the stuff you send doesn't get to where it needs to go. It's frustrating to try to do very much for these people, because so many people are willing to take away what they have. That's just the nature of human beings, I guess. . . . The people in power have a lot more to say than people not in power. (Interview #13)

Some have suggested that these problems of graft and corruption are just a cost of doing business in Haiti and so need to be factored in as such. By paying "gratuities" and enrolling key players within the twinning network, one local businessman in another Grand Rapids parish has made getting sea containers to Haiti intact "an art." And Doug now helps coordinate sea container shipments from Grand Rapids to Haiti through this man, rather than through PTPA. As he puts it, "Bruce has gotten it down to an art. He can get containers in and out in two months. While PTPA was sending them, they would just be opened up on streets. It's much more organized now than what the national end is doing."

Interestingly, despite having access to this new "streamlined" import system, St. Robert has not shipped any containers through Bruce. There seems to be some hesitation about the best way to proceed with containers, perhaps because committee members are still smarting from the loss of so much equipment from the last shipment made. At any rate, like development professionals more broadly, committee members at St. Robert have been frustrated by what they see as a disruption in the chain linking them to their intended beneficiaries. The system is currently viewed as problematic and in need of transformation.

St. Robert committee members have been frustrated by other aspects of the twinning, as well. As discussed in prior chapters, the relationship between the committee and the current head of Our Lady, Father Yvens, has been strained, not in the least because of Father Yvens's perceived poor accounting of how he is spending twinning funds. The problem with the church pews, described earlier, escalated the tension between the two parishes, and Father Yvens's behavior since then has been considered somewhat strange and sometimes suspicious.

In conventional development endeavors, formal accounting is a necessary and non-negotiable condition of receiving development aid. The recipients of that aid—or at least those tasked with delivering the aid—are required to provide an accounting of how funds have been used. Without such accountability, aid will not be dispersed.

In the context of twinning, these lines are less clear. Again, stemming from the idea that two parishes are coming together in equal partnership with one another, the donor parish is not supposed to be in a more powerful position than the recipient parish. As seen earlier, this ideal unevenly translates into practice. Nonetheless, the voiced ideal does set some parameters on how demanding some St. Robert committee members feel they can be. In talking about the accounting reports coming from Haiti, one woman remarked, "We're supposed to get accounting every six months; they do it when they feel like it. And it's down to the penny, so you know [the reports are not completely accurate]" (Interview #8).

This sense that Father Yvens makes an accounting of twinning funds only when he feels like it has been a cause of tension between committee members themselves. Some feel they should demand more rigorous accounting before additional funds are dispersed, and others feel that funds should continue to flow to Haiti despite what is considered shoddy and intermittent accounting. In talking about "not getting very much information from Father Yvens"—specifically regarding the diminution of the food project, where students were being fed only 2 to 3 days a week rather than 4—at one committee meeting, the following exchange took place:

Committee member #1: The only way to get accountability is to withhold the money. It gets me in my belly thinking of children going hungry.

Committee member #2: It's the Haitian tradition—everything runs through the priest. We've had more success with the microloan committee.

Committee member #3: It's contrary to Haitian culture [to skirt the priest's authority]. The priest is second to God.

Committee member #1: Father does not like being in that parish.

Committee member #4: If we want to get the money into the food program, [we have to set up the program differently].

Committee member #2: Father would be insulted. He likes to control the money.

Committee member #4: But the money's not being used for what it's supposed to be. Maybe we need to find an alternative.

Committee member #2: He's proud of the system he's worked out . . . .

Committee member #5: Maybe we could ask [the Bishop of Gonaïves] for a transfer [for Father Yvens]?

Committee member #6: We can't ask that. How would it look if
someone from the outside asked for Father Lou's [St. Robert's
head pastor] removal?
Committee member #5: Jean [former head pastor of Our Lady] sees
the Bishop daily. . . .

There were calls later in the meeting for sending only a small portion of the $20,000 allotted for the food project, for sending the full
amount but warning that receipts really were needed, and for sending 2
months' worth and withholding the remainder of the funds until receipts
were received. Some suggested requiring Father Yvens to show some evidence that food was really being purchased and prepared for the students. "Show us some pictures, some evidence of them eating" suggested
one committee member.

After deciding to send a portion of the $20,000 allotted for the food
project, the committee proceeded to another contentious topic: the
"doubling up" of twins by Our Lady. As one woman reported, "Father
Yvens wrote to Theresa Patterson two summers ago, asking to be
twinned, thinking we wouldn't find out about it." Although Theresa
reportedly declined to assign him another twin, Father Yvens was able to
find his own supplemental twin in a Baltimore parish. This information
came through "secret sources" rather than Father Yvens himself.
Moreover, the Baltimore parish—aside from the head of its Haiti
Committee—is unaware of St. Robert's involvement with Our Lady.
And the head of that committee does not want St. Robert to tell the
larger Baltimore parish of the double twinning.

Since learning about the duplicate twinning, St. Robert has
attempted to work with the head of the Baltimore committee, though
with little success. Labeling him "cagey," one woman on the Haiti
Committee expressed her confusion about the secrecy surrounding his
twinning. Said another, "If I were a member of the Baltimore parish, I'd
want to know [about us here at St. Robert]!" St. Robert's Haiti
Committee has decided against contacting the Baltimore parish, opting
instead to continue working only with its committee head, so as to not
disrupt the financial flows Father Yvens is receiving from Baltimore.

Despite these revelations about the lack of accounting, the scarcity in the food project, and the "double dipping" into twinning funds, one woman at the meeting returned to the earlier debate about how much money to send Father Yvens for the food project: "I'd like to send the larger amount." In a frustrated and irritated tone, another responded, "How often do we have to get kicked in the head? We're throwing money down a pit while the kids still aren't eating!"

These types of interchanges are typical of twinning meetings, where there are no clear answers to the many questions raised by committee members. Indeed, almost a year after the committee meeting just detailed, another meeting included the following exchange.

Father: My concern is accountability.

Committee member #1: I don't know that we'll ever get an accounting. We have two different geographies, cultures, languages.

Father: I said accountability, not accounting.

Committee member #2: Why, there's always overhead. We're trying to get the money directly to the people. On the other hand, we could pay someone $30,000 year to live there, to have a person on the spot [to let us know what's really going on.]

Committee member #3: Every group that goes down is both frustrated and impressed with what they find.

Committee member #1: Do we really not trust the parish and the priest? We give them the money—do we need to monitor how it's spent?

As these exchanges demonstrate, there is no consensus on what accountability might be or whether it is really necessary. Despite proclamations that "we control the finances, so they have to jump through the hoops," as one woman commented to me in another context, the reality is that there is little agreement on what those hoops should look like and who precisely should do the jumping. The impulse to create a system of accountability, however, intends to promote a new form of subjectivity in Haiti, one that is "auditable."

> To be audited, an organisation must actively transform itself into an auditable commodity; one structured to conform to the need to be monitored. . . . In contemporary partnerships, various types of auditing technologies are instruments of a new form of governance and power, designed . . . [to create] new kinds of subjectivities, of self-managed individuals and states who render themselves auditable. (Abrahamsen 2004:1463)

As of 2005, Father Yvens had managed to avoid being subjected to much scrutiny and resist becoming unambiguously "auditable." Despite the displeasure and disapproval that those most active on the Haiti Committee feel about this, they continue to support Father Yvens financially.

Would the "fungibility" of St. Robert's aid be considered corruption in conventional development circles? Would Father Yvens's accounting sheets—balanced to the penny as they are—be eyed suspiciously? Would aid continue to flow to Our Lady, even when duplicate projects and funding from other sources were likely possibilities? The debates that continually occur at committee meetings—including concerns about accountability—are in many ways distinctive of this type of development initiative. Implored to respect, trust, and collaborate with its twin in Haiti, St. Robert's committee faces numerous challenges that have no easy solutions. Thus, although both conventional and lay initiatives worry about the presence and effects of corruption on projects and beneficiaries, only twinning agonizes over how to handle them. Like the failures of the Haitian state, the perceived failures of the local leadership do not result in marginalization or exclusion from aid regimes in twinning. They cause tension among those on the Haiti Committee, but aid continues to flow as members attempt to forge agreeable solutions.

■ "Hegemonic Discourse" and Twinning

As examined in Chapter Three, many post-structuralist scholars agree that a hegemonic development discourse exists:[3] one preoccupied with (abnormal) poverty and its elimination via the rational, technological application of (Western) scientific knowledge (Escobar 1995). The dis-

course allows certain development "professionals," those with specialized and expert knowledge, to "set the rules for the game," to define
what is rational and possible. And, in the process, it allows those in the
global north to justify interventions into the south. Moreover, despite
being "experts," development professionals often have an incomplete—
and sometimes wholly inaccurate—understanding of the historical and
political contexts in which they work and the people they are endeav-
oring to develop (Ferguson 1994).

   This book is an exploration of development as it is conceived,
designed, and implemented by those outside formal development agencies—whether state-sponsored or nongovernmental—those who generally would not be considered development experts and who have not
been formally indoctrinated with a hegemonic development discourse.
One question this book attempts to answer is "What is the relationship
between the entrenched hegemonic discourses characterizing conventional development initiatives and those of lay development?"

   To consider the question here, I will break it down into a couple of
statements addressing the concerns many scholars have raised about
hegemonic development discourses. I evaluate these statements in terms
of their applicability to parish twinning.

Development Depoliticizes Poverty

Some have argued that development is, in many ways, a sleight of hand
that magically diverts attention from the *structural* features undergirding
global poverty and instead focuses it on *technical* features that can be
quantified, measured, and evaluated (Ferguson 1994; Escobar 1995).
From this perspective, poverty exists because something is perceived to
be lacking—or abnormal—about the nation, society, or group labeled
poor. Thus, rather than addressing issues of power and domination, the
global division of wealth, structural inequality, and the like, development
instead tends to treat poverty as a technical problem that can be resolved
through certain interventions, such as increasing industrialization, promoting trade, enhancing agricultural efficiency, reducing disease, and
building roads.

   With this understanding post-structuralists critique development
for not focusing on the structures and processes that enable some to ben-

efit from the global and local orders while others are exploited and oppressed by them. Furthermore, by ignoring these features, development is able to cast poverty in apolitical terms, calling for solutions that are not threatening to elites and other power brokers. Of course, not all development scholars have ignored the political, social, and economic structures promoting and maintaining poverty. Feminist scholars in particular have focused intensely on the structural features of oppression (for example, see Moser 1993; Sen and Grown 1987; Young 1993), although few have been successful at translating such analysis into structurally transformative development projects. This may be for reasons noted by Black (1999): Those institutions and individuals successfully focusing on "important" work—such as land reform, for example—are also those most likely to be quickly suppressed. Such work draws a ready and negative reaction from privileged classes, whose interests may be threatened. Changing structures is difficult; handing out new high-yield seeds, by contrast, is relatively easy.

As discussed in the previous chapter, twinning likewise does not focus on the structural features underpinning Haiti's poverty. In a manner reminiscent of Ferguson's (1994:37) analysis of the ways in which the World Bank frames Lesotho, where "the colonial past is a blank, economic stagnation is due to government inaction, and 'development' results from 'development projects,'" many St. Robert's Haiti Committee members have little or no knowledge of Haiti's history, its position in the global political economy, or its past interactions with development regimes. Although many are critical of the divisions cleaving Haitian society along "elite" and "peasant" lines, committee members tend not to know why these cleavages exist, how they came to be, or how they might be addressed or undone. Likewise, although some mentioned the "indemnity" that Haiti was forced to pay in exchange for political and economic recognition following its independence in the early nineteenth century (see Farmer 1994), no one suggested that this was relevant for understanding why Haiti continues to be poor today. Rather, the government—conceived of primarily as an isolated entity apart from regional or global forces—was blamed for its inadequacies and as the fomenter of Haitian poverty. Even with this explanation, nothing in St. Robert's program endeavors to transform—or even address—what it considers to be the failures of Haiti's government. No, the task is simply too large, too overwhelming. Moreover, as in conventional development, some believe twinning is not supposed to be overtly "political."

The reality is, of course, that twinning does have political overtones, sometimes overtly. For example, when groups first travel to Haiti and stay at the PTPA guesthouse in Port-au-Prince, a guide takes them on a tour of "the stations of the cross." These are sites throughout the city where political persecution and violence have occurred, especially that targeting Haitian social justice advocates. Aside from giving twinning participants a platform from which to critique Haiti's elite, however, these tours are largely disconnected from twinning's daily activities, in part because some openly reject their political overtones:

> They had the stations of the cross, fourteen places where horrible things happened, so that Aristide came to power. Well, anything I had ever seen or read about Aristide, he was a crook. And this was obscene, ridiculous. But our group was very much involved in that. But I felt there was undue involvement in politics that I didn't agree with. It's one thing to do Christian service and brotherhood. And it's quite another to be involved in politics. (Interview #9)

To tease this sentiment out a little more, consider that several in the twinning program hold Mother Theresa as a model to emulate: Mother Theresa, who devoted her life to the poor, living and working among them and sacrificing her own material comfort. Yet some scholars have criticized Mother Theresa for her myopia, for herself failing to address the larger conditions encouraging and maintaining poverty among the groups with whom she was working. Her efforts were so widely esteemed and supported, some allege, precisely because they posed no threat to existing hierarchies; they in no way challenged the status quo. Instead, Mother Theresa's work served to blunt the structural violence impinging on people's lives, thereby shifting the focus to caring for the poor and downtrodden rather than challenging the conditions that shaped their vulnerability. Certainly, the same criticism could be leveled at those working in twinning. One response, of course, is that the world needs both kinds of approaches to remedying poverty: those that revolutionize oppressive structures and those that focus on caring for the oppressed (Shaw 2005).

Perhaps, then, my concern with twinning's lack of attention to structural factors is not fair, because the objectives of those active in twinning are clear; their intention is to save the individual starfish, not clear the beach of them. And this thinking has parallels in more conventional initiatives. In particular, many mainstream participatory development approaches have been criticized for adopting an overly "local" orientation—one that precludes engagement with macro-level features (Cooke and Kothari 2001). As Mohan and Hickey (2004:61) suggest, participation has been castigated for encouraging "fragmentation rather than multi-scaled strategies." Yet those who respond to such criticism maintain that a focus on the local level need not be isolating. For example, Cornwall (2004), Gaventa (2004), Hickey and Mohan (2004) and all examine the ways in which citizenship and "space" can be transformed and transforming in order to allow for local-level action to pierce exploitive structures—especially via democratic practices. This suggests that twinning might be able to maintain its local focus while also extending its analysis and action into the realm of more structural features.

As discussed in the last chapter, although committee members tend to define development in diverse terms, they also generally agree that development should "develop people" and be locally grounded. I am not saying this focus is good or bad, right or wrong, but it is consistent with a broader reconceptualizing of development as the empowerment of the poor, whereby they can become "partners rather than recipients; the active creators of their own future and development . . . no longer simply victims but subjects to be empowered" (Abrahamsen 2004:1460). This is a new form of governmentality, wherein the poor are constituted as active agents in their self-management. I also am suggesting that by concentrating so intently on the local level and framing their projects primarily around addressing Haitian poverty through food aid and education, the St. Robert's Haiti program does—like conventional development—reduce Haiti's challenges to a series of "problems"—partialization, in Poppendieck's (1998:307) terms—that can be addressed through seemingly apolitical solutions, though in this case delivered via caring, committed brothers and sisters of the Catholic faith. Haitian "underdevelopment" then becomes manageable as a series of identifiable problems to "fix," with solutions modeled on the application of Western knowledges and scientific understandings of the world, attained through formal education. Indeed, many on St. Robert's Haiti Committee see their twinning program as equipping Haitians with the skills and training they need to assess their situations and forge their own solutions to the problems of poverty. Meanwhile, the structural features of Haiti's inequity, oppression, and position in the world economy are largely ignored.

The Poor Are "Backward"

In a similar vein, conventional development discourses traditionally conceive of those targeted for development as somehow deficient or delinquent, as in need of external "salvation." Again, rather than situating poverty or powerlessness within a wider framework addressing issues of structural inequality, these discourses suggest the need to reconfigure the poor. Escobar (1995:41), for example, argues that "Development proceeded by creating 'abnormalities' (such as the 'illiterate,' the 'underdeveloped,' the 'malnourished,' 'small farmers,' or 'landless peasants'), which it would later treat and reform." That is, rather than reflecting "truth" or "reality," discourses—in this case, development discourses—construct "the poor" as objects of knowledge that can be intervened upon and managed.

Indeed, Escobar's (1995:23) assertion that "management of poverty called for interventions in education, health, hygiene, morality, and employment and the [instilling] of good habits of associations, savings, child rearing and so on" is strikingly descriptive of the very nature of St. Robert's twinning. As discussed in earlier chapters, twinning participants assess, label, and attempt to address what is seen to be lacking among Haiti's poor: adequate food, environmental quality, jobs, education, medical knowledge. But, perhaps more tellingly, some also attribute these problems to the deficiencies of Haitians themselves, conceiving of the Haitian peasantry as uncultivated, uneducated, and illiterate.

These constructions are not unique to committee members at St. Robert. They are fundamental to the configuration and exercise of development more broadly. Escobar (1995:110) calls such practices "labeling," whereby the "whole reality of a person's life [can be] reduced to a single feature or trait . . . [and] the person is turned into a case." Again, this diverts attention from the structural forces impinging on peoples' lives and instead focuses on explanations deriving from characteristics internal to the poor, which can be treated through some technological fix (Escobar 1995:110). James Ferguson (1994), for example, considers how those "targeted" for development projects in Lesotho are necessarily defined in ways necessitating outside intervention: as "backward" subsistence farmers, as cut off from markets and the modern cash economy, and as adhering to anachronistic, "traditional" livestock customs because they lack knowledge and technical inputs. Ferguson deftly deconstructs these "myths," demonstrating how, in reality, these farmers have been deeply embedded in a modern, capitalist reserve labor economy and noncommercial livestock practices.

Similarly, Jennie M. Smith focuses her analysis on professional developers' construction of peasants in Haiti. In considering the ways in which "aiders" have conceptualized the "aided" in Haiti, Smith (2001:31) sketches four traits that tend to be attributed to Haitians as explanations for their poverty:

> a preference for dependency on more powerful others (a dependency mentality, or, as it is sometimes called, a slave mentality); a fatalism leading to apathy and resignation; an inability to think analytically or critically about their situation; and a chronic resistance to working cooperatively and effectively in the interest of the common good.

Smith's descriptions, in fact, are closely aligned with stereotypes held by many on St. Robert's Haiti Committee. Committee members widely view Haitians as less motivated than Americans, resigned to their poverty, unable to think critically, and selfish. Said one Haiti committee member: "I used to hear people speak of problems who'd been involved in Haiti before. They spoke of ingrained attitudes. I thought they were being awfully negative. But now I see some of those issues are there and have to be overcome" (Interview #1).

How did these broader stereotypes come to the attention of St. Robert's Haiti Committee? Certainly Tom—introduced earlier as the director of a forestry and agricultural extension project that St. Robert partially funds—is to some extent responsible. Tom runs an officially recognized nonprofit, partakes in development training seminars, reads development texts, and interacts with others in Haiti who work in "official" development channels. This puts him in contact with other development professionals, many of whom are likely to hold views similar to those analyzed by Smith. Moreover, Tom is vocal about what he views as the shortcomings of the Haitian peasantry, particularly their preference for "handouts," their inability to think critically, and their apathy. For example, in talking about the inadequacies of the Haitian educational system, Tom decries what he sees as the failures of learning "by rote":

> They cannot problem-solve. If you can't problem-solve, how can you have community development? I asked a group one time why the river ran brown after it rains. They couldn't answer, couldn't even begin to guess. Even Jean-Rony, who's at the top of his class in high school, didn't know. They weren't taught why and so they didn't know. They couldn't go any farther than that.

Tom is an influential force among some on the committee because he actually lives in Verrettes for most of the year. He is able to claim knowledge about the area, "culture," and needs that others on the committee cannot. And this gives him a platform from which to espouse his particular visions, which are more closely linked to conventional development initiatives. When Tom is in Michigan, he often attends Haiti Committee meetings, if they are scheduled. And he stays in email contact with several committee members while in Haiti. The point is that Tom is exposed to the conventional stereotypes of Haitians, and in his experience, they ring true. He then is able to communicate these ideas to others on the committee, with whom they likewise resonate.

Many scholars argue that these conceptualizations and constructions of the "developing" are fundamental to development's discourse and practice (Crush 1995; Escobar 1995; Esteva 1992; Ferguson 1994). I agree, and I suggest that such discourses also characterize the ways in which some St. Robert committee members imagine Haitians and their communities. They provide constructions that at once explain what is happening in Haiti—Haitians are uneducated and hence unable to forge solutions to their problems—and also provide a remedy—through St. Robert's sponsorship of educational programs, Haitians will be able to find jobs and provide for themselves.

But the situation in twinning is, in fact, more complex than Escobar and others posit for development. In twinning, as we have seen, Haitians not only are regarded as exhibiting characteristics that must be repudiated—and, more important here, must be "fixed"—but also are held up as models to emulate. That is, committee members tend to simultaneously frame Haitians in terms of both deficiencies and righteousness. Haitians' perceived greater spirituality, commitment to family, simpler living, freedom from materialism, and the like provide inspiration for some on the committee to rethink their own values, ways of life, and priorities. That is, Haitians, by virtue of their poverty, offer committee members alternative visions for being in the world, alternative models of reality. These are powerful lessons for middle-class and upper-middle-class committee members, who suddenly find themselves questioning the otherwise unrecognized and unchallenged features of their own lives: the importance of work, money, accumulation, consumption, and material comfort.

■ Professionalizing Knowledge for the Exercise of Power

At its most basic, the hegemonic development discourse is thought to be a construct through which poor countries are "known, specified, and intervened upon" (Escobar 1995). Anti-development scholars argue that Western models of development arose from the creation of a constructed and specialized knowledge about the global south. This knowledge was predicated upon notions of poverty and the need to correct its "abnormalities" (for example, illiteracy and overpopulation). Institutionalizing a cadre of "experts" to address the "problem" of underdevelopment set the stage for the exercise of power over that object: the global south. Through the hegemony of norms and values, development discourses convinced the global south of their own "underdevelopment" and promised them a better life through outside intervention in their economies and societies. And in the process, not only were jobs created for the Western middle class, but Third World countries were brought back under (post-) colonial control and administration.

Post-structural discourse analysts suggest that professionalized knowledge is one way in which this power is exercised and reproduced. But how do we know when knowledge is "professionalized"? What exactly does that mean? Or, even more basically, what is knowledge? Arce and Long (1992:221) suggest that knowledge is not simply an accumulation of facts that are learned or discovered but, rather, is a way of "construing the world"; it is constructive and is "constituted by the ways in which people categorize, code, process and impute meaning to their experiences." That is, knowledge is the way people make sense of and give meaning to their lives. Knowledge, according to Arce and Long, is destructive as well, because it destroys other possible frames through which to see the world.

Robert Chambers defines "normal professionalism" as the thinking, values, methods, and behavior dominant in a profession or discipline. He suggests that it is both stable and conservative (Chambers 1993:3). Indeed, it is on the basis of specialized training—"diploma disease" (Chambers 1993:3)—and experience that development professionals are able to position themselves as experts within development institutions. They are granted legitimate claim to development knowledge and have license to design and deliver projects. Their authority as experts is recognized and rewarded by those within the conventional development apparatus. Rooted in Enlightenment thinking, professional knowledge/expertise depends on "Western scientific knowledge . . . as . . . universally valid and applicable to all," even though only some are granted "expert" status to produce it (Parpart 1995:222–223; Crewe and Harrison 1998). Consequently, development practitioners overvalue knowledge obtained via formal education, while undervaluing and discounting knowledge acquired in other ways.

> Development practitioners (and scholars) [tend] to undervalue
> knowledge that comes from living in poverty, from working out
> solutions to daily life in specific, often difficult locales, and from
> cultural traditions that have provided basic but adequate sur-
> vival patterns for hundreds of years. (Parpart 1995:229)

Or, to put it more bluntly, "Rural development is a process whereby affluent urban-dwellers teach poor peasants how to survive in the countryside without money" (Black 1999:10).

Development experts craft the discourses by which development can be "known" and discussed. Dorothy Smith suggests that professional discourses offer

> the categories with which facts can be named and analyzed and
> thus have an important role in constituting the phenomena
> that the organization knows and describes. Facts are presented
> in standardized ways. In this sense, facts are an aspect of social
> organization, a practice of knowing, that, through the use of
> ready-made categories, construct an object as external to the
> knower and independent of him or her. (Escobar 1995:107)

Like all discourses, those characterizing St. Robert's twinning are "category-driven," presenting "facts" about Haiti and Haitians in fairly standardized ways. Haitians are poor, uneducated, illiterate, oppressed by the government, and in need of external intervention. Whether or not these "facts" are "true" is irrelevant; rather, the constructions themselves reveal how those on the Haiti Committee are able to—indeed, are compelled to—configure Haiti and Haitians as deficient and "abnormal," how Haitians are defined in terms of what they lack.

And yet, as previously mentioned, although Haitians are constructed in traditionally "developmentalist" terms as deficient and abnormal, twinning simultaneously casts Haitians as pillars of hope and inspiration, as models to emulate in some ways. There is a real sense among some on the St. Robert Haiti Committee—and it is explicitly stated within PTPA promotional literatures—that Haitians have something to teach Americans about simplicity of faith, uncomplicated living, and the importance of family. Nevertheless, just like the more negative assessments, these more positive spins are merely constructions invented according to the imaginations of those active in twinning. Again, I am not interested in whether such assessments are "true"; indeed, scholars such as Jennie Smith (2001) explicitly maintain that Haitians *do* have something to teach Americans about these things. Rather, my interest here is in the ways in which such constructions are related to, buoy up, and challenge hegemonic development discourses. And in this case, they tend to stem from the inherent "othering" that development entails. Because of their poverty, Haitians are cast as fundamentally *different* from U.S. twinning participants. That is, Haitians' poverty provides the framework through which the St. Robert Haiti Committee members make sense of Haitians, both as models of inspiration and as examples of qualities that must be repudiated. Whether they are esteemed for their focus on family, greater spirituality, and lack of materialism, or chastised for their illiteracy, laziness, evasiveness, or dishonesty, Haitians are understood in terms of their poverty—in terms of what it gives them, what it denies them, and why it exists.

From their positions of relative power and privilege, St. Robert's Haiti Committee members are largely able to establish the parameters of twinning and development in Haiti. Their representations inform the rest of the parish about who Haitians are, what their lives are like, and what the best way is to "improve" them. The authority and "expertise" of committee members seem to be accepted to a degree, as evidenced by the continued financial support the twinning program enjoys at St. Robert, both in terms of individual contributions and in terms of allocations from the church's annual budget.

Once funding is arranged and access to "the people" is secured through twinning networks, there are relatively few barriers for those wishing to engage in Haitian development. The Haitian state allows foreigners, their goods, and money into the country without too much red tape. Geographically, getting to Haiti is simple, quick, and relatively inexpensive. Through twinning, in-country networks are established to assist with internal travel. Indeed, the ease of entering into Haitian development might help explain why Haiti in general is so intensely subject to the development "gaze." Although reliable numbers are impossible to find, estimates of the number of NGOs currently working for development in Haiti range from 2000 to 10,000 (World Bank 1998b), even though Haiti's population is only around 8 million and its territory about the size of Massachusetts. Assessing this state of affairs, Tom lamented what he considers to be the overly facile entry of nonexperts into Haitian development:

> In other countries, like Africa [sic], people who go there to work must have all these ideas, they're experts. But Haiti is so close, you have all these people who go thinking they know—neophytes—who think they know where they're going, what they're doing.

Despite Tom's skepticism, it is certainly legitimate to ask whether those on St. Robert's Haiti Committee are development experts or even specialists, as Cassie asserted. Certainly, when held to the "diploma" standard, they are not. They are not educated in development economics or related fields. They have not enrolled in special development courses. They will not be showing up for work at the World Bank or giving papers at conventional development conferences.[4] They do not make a living from their development activities. At the same time, however, they have experiential knowledge grounded in twinning networks and in Haiti. And they parlay this knowledge into projects, presentations, and practice. Some also read academic articles related to Haiti, including works by Paul Farmer, and draw selectively from them in framing critiques of Haiti's predatory state, for example. Thus, although lay development practitioners might be marginalized within conventional development regimes, they certainly have "space" enough outside the "development machine" to exercise their knowledge and practice of development.

But what about the intentional (or at least intended) "mutuality" of twinning—the idea that St. Robert and Our Lady are "equal partners" in twinning? And what about the fact the most of the projects established in Verrettes originate in suggestions made by the priests there? Addressing similar "partnerships," Parpart (1995:240) has noted,

> Cooperation based on equal partnerships between Northern (and some Southern) experts is rare and difficult. Most partner-

ships between North and South have focused on transmitting information from the North to the South, or from Southern experts to the poor. Many have been fraught with "tensions and conflicts" and have failed to produce the expected benefits.

This seems largely to be the case with St. Robert's twinning, where, although they try to be attentive to differences in power and culture, committee members ultimately value their own knowledge systems and expertise above those of Haitians. That is, despite a voiced concern with building a give-and-take relationship, the practice of twinning is often a one-way street. Committee members often speak of twinning as more about their giving to Our Lady, with little benefit to themselves. The relationships between the parishes and between the individuals representing them are largely framed by the "experts" on St. Robert's Haiti Committee and center on projects in Haiti, funding, accountability, and "helping" Haitians. St. Robert's committee members, then, are largely setting the rules of the twinning and determining how it can be imagined and practiced. The priests in Haiti *do* resist the management systems imposed by St. Robert (their not providing regular accounting, their asking that St. Robert not visit Our Lady, and their refusing to help in my research for this book may be seen as examples of this resistance). But ultimately, the encounters between the two parishes are bound by the rules established by St. Robert. The St. Robert Haiti Committee's discourses on development and Haiti "represent the world as it is for those who rule it, rather than as it is for those who are ruled" (Escobar 1995:108). At the end of the day, then, St. Robert's twinning—even though it is a lay initiative outside of the conventional professional sphere—constructs "expert" discourses that both legitimize their intervention in Verrettes and provide a rationalization for their management of the program.

■ Twinning as Counter-Development?

As discussed in earlier sections, anti-development scholars reject development as a theoretical and practical enterprise, "not merely on account of its results but because of its intentions, its world-view and mindset"

(Nederveen Pieterse 2000:175). Instead, they imagine a "post-development" era, where "the centrality of development as an organizing principle of social life would no longer hold" (Escobar 2000). There are two different ways in which this transformation—or, more precisely, this "undoing" of development—might proceed: from anthropologists' radical disengagement from development (for example, Sachs 1992) or from their active involvement in and attempts to subvert development (for example, Gardner and Lewis 1996).

In both cases, post-development scholars suggest that anthropology of development analyses should "call attention to diversity, highlight alternatives, show interconnectedness, and uncover the complexity of social and economic life" in order to challenge development's key assumptions and representations and provide alternative ways of seeing (Gardner and Lewis 1996:50). One way to do this, they suggest, is by looking at alternative visions of development or counter-development as they are (re)created at local-level "interfaces," where individuals with differing interests, resources, and power come together (Arce and Long 1992). I agree, which is why this project explores parish-to-parish twinning, where "grassroots" communities come together to forge relatively novel approaches to development and cross-cultural collaboration. Although twinning clearly exemplifies the diffusion of development thinking outside of official development institutions, a question hangs over this project: Does twinning constitute counter-development? Is it "alternative development," an alternative to development, or something entirely different? In formulating such questions, I am referring to development in its hegemonic sense, as the "set of statements" outlined in Chapter Three: (neo)evolutionary concepts of progress; the West as "advanced"; preoccupation with poverty; technical application of Western, scientific knowledge; emphasis on growth.

One way to tackle this question is to consider twinning within a broader context of NGO-ization and the "revolution" NGOs were supposed to unleash within the development world (Fisher 1997). Some suggest that NGOs have been idealized as "doing good" because they are thought to be motivated not by politics and profits but by other factors—such as religiosity, charity, and humanism. Both critics of development—such as those in the anti-development camp—and development's supporters have hailed NGOs as the solution to development's failures. NGOs are understood by some as more efficient than government programs, as better at providing welfare services, and as a way to overcome the "bad policy environments" of rogue states. Others suggest that NGOs—and grassroots organizations, in particular—are vehicles for resisting and altering power relationships, that they can transform state and society through their ability to politicize issues and magnify "subjugated knowledges" (Fisher 1997:6). Although the purpose of this book is not to evaluate the efficiency or success of twinning's programs in Haiti—but rather to assess twinning as it is related to broader initiatives within the development regime—it seems clear that twinning would not fulfill the hopes of either camp.

Like conventional development, twinning participants are very interested in trying to measure the "effectiveness, accountability, disbursement rates, and 'visible impact' of their programs" (Rew 1997:91). Yet St. Robert finds it exceedingly difficult to get a clear understanding of the "on the ground" needs in Verrettes, to know whether the project's "goals" are being achieved, or to complete any sort of comprehensive project evaluation. As mentioned at one meeting, the committee often takes a "flying leap into the darkness" in trying to design, deliver, and assess how their twinning relationship is actually working in Verrettes.

This stems in large part from the very structure of St. Robert's twinning, where development is the focus but the typical development apparatus integral to "measuring success" is missing. Twinning is driven by volunteers, many of whom are enmeshed in busy professional careers. These volunteers donate their time, talent, and money, and this keeps "administrative" staff salaries to a minimum. But the result is twofold. First, only a handful (more realistically, only a few) invest considerable time in making the twinning work. The program began at St. Robert as a result of the efforts of one particularly dedicated and inspiring woman, and it continues to be directed by only a few individuals. Second, this not only creates an institutional "weakness" (if those most active on the committee needed to halt participation, few others would be able to pick up the reins) but also centralizes decision making, restricting power to just a few people, whose choices may or may not represent the wishes or desires of the larger St. Robert parish.

The local-level orientation of twinning also tends to obfuscate, or render irrelevant, the "systems" in which twinning occurs. That is, issues of power, authority, inequity, and the like tend to be overshadowed by the intense focus on meeting individual needs in Verrettes. The macro-level context is not being—and cannot be—addressed via twinning networks, as twinning currently is practiced. Significantly, this is a criticism that has been leveled at NGOs in general, particularly at those that employ participatory strategies:

> [NGOs' principal] weakness is that they have difficulty coming to grips with, and then addressing, the processes and relationships underlying rural poverty. . . . Much NGO work is conducted in isolation from wider policy issues. (Farrington and Bebbington 1993:184; see also MacDonald 1995)

Recognizing twinning's limitations, one man said he was not going to change the world through twinning, maybe only make a few people's lives better. This may certainly be true, but others have raised concerns about the problems such programs engender. Blunting the negative effects of the current social order may pacify the "oppressed" and undermine their political potential (Ferguson 1994). In her study of the U.S. food-banking system, for example, Poppendieck (1998) suggests that food banks ultimately have a negative effect on the poor, because, like development, they turn hunger into a technical problem "appropriately" managed via private interventions. Food banks shift the focus from the underlying causes of hunger to its manageable solution. As one food bank worker commented, "In the worst analysis, [food banking] is an awful thing—what we're doing is allowing an oppressive system to continue" (Poppendieck 1998:268).

Twinning, even though it is a Catholic project, in many ways reflects these trends in "secular" social service delivery. But it also fits within a broader trajectory identified by Wuthnow as characteristic of American religious projects more generally, which are concerned with "caring for the needy and contributing time to help with community service projects" but are also "intensely individualistic . . ., skeptical of people who are not self-sufficient, and driven by such self-interested motives as greed, materialism, and excessive consumerism" (Wuthnow 2004:21).

This is true of twinning, where—as in other religious programs— participants are encouraged to "think compassionately about the poor, but they also channel this thinking in individualistic ways that may encourage charity more than public advocacy on behalf of the poor." Unlike the mainstream religious initiatives that Wuthnow identifies, Catholic liberation theology is a radical critique of power structures focused on transforming "social institutions, not individuals." But, despite the rhetoric evident in its literature and the liberation theology prompting Theresa Patterson's activism, St. Robert's twinning does not extend itself into Catholic liberation theology discourse or practice.

Faith-based and voluntary efforts that are less radical than liberation theology—such as twinning, World Vision, and Christian Care (Bornstein 2005)—find more acceptance; indeed, they are rather fashionable in the early 2000s. In 2001, President George W. Bush established the Office of Faith-based and Community Initiatives to "strengthen and expand the role of FBCOs [faith-based community organizations] in providing social services" (Office of the Press Secretary 2001:webpage). The United Nations declared 2001 the International Year of Volunteers to help encourage and support "volunteer service," which the UN defines as "as non-profit, non-wage and non-career action that individuals carry out for the well-being of their neighbours, community or society at large" (UN 2006:webpage).

Within this context, one could argue that twinning's "instrument effects" (Ferguson 1994) do encourage participants to think compassionately about Haiti's poor but then channel this thinking into charity rather than transforming social institutions (Wuthnow 2004:21). In the context of a weak—but predatory—state where social service delivery is otherwise nonexistent, twinning provides Haitian parishes access to external funding through which to provide food, medicine, education, water, and other goods and services to their parishioners. It also provides priests with new vehicles, fancy rectories, and other amenities they might otherwise lack. But in the process of building these relationships, identifying local-level problems, and forging solutions, the focus shifts from the underlying and structural forces that cause suffering among Haiti's people to managing them through seemingly apolitical interventions. In effect, twinning can serve to depoliticize poverty, just as Ferguson (1994) suggests "development" more broadly does in Lesotho. However, in contrast to Ferguson's analysis, twinning does not prop up the power of the Haitian bureaucratic state. Although it is constrained by the state in certain instances (for example, travel visas, customs), twinning largely operates outside of state channels and is explicitly critical of the Haitian government. That said, many twinning participants hope that a Haitian government modeled on the U.S. government will emerge, and by encouraging a "citizen" subjectivity among Haiti's twinning participants, St. Robert hopes to encourage the development of a neoliberal Haitian government sometime in the future.

Twinning, in large part, skirts the state, opting instead to work directly with grassroots communities. Yet MacDonald (1995:6) suggests that such people-to-people linkage may, in fact, be more "dangerous" than aid conventionally routed through the state, because it "penetrates the very fibers of the community, creating new forms of clientism and cooption." Erica Bornstein (2005) discovered this when tracing the impacts of child sponsorship programs in Zimbabwe, where direct funneling of money to sponsored children upset traditional family structures and generated community conflict between those who received aid and those who did not. Similar discord has arisen in Haiti among sponsorship students and their communities. Some priests in Haiti have responded by refusing to divulge the names of sponsorship funds recipients. Instead, they decide which students require help and then pay the fees for those children without revealing to the community who has benefited and who has not.

One result is that twinning further concentrates the power of priests in Haiti. Haitian priests are already in quite powerful positions vis-à-vis their parishioners. Twinning gives priests access to relatively large sums of money, over which they exercise some discretion, even when the funds are earmarked for specific purposes (for example, feeding school children). In parishes outside of Verrettes, I personally have seen veritable "rectory castles" constructed with U.S. donations and have found stockpiles of supplies and other "goodies" shipped for specific people but never delivered to them by priests. And remember that part of the money sent by St. Robert for the purchase of pews was spent on a backyard renovation project at the Verrettes rectory, where a gate and walkway were constructed to shield the priests from the weather as they walked from the rectory to the church—and, some speculate, to shield them from the prying eyes of parishioners. This, too, is an irony of twinning. Such assertions of "agency" on the part of priests diminish the control that U.S. Haiti committees have over Haitian priests. And at the same time, they expand the distance between the priest and his flock. Largely left out of the equation are those whom twinning is intended most to engage: parishioners in *both* locations. And yet, are priests better able to speak for local people than others might be? That is, even taking into account the power and authority that priests have vis-à-vis many others locally, does their presence in communities, engagement with locals, and likely concern for their parishioners make them—though perhaps not ideal advocates—better spokespersons than development professionals from Port-au-Prince or abroad?

Another question one might ask is whether programs such as twinning are inherently demeaning. Returning to this notion of professionalizing knowledge, I would argue that twinning—like conventional development—requires a "logical framework. But, in the adoption of these terms and frames of reference, they become the property of the developers, not the developed" (Kaufmann 1997:120). By constructing Haitians as deficient, twinning committee members configure a framework whereby they can "save" Haitians, they can "better" them through providing education and making them employable. The frames of reference that Haiti Committee members necessarily use are their own; they compare, judge, and imagine Haitians from their own perspective as middle-class, white American suburbanites. In fact, some have argued that such attempts to help others are really little more than affirmations of one's own position and superiority (Gronemeyer 1992). "Help is extended for the sake of the achievements of one's own (Western) civilization. It serves to confirm and secure the standards of normality" (Gronemeyer 1992:61). This might be partially true of twinning, where the twinning committee's own experiences do serve as the template for imaging a different Haiti. For example,

> The first day Father [Alexis] was with us, we met . . . for a potluck. We asked if the Haitians have potluck suppers. He said, "The Haitian people do not have potlucks because they don't eat every day." I have NO IDEA of what this would be like; I can't even imagine not having three meals a day (unless I choose not to eat). (*Weekly Bulletin*, 4/26/1998)

Gronemeyer (1992) also argues that "help" generally can be characterized in three ways: self-confident, superior, and self-congratulatory. And to a degree, these elements do characterize St. Robert's twinning. For example, in commenting about matching St. Robert and Our Lady, Doug said, after returning from the first trip the St. Robert committee made to Haiti, "I got 'em back, and they took the ball and ran with it. There are lots of professionals there, so they know how to work [to get things done]." There is an air of self-confidence that derives from those on the committee being well educated and relatively affluent; they are not afraid to push for what they think is in the best interest of St. Robert and Verrettes (a prime example is their contacting the bishop to protest Father Jean's transfer from Our Lady). But this self-confidence occasionally hints at notions of superiority and self-congratulation, as well. A recent correspondence regarding Father Yvens's impending travel to the United States—and his decision to send an assistant priest in his stead—drives home the point: In a memo to themselves, the Haiti Committee noted that they had "graciously agreed" that the assistant priest could visit Ada instead of Yvens. Although Cassie has assured me that the memo was "tongue in cheek," it nonetheless suggests that committee members recognize themselves as more powerful than the priest in Haiti and that they see—and explicitly self-label—their intentional tempering of this power as "gracious."

That aura of *noblesse oblige* aside, I do not think twinning is inherently demeaning. Indeed, in its rhetoric, twinning is quite the opposite: It attempts to build bridges, find commonalities, appreciate differences, and share resources and "gifts." Difficulties arise, however, at the intersection of twinning and development, with the pressure to manage programs, evaluate successes, and account for money.

To return to the question framing this section, what is twinning? Is it development as usual, alternative development, an alternative to development, or something else? From my perspective, I would argue that twinning is an alternative to the conventional development apparatus. John Martinussen (1999:291) suggests that alternative approaches to development come in two varieties: (1) a redefinition of development's goals (rejecting the hegemonic discourse of economic growth as an end in itself and instead advocating welfare and human development), and (2) a shifting of development toward civil society (emphasizing local communities as a means for promoting human well-being). Twinning is considered here an "alternative" because it incorporates both of these elements.

Twinning—based on Catholic notions of doing good and helping Haitians—challenges certain discourses and practices of the conventional development discourse, specifically its emphasis on economic growth. Instead, twinning focuses on meeting basic needs in Haiti. Framed by ideas of mutuality and by attempts to be conscious of power differentials between the two parishes, twinning aspires to cultural sensitivity and builds "relationships" between individuals and parishes. And it explicitly works through "grassroots" pairings, rather than through the state, to bring individual communities together in mutually rewarding relationships.

At the same time, however, twinning fails as an alternative to development, at least as imagined by Escobar (1995) and Nederveen Pieterse (2000), because it does not attempt to "undo" development in Haiti. Rather, it intends to extend its reach there, to "bring in" those who are perceived as having been neglected by more formal development initiatives. Twinning fails as an alternative *to* development, because in its "intentions, world-view, and mindset," it is very much characterized by belief *in* development and is invested in promoting its spread throughout Haiti. As in conventional initiatives, many of those on the Haiti Committee subscribe to the view that Haitians are impoverished, uneducated, and "diseased" and that these realities can be mitigated—even if not eliminated—through local-level parish partnering. The fact that these are "nonprofessionals" undertaking development does not radically alter the frames of reference (Western, middle-class standards and

Enlightenment thinking), the projects they fund, or their intention to manage the projects under way.

Why might this be? I would like to suggest that development, in fact, rests not on an exclusionary "expert discourse" but on a larger modernist worldview held by middle-class Americans, particularly the "affluent middle class" (Plotnicov 1990:16), writ large. Lay developers, such as those involved in Catholic parish twinning, are not simply absorbing the discourses of professional developers. The flow of knowledge is not from development experts to lay developers and then down to the developed. Rather, professional developers are themselves beholden to the middle-class visions they bring to their development expertise. Thus knowledge flows both "up" to conventional institutions and "down" to those targeted for development. The expertise that emerges in twinning—the specialized knowledge that lay developers draw on to legitimize their interventions—rests on their grounded knowledge of what it means to be middle-class (that is, "developed").

Thus, although the development discourses explored here as part of the operation of the Haiti Committee at St. Robert in large part reflect and buoy discourses described by post-structural scholars as hegemonic, perhaps St. Robert's Haiti Committee—because it is peopled by "manager–professionals," in Leonard Plotnicov's (1990:16) terms—is not in the grip of the developmentalist ideas of the hegemonic development apparatus. Perhaps, instead, the development apparatus is better understood as one particular exercise of modernity. That is, development does not monopolize modernist discourses. Rather, modernity is the larger project to which development is attached. Development, then, is the site of struggle, the practical application of modernity. Those at St. Robert, despite being "outside the formal dimensions of the aid industry," are able to replicate, rework, and repeat many of the discourses and practices of development because both conventional and lay approaches rest on similar ideas: notions of superiority, accountability, and professional expertise. What it means to be a member of the "affluent middle class" is largely what it means to be developed. In many ways, St. Robert's Haiti Committee members are the living embodiment of their modernist agenda for Haiti.

■ Notes

1. There are eight UN Millennium Development Goals: (1) Eradicate extreme poverty and hunger. (2) Achieve universal primary education. (3) Promote gender equality and empower women. (4) Reduce child mortality. (5) Improve maternal health. (6) Combat HIV/AIDS, malaria, and other diseases. (7) Ensure environmental sustainability. (8) Develop a global partnership for development (UN 2005).

2. The U.S occupation of Haiti from 1915 to 1934 has been described as an exceptionally brutal period in Haiti's history. The United States imposed marshal law, censored newspapers, favored light-skinned elites for key administrative positions, and rewrote Haiti's constitution to allow for foreign ownership of land. The "U.S.-built" roads were actually constructed using corvée labor extracted from Haiti's peasantry. (See Schmidt 1995.)

3. There is disagreement, of course, about the extent to which such a discourse is monolithic and impervious to challenge or change.

4. Nevertheless, PTPA has sponsored conferences for individuals and parishes active in the twinning program. For example, in June 2003, PTPA sponsored the "Medical Mission Conference" in Indianapolis, Indiana. Paul Farmer and several other healthcare specialists sponsored sessions on topics such as "Voodoo and Its Effects on Healthcare" and "Organizing a Surgical Team." A conference held by PTPA in Nashville in September 2004 drew St. Robert's participation, including as "expert" presenters.

CHAPTER SEVEN

Conclusion

In a context where globalization, neoliberalism, and a crisis in foreign aid are increasingly shifting "development" from a government project to a private one, this book has provided an in-depth look at Catholic parish twinning as one increasingly important manifestation of development's privatization. Taking as its central concern how lay initiatives such as U.S.–Haiti parish twinning are related to conventional development discourses and practices, this project has explored in detail what development means for those active in St. Robert's Haiti twinning program, which has partnered with Our Lady of the Nativity parish in Verrettes, Haiti, since 1995.

One question guiding the book has been: What is development? What does it mean, how is it constructed, what are its goals — to these noncredentialed "lay" developers? I have argued that development, though defined in diverse terms by committee members, generally is constructed to mean two things: developing people (by educating them, providing opportunities for them to better themselves, and promoting self-sufficiency) and locally grounding development (so that it responds to local aspirations and needs). These constructions translate unevenly into practice, however, in part because accessing and assessing the local has been exceedingly difficult given the language barriers, geographical distance, and cultural differences separating these two parishes. The structure of twinning—with Haiti committees directing U.S.-based twinning activities and priests in charge of twinning in Haiti—means that a relatively few people are charged with "speaking for" parishioners in each location. It is not clear, for example, to what extent priests are able or willing to accurately gauge the needs of their parishioners or whether the work of the Haiti Committee represents the wishes of the larger congregation. The result is a "people-to-people" relationship that remains, in many ways, generated "from the top down" rather than from the "grassroots" up, even though that "top" is much nearer the people than one that might be configured from Port-au-Prince or Washington, DC.

The twinning between Our Lady and St. Robert takes a micro-oriented perspective, focused on helping individuals within one relatively small community. Thus, rather than locating Haiti's poverty or its "underdevelopment" within a structural and historical framework, those on the Haiti Committee concentrate their efforts and analysis whole-heartedly on the local level, where problems seem more readily identifiable and treatable. The projects that St. Robert funds and Our Lady implements attempt to blunt the effects of poverty, deprivation, and oppression, rather than to alter or dismantle the larger forces undergirding these problems. They also attempt to "responsibilize" citizens to fulfill their human potential by enrolling specific individuals in school or offering them microcredit.

Twinning's mandate to respect the unique gifts that each parish possesses, while practicing a "noncontrolling mutuality" in the the parishes' relationship with one another, has proved exceedingly difficult for St. Robert. In part, this stems from the development-oriented nature of the partnership with Our Lady. With large sums of money flowing from St. Robert to Our Lady, the Haiti Committee feels compelled to "protect the intentions" of their donors and the intended recipients. That is, it expects the money it sends to Haiti to be used for specified purposes. Haitian priests have sometimes resisted these prescriptions, and their discretionary use of that money has generated real tension between the two parishes, thereby straining their collaboration.

A second question the book explores is: What relation do private, nonprofessional initiatives have to the entrenched institutionalized development apparatus criticized by anti-development scholars? I suggest that twinning in many ways strongly reflects dominant development discourses, though in other ways it challenges them. On the one hand, St. Robert's twinning invests in the idea of Haiti's "underdevelopment." Identifiable in Haitians' high levels of illiteracy, lack of formal education, malnutrition, disease, unemployment, and other "abnormalities," Haiti is readily acknowledged as "the poorest country in the Western Hemisphere." Moreover, these defining features of Haiti's underdevelopment are explained in conventional terms: the result of "bad government," Haitians' lack of education, poor leadership. The result—as in conventional initiatives—is a depoliticization of poverty, as it is approached primarily on technical rather than structural terms. Haiti's challenges are transformed into a series of "problems" that can be (at least partially) addressed through targeted apolitical interventions that leave the status quo unchallenged.

Twinning also tends to frame Haiti's peasantry in developmentalist terms: as non-analytical, evasive, uneducated, and resigned to poverty. Such conceptualizations of the poor are central to development, more generally, providing easy explanations for poverty—locating it among the deficiencies and abnormalities of the poor—while also making its solution seem self-evident. I believe that they serve the same function for St. Robert's Haiti Committee, which assumes that problems of poverty can be mitigated or overcome by first identifying Haitians' deficiencies and then engaging Haitians in their own self-improvement.

Unlike conventional discourses and practices, however, twinning also constructs Haitians in positive moral terms. By thinking about Haitians in terms of a shared Catholicism, committee members see Haitians as alternative models for "being in the world." They imagine Haitians as embodying a deep and authentic spirituality that stems from a focus on family and freedom from rampant consumption and materialism. They identify a *joi de vivre* among Haitians that they attribute to the Haitians' "simpler" lives. That is, Haiti Committee members tend toward a dual construction of Haitians, as models both to emulate and to repudiate. In any case, the St. Robert committee members imagine that Haitians are very different from themselves, and they see the differences as rooted in Haiti's poverty.

Escobar (1995:23) asserts that the "Third World can scarcely be thought about in any other terms than its essential trait: poverty." This is largely true in twinning networks. Indeed, poverty was the most often cited characteristic of Haiti that came to people's minds during free-listing exercises, and even the positive traits that committee members attribute to Haitians are framed in relation to Haitians' poverty: Haitians are able to be joyful, dignified, and happy *despite* poverty, while being more family-oriented, spiritual, and less materialistic *because* of it. In any case, poverty provides the framework for understanding "who Haitians are," as they embody both qualities to emulate and deficiencies. But Haitians are also thought about in racial terms—as "Blacks" who are different from both white U.S. twinning committee members and African Americans.

Finally, the book has considered how twinning might be best understood: Is it another manifestation of the hegemonic development apparatus or something different? I have framed twinning as "alternative development," because even though it is in many ways firmly entrenched within conventional development thinking, twinning in some ways skirts it, as well. For example, contrary to Escobar's (1995:44) assertion that all development was (and is) merely "a top-down, ethno-centric, and technocratic approach, which treated people and cultures as abstract concepts, statistical figures to be moved up and down in the charts of 'progress,'" I have found twinning to be intensely focused on local-level interactions between Our Lady and St. Robert. Members of the St. Robert Haiti Committee focus on individuals, on schools, and on Verrettes—on the particulars, such as whether school children are eating lunch—rather than on rising income levels or other conventional development markers. Perhaps this is not for lack of desire, however. Social scientific knowledge often provides the basis for "charting progress." And, as I have discussed, this is precisely the type of knowledge that St. Robert's twinning participants find it difficult to obtain. They want to know how many graduates are finding jobs, how many microcredit borrowers are paying their loans, how many children are excelling in school. But without the appropriate managerial apparatus in Haiti to gather these data, twinning committee members often feel they are taking a "flying leap into the darkness." Thus, perhaps because it has been unable to formulate "charts of progress," twinning aspires to help Haitians become self-sufficient, to meet their own basic needs, and to have choices. Yet committee members see this help as ultimately leading Haitians to particular types of market-based activities, such as laboring as an auto mechanic. In this way, twinning *is* about integrating poor Haitians into larger economic systems based on capital and exchange.

Twinning rhetoric intends to be critical of power differentials between partnered parishes, and it advocates relationships that are mutually beneficial and rewarding for both parties. Indeed, both St. Robert and Our Lady seem to be "getting something out of" twinning (for the Americans, a sense of doing good, meeting their Christian service obligations, finding new models for being in the world, and having opportunities for travel; for Haitians, access to goods and services). But even so, power differentials between the two parishes actually seem to be extended via twinning. In the more overt manifestations of this, St. Robert's participants attempt to impose a system of accountability in Haiti, where priests keep, and produce upon request, an "auditable" reporting of their spending. Moreover, priests are vulnerable to sanction for using the money in ways not intended by the donors. Priests, however, attempt to evade these management practices—for example, by not providing the required accounting. Such resistance meets with a mix of frustration, suspicion, and bewilderment among the St. Robert committee members. But funds often continue to flow, as the Haiti Committee attempts to design and impose an agreeable system for monitoring spending in Haiti.

Twinning at St. Robert invests in the idea of development and in its spread throughout Haiti, attempting to "bring in" those who have been marginalized by formal development regimes. For this reason, twinning fails to be an alternative to development. Rather, seeing poverty as indicative of Haiti's underdevelopment and its lack of "good governance," St. Robert's twinning committee attempts to equip Haitians with the skills and resources necessary to mitigate economic vulnerability and one day to become successful in the market economy. These are the more covert exercises in power. St. Robert's committee members focus on education so that Haitians can "analyze their own situations," forge their own solutions, and eventually, it is hoped, land formal-sector jobs.

Twinning, in short, seeks to prepare Haitians to be integrated into larger economic systems, where they can access food, water, shelter, and other necessities. It encourages Haitians to become "empowered . . . to act on their own behalf" (Cruikshank 1999:39), and in so doing, it attempts to encourage Haitians' willing participation in their own development.

In basic terms, twinning might simply be labeled a faith-based NGO, led by volunteers rather than development professionals and serving as an alternative to "top-down," state-directed development. Despite the fact that twinning depends on lay developers, the parallels with professional NGO initiatives are clear: The frames of reference are similarly Western and middle-class, the projects they fund are mainstream, and their desire to create efficient projects that can be assessed in terms of effectiveness is overt. Like conventional development, twinning promotes neoliberal economies structured around education, waged work, and self-improvement.

Twinning does not fall entirely within conventional discourses, at least as identified by Escobar, Rist, Ferguson, and others, but neither does it fall much outside them. These lay developers call forth contested notions of what development means and how it should proceed, and they attempt to create models for social justice to stand in solidarity with Haiti's poor. In the process, they question their own cultural values and find inspiration in the alternative ways of being that Haitians present. But with its intense focus on cultural difference, local-level action, and correcting deficiencies, twinning seems to remain an alternative form *of* development, without articulating an alternative *to* development. Rather, like conventional initiatives, twinning tends to reduce Haiti's challenges to a number of "problems" to fix, while ignoring and depoliticizing the structural features undergirding Haiti's poverty. In short, twinning exemplifies the "decentering of power into more diffuse sites" (Abrahamsen 200:1459) where "average" Americans become "responsibilized" to become developers and, consequently, becoming responsible for "responsibilizing" Haitians to engage in their own self-improvement and development.

This leaves the perplexing question of what—if anything—should be done. While this research does not investigate the impact of twinning "on the ground" in Haiti, it does raise several concerns about the forms it takes among participants in the United States. As a scholar concerned about power and resource imbalances separating the wealthy from the poor, I have asked myself whether twinning is something that should be "subverted." In the spirit of Escobar, Sachs, and other anti-development scholars, I wonder whether I should be working to dismantle or undermine twinning. Is twinning an imperialist project? Or does it affirm a "common humanity" (admittedly, a problematic concept; see Abu-Lughod 1993) across the United States and Haiti?

I do not have a clear answer to this question, but I suspect it probably lies somewhere in the middle; twinning is both a "humane" and an imperialist project, neither fully one nor the other. In some ways it resembles the "humane 'imperialism'" noted by the Comaroffs (1991:309) in their analysis of British colonial missionization in southern Africa. The "sending of humble men on heroic missions . . . to save Africa" partially describes twinning. There *is* an impulse to "save" Haitians, though not (primarily) from the horrors of savagery or the worship of "false idols," as in traditional missionary activities. Rather, these "average" Americans want to help "rescue" Haitians from poverty, while also valuing the models of spirituality and simple living that Haitians offer. Necessarily, such interventions are exercises of power, although U.S. participants have not understood them as such.

That said, my goal here is *not* to undermine twinning or to encourage its "death." Rather, I want to start a conversation about how twinning might be constituted differently, so that it exists less as development. Like many others, I wrestle with the question of how to counter hegemonic forces that work in the interest of the status quo, how to refashion relationships in ways that are more self-conscious about the operation of power. I agree that grassroots collaborations have the potential to revolutionize structural inequality (Farmer 2004) and perhaps offer "alternative representations and practices" (Escobar 1995:213) by bringing together differing systems of attitudes, values, and beliefs that challenge or oppose "common sense" understandings. With its roots in liberation theology, twinning might hold potential for doing this, but not in its present form. In fact, there are currently many problematic aspects to twinning, particularly as its theories and practices converge with conventional development initiatives. I have raised them herein not because I have the answers; I do not. But I hope my analysis makes a contribution not only to scholarly thinking about international development but also to the practical reworking of twinning in ways that can recognize and subvert the differences in wealth, power, and opportunity that separate the United States and Haiti.

■ Contributions and Considerations

Anthropology of development is concerned with the analysis of development as a cultural, economic, and political process (Grillo and Stirrat 1997). In particular, post-structural anthropology of development scholars are interested in power and knowledge and their operation within the development field. This includes "denaturalizing development in order to deconstruct its modes of operation, the languages used to define it, the role of power in structuring its form and goals, and its intended and unintended effects on individuals and communities" (Sachs 1992; Gardner & Lewis 1996; Ferguson 1994).

This has generated an important body of literature that "stands apart" from the development apparatus, objectifies it, and critiques it. Many of these analyses have deconstructed hegemonic, institutional-level development aid discourses (Gardner and Lewis 2000; Moore 2001) and illuminated the ways in which these entrench bureaucratic state power (Ferguson 1994) and limit participants' conceptualizations of "what is possible" (Escobar 1995). From such understandings, scholars have argued that development—as one way in which power is exercised (Escobar 1995; Rist 1997; Sachs 1992)—uses specialized (professionalized) discourses to craft the Third World as an object of knowledge to be intervened in and controlled. By setting limits on what people are able to think about the world and its operations, such discourses create spaces, particularly within institutions, where only some people—those deemed experts—have authority and legitimacy. Others, in effect, are locked out (or at least constrained) from creating alternative discourses and practices. This produces a view of the "Third World" as poor, backward, and in need of external intervention and guidance. From this perspective, it is assumed that the underdeveloped can "progress" toward Western advancement/development through the application of scientific knowledge to promote economic growth.

In contrast, this project has argued that development knowledge is in many ways becoming "deprofessionalized." Because globalization and neoliberalism are encouraging the privatization of development delivery, ordinary citizens (that is, lay developers) are increasingly taking over the design and delivery of international development. Until now, little research has documented or examined in depth what these lay knowledges look like, how they are deployed, or how they connect with or diverge from "expert" knowledges, even though similar questions have been of primary concern to anthropology of development scholars deconstructing conventional development initiatives (for example, Arce and Long 2000; Gardner and Lewis 1996; Grillo and Stirrat 1997).

Development, in this new privatized form, does not rest simply on an expert discourse based in conventional economics. Yet, in many ways, twinning replicates the discourses and practices of conventional development, despite most participants having no formal training in or professional experience with it. This, I suggest, is not because lay developers merely are absorbing expert discourses. The flow of knowledge is not simply top-down, emanating from development experts, passing to lay developers then onto the developed. Instead, there is a shared grounding in Western middle-class values that links both professional and lay developers and results in similar discourses and practices, despite the absence of formal "indoctrination" in development thinking among twinning participants. What it means to be "developed" reflects and buoys an understanding of what it means to be "modern" and middle-class: financially secure, educated, rational, ambitious, employed.

That professional and lay developers are linked by a middle-class modernist worldview suggests that the conventional development apparatus itself may be less beholden to expert discourses than was originally conceived. Rather than having only professional expertise framing its discourses and practices, conventional development is constrained by the middle-class visions that developers hold. From this perspective, the development apparatus can be understood not as the preeminent hegemon but, rather, as merely one expression of hegemonic modernity.

That is, conventional development does not originate or monopolize modernist discourses and practices. Rather, modernity finds its expression in conventional development. And, as we have seen, it also finds its expression in "lay" development as a new form of governmentality. The discourses and practices of conventional and lay development converge in many ways because modernity is the larger project to which development—in myriad forms—is often attached. Development—be it lay or conventional—becomes the site of struggle, the practical application of modernity.

Those at St. Robert replicate, rework, and repeat many of development's discourses and practices because both conventional and lay approaches rest on similar ideas: notions of superiority, accountability, and professional expertise. In many ways, to be a member of the "affluent middle class" is to be "developed." St. Robert's Haiti Committee members embody what it means to be modern, to be developed. This is the source of their expertise. They are experts at being "successful" Americans; they work hard, value education, and see that they are materially and financially rewarded for their efforts.

This project—which responds to Arce and Long's (2000) call for greater attention to development discourses at the "local level" and to Gardner and Lewis's (2000) insistence that such studies extend beyond the "formal dimensions of the aid industry"—situates itself at a relatively new intersection, where development, religion, and NGO-ization meet. To date, few anthropological studies have examined this convergence (for example, Bornstein 2005; Occhipinti 2005). Moreover, few studies have looked specifically at the lay dimensions of this junction. Yet, as globalization and neoliberalism reconfigure states, privatize social services delivery, and permit relatively quick and convenient communications and travel across the globe, faith-based programs such as parish twinning exemplify development's reconfiguration. Far from spelling the "death of development" (Sachs 1992; Esteva 1992), projects such as twinning demonstrate not only that belief in development (Rist 1997) is still very much alive, but also that lay men and women have both the resources and the determination to do it. And yet, understanding of these processes, their effects, and their connections to the conventional development apparatus is sorely lacking. As an example of the new, fractured, privatized forms that development is assuming, this study of twinning has served as an entry point for understanding one manifestation of development's privatization. I hope others will extend this analysis by considering the links between lay and conventional initiatives in other forms and other locations.

General Interview

Background Information—Individual

1. Interviewee Name:
2. Could you tell me a bit about yourself? Your family? What do you do for a living?
3. If you grew up Catholic, how would you describe your own experience of growing up Catholic (for example, your family's relationship to the church, your religious education and involvement with church activities, etc.)? If you did not grow up Catholic, how and why did you become a Catholic?
4. To you, what are the most meaningful aspects of being a Catholic? Are there facets of being a Catholic or of the Catholic Church that you find troubling or problematic?
5. Do you have any Catholic heroes or heroines or people who serve as role models for you?
6. What do you think of the direction of the Catholic Church, post–Vatican II?
7. Growing up, were you or your family involved in any social organizations or social issues? Are you involved in social organizations or issues now, other than Haiti twinning?

8. When you were growing up, what experiences or interactions did you have with other cultures or races?

Local Context

9. How long have you been a member at St. Robert? Why did you join the parish?
10. How would you describe St. Robert, as a parish?
11. How does the leadership style of Father Lou compare to other priests you've known?
12. How would you describe Sister JoAn's involvement in St. Robert?
13. What's the role of the laity in leading St. Robert?

Involvement in Twinning

14. How did you personally become involved in Haiti twinning?
15. In what ways have you participated in the twinning program?
16. Are you still active? Why (not)?
17. What personal rewards or fulfillment did / do you get out of twinning? Any frustrations?
18. As a church community, how does St. Robert benefit from being a part of the Haiti program? And, how does Our Lady in Verrettes benefit? Are there any drawbacks for the churches?

Notions of the "Third World" and Haiti

19. When you think of Haiti, what are the first five words that come to mind?
20. What did you know about Haitian history and culture before joining the twinning? Did you know any Haitians or Haitian Americans? What have you learned since?
21. In what ways would you like Haiti to be more like the U.S.?
22. In what ways would you like the U.S. to be more like Haiti?
23. What do you think of Haitian Vodou?
24. What's your favorite memory of traveling in Haiti? Worst?
25. How did you respond to requests for money?

26. Why do you think Haiti is so poor?

27. What do you think can be done to help Haiti out of poverty?

28. Some people contend Haiti's poverty stems from its legacy as a slave colony. What do you think of that? What do you think of similar explanations of African-American poverty in the U.S.?

29. Do you see any parallels between the unrest in Haiti and that in other parts of the world, for example Iraq or Afghanistan?

30. What role should the U.S. government play in other parts of the world? What about U.S. churches or non-profits?

31. What does "good government" mean to you? Is "good government" possible everywhere in the world? Why (not)?

Development, Missionization, and Twinning

32. What is the purpose of the twinning program?

33. Why does twinning focus on Haiti, in particular?

34. Do you think of twinning as missionary work? In what ways or why not?

35. When you think about what it means for a community to be "developed," what things come to mind?

36. Can you think of any "Third World" countries that would be considered "developed" by your definition?

37. Does the twinning aspire to develop Verrettes in any way? How so?

38. Under what—if any—circumstances do you think Haiti–U.S. parish twinning would no longer be necessary?

39. What role—if any—do you think the U.S. government should play in Haiti?

St. Robert Programming

40. Could you talk a bit about the different programs St. Robert sponsors in Verrettes?

41. Why did St. Robert decide to establish these programs?

42. What happens when the priests in Haiti request something St. Robert thinks is undesirable or unnecessary?

43. Are there programs or projects you'd like to see St. Robert sponsor in Haiti? In the U.S.?

44. Do you think any of the existing programs should be dismantled? Why (not)?

Conflict and Cooperation

45. Could you talk a little about what the Haiti Committee is and its purpose?

46. What's the role of the priests—both in the U.S. and Haiti—in twinning decision making? What is Sr. JoAn's role?

47. What happens when there are differences of opinion about the twinning program?

48. Are there differences that can't be overcome?

Bettering Twinning

49. What suggestions do you have for strengthening the St. Robert–Verrettes twinning?

50. What do you think are the most important "lessons" that St. Robert has learned since beginning the twinning?

51. What advice would you give parishes interested in joining the twinning program?

Works Cited

Abrahamsen, Rita. 2004. The power of partnerships in global governance. *Third World Quarterly* 25, no. 8:1453–1467.

Abu-Lughod, Lila. 1991. Writing against culture: Recapturing anthropology. In *Recapturing anthropology: Working in the present.* Santa Fe, NM: School of American Research Press.

Abu-Lughod, Lila. 1993. *Writing women's worlds: Bedouin stories.* Berkeley, CA: University of California Press.

Adam, Barry D. 1993. Post-Marxism and the new social movements. *Canadian Review of Social Anthropology* 30, no. 3:316–336.

Agarwal, Bina. 1992. The gender and environment debate: Lessons from India. *Feminist Studies* 18, no. 1:119–158.

Ammerman, N. T., J. W. Carroll, C. S. Dudley, and W. McKinney. 1998. In *Introduction. Studying congregations: A new handbook.* Nashville, TN: Abingdon.

Appadurai, Arjun. 1991. Global ethnoscapes: Notes and queries for a transnational anthropology. In *Recapturing anthropology: Working in the Present.* Santa Fe, NM: School of American Research Press.

Appardurai, Arjun. 2001. *Globalization.* Durham, NC: Duke University Press.

Arce, Alberto and Norman Long. 1992. The dynamics of local knowledge: Interfaces between bureaucrats and peasants. In *Battlefields of*

215

knowledge: The interlocking of theory and practice in social research and development. London, New York: Routledge.

Arce, Alberto and Norman Long. 2000a. Reconfiguring modernity and development from an anthropological perspective. In *Anthropology, development and modernities: Exploring discourses, counter-tendencies and violence.* New York: Routledge.

Arce, Alberto and Norman Long. 2000b. *Anthropology, development and modernities: Exploring discourses, counter-tendencies and violence.* New York: Routledge.

Bates, Eric. 1995. What you need to know about Jesse Helms. *Mother Jones.* May/June. Available online.

Bauer, Peter. 1995. Foreign aid: Central component of world development? In *Development studies: A reader.* New York: Oxford University Press.

Bebbington, A.J. and G. Thiele. 1993. *NGOs and the state in Latin America: Rethinking roles in sustainable agricultural development.* London: Routledge.

Bell, Beverly. 2001. *Walking on fire: Haitian women's stories of survival and resistance.* Ithaca, NY: Cornell University Press.

Belshaw, Deryke, Robert Calderisi, and Chris Sudgen, eds. 2001. *Faith in Development: Partnership between the World Bank and the Churches of Africa.* Washington, DC: World Bank Publications.

Best, Steven and Douglas Kellner. 1991. *Postmodern theory: Critical interrogations.* New York: Guilford Press.

Black, Jan Knippers. 1999. *Development in theory and practice: Paradigms and paradoxes.* Boulder, CO: Westview Press.

Bodley, John. 1982. *Victims of progress.* Mountain View, CA: Mayfield Publishing Company.

Boone, Peter and Jean-Paul Fauget. 1998. Multilateral aid, politics and poverty: Past failures and future challenges. In *The global crisis in foreign aid.* Syracuse, NY: Syracuse University Press.

Bornstein, Erica. 2001a. The verge of good and evil: Christian NGOs and economic development in Zimbabwe. *POLAR: Political and Legal Anthropology Review* 24, no. 1:59–77.

Bornstein, Erica. 2001b. Child sponsorship, evangelism, and belonging in the work of World Vision, Zimbabwe. *American Ethnologist* 28, no. 3:592–622.

Bornstein, Erica. 2005. *The spirit of development: Protestant NGOs, morality, and economics in Zimbabwe*. Stanford, CA: Stanford University Press.

Boserup, Esther. 1970. *Women's role in economic development*. London: George Allen & Unwin.

Bovard, James. 1986. The continuing failure of foreign aid. *Policy Analysis* 65, January 31. Available online.

Bowen, J. 1998. *Foreign aid and economic growth: A theoretical and empirical investigation*. Brookfield, VT: Ashgate.

Brautigam, Deborah and Michael Woolcock. 2001. *Small states in a global economy: The role of institutions in managing vulnerability and opportunity in small developing countries*. Helsinki: World Institute for Development Economics Research/United Nations University.

Burnside, Craig and David Dollar. 1997. Aid, policies and growth. *Policy research working papers*. Washington, DC: World Bank.

Burnside, Craig and David Dollar. 1998. Aid, the incentive regime, and poverty reduction. *Policy research working papers*. Washington, DC: World Bank.

Bush, George. 1989. Inaugural address of George Bush. January 20. Available online.

Candland, Christopher. 2000. Faith as social capital: Religion and community development in southern Asia. *Policy Sciences* 33, 355–374.

Caribbean Development Bank. 2000. Aid effectiveness in the Caribbean: Revisiting some old issues. *Staff Working Paper Series* No. 3.

Carroll, Thomas F. 1992. *Intermediary NGOs: The supporting link in grassroots development*. Bloomfield, CT: Kumarian Press.

Castor, Suzy. 1988. Femme et participation sociale. In *Theories and pratiques*. Port-au-Prince, Haiti: CRESFED.

Central Intelligence Agency (CIA). 2005. CIA world fact book: Haiti. Available online.

Chambers, Robert. 1993. *Challenging the professions: Frontiers for rural development*. London: Intermediate Technology.

Chambers, Robert. 1997. *Whose reality counts? Putting the first last*. London: Intermediate Technology.

Chambers, Robert. 2005. *Ideas for development*. London: Earthscan.

Chomsky, Noam, Paul Farmer, and Amy Goodman. 2004. *Getting Haiti right this time: The U.S. and the coup.* Monroe, ME: Common Courage Press.

Cima, Lawrence R. and Thomas L. Schubeck. 2001. Self-interest, love, and economic justice: A dialogue between classical economic liberalism and Catholic social teaching. *Journal of Business Ethics* 30:213–231.

Collier, Paul and David Dollar. 2001. Can the world cut poverty in half? How policy reform and effective aid can meet the international development goals. In *Aid effectiveness research.* Washington, DC: World Bank.

Comaroff, Jean and John L. Comaroff. 1991. *Of revelation and revolution, Vol. 1: Christianity, colonialism, and consciousness in South Africa.* Chicago: University of Chicago Press.

Comaroff, John L. and Jean Comaroff. 1997. *Of revelation and revolution, Vol II: The dialectics of modernity on a South African frontier.* Chicago: University of Chicago Press.

Cooke, Bill and Uma Kothari. 2001. *Participation: The new tyranny?* London and New York: Zed Books.

Cornwall, Andrea. 2004. Spaces for transformation? Reflections on issues of power and difference in participation in development. In *Participation: From tyranny to transformation?* New York: Zed Books.

Crewe, Emma and Elizabeth Harrison. 1998. *Whose development? An ethnography of aid.* New York: Zed Books.

Cruikshank, Barbara. 1999. *The will to empower: Democratic citizens and other subjects.* Ithaca, NY: Cornell University Press.

Crush, Johnathon S. 1995. *Power of development.* London and New York: Routledge.

Demas, W. G. 1997. *Critical issues in Caribbean development: West Indian development and the deepening and widening of the Caribbean community.* Kingston, Jamaica: Ian Randle Publishers.

Devarajan, Shantayanan, David Dollar, and Torgny Holmgren. 1999. Aid and reform in Africa. In *Aid effectiveness research.* Washington, DC: World Bank.

Devarajan, Shantayanan and Vinaya Swaroop. 1998. The implications of foreign aid fungibility for development assistance. *Policy research working papers.* Washington, DC: World Bank.

DeWind, Josh and David H. Kinley III. 1998. *Aiding migration: The impact of international development assistance on Haiti.* Boulder, CO: Westview Press.

Dolan, J. P. 1992. *The American Catholic experience: A history from colonial times to present.* Notre Dame, IN: Notre Dame University Press.

Duffield, Mark. 1994. Complex emergencies and the crisis of developmentalism. *IDS Bulletin: Linking Relief and Development* 25, no. 4:37–45.

Dupuy, Alex. 1989. *Haiti in world economy: Race, class, and underdevelopment since 1700.* Boulder, CO: Westview Press.

Dupuy, Alex. 1997. *Haiti in the new world order: The limits of democratic revolution.* Boulder, CO: Westview Press.

Edwards, Michael and David Hulme. 1996. *Beyond the magic bullet: NGO performance and accountability in the post–cold war world.* West Hartford, CT: Kumarian Press.

Egbue, N. G. 2006. Africa: Cultural dimensions of corruption and possibilities for change. *Journal of Social Science* 12, no. 2:83–91.

Ehlers, Tracy Bachrach. 1990. *Silent looms: Women and production in a Guatemalan town.* Austin, TX: University of Texas Press.

Ehrenreich, Barbara. 1990. *Fear of falling: The inner life of the middle class.* New York: Harper Perennial.

Escobar, Arturo. 1988. Power and visibility: Development and the invention of management of the Third World. *Cultural Anthropology* 18, no. 4:428–443.

Escobar, Arturo. 1991. Anthropology and the development encounter: The making and marketing of development anthropology. *American Ethnologist* 18, no. 4:658–682.

Escobar, Arturo. 1995a. *Encountering development: The making and unmaking of the third world.* Princeton, NJ: Princeton University Press.

Escobar, Arturo. 1995b. Imagining a post-development era. In *The power of development.* London and New York: Routledge.

Escobar, Arturo. 2000. Beyond the search for a paradigm? Post-development and beyond. *Development = Developpement = Desarrollo* 43, no. 4:11–15.

Esteva, Gustava. 1992. Development. In *The development dictionary.* London: Zed Books.

Evans, Peter. 1992. The state as problem and solution: Predation, embedded autonomy, and structural change. In *Politics of economic adjustment.* Princeton, NJ: Princeton University Press.

Farmer, Paul. 1992. *AIDS and accusation: Haiti and the geography of blame.* Berkeley, CA: University of California Press.

Farmer, Paul. 1994. *The uses of Haiti.* Monroe, ME: Common Courage Press.

Farmer, Paul. 2004. What happened in Haiti? Where the past is present. In *Getting Haiti right this time: The U.S. and the coup.* Monroe, ME: Common Courage Press.

Farmer, Paul, Mary C. Smith-Fawzi, and Patrice Nevil. 2003. Unjust embargo of aid for Haiti. *Lancet.* 361:420–423.

Farrington, John and Anthony Bebbington. 1993. *Reluctant partners? Non-governmental organizations, the state, and agricultural development.* London: Routledge.

Ferguson, Anne and Bill Derman. 2000. Writing against hegemony: Development encounters in Zimbabwe and Malawi. *Development encounters: Sites of participation and knowledge.* Cambridge, MA: Harvard Institute for International Development, Harvard University.

Ferguson, James. 1994. *The anti-politics machine: "Development," depoliticization, and bureaucratic power in Lesotho.* Minneapolis, MN: University of Minnesota Press.

Ferguson, James and Akhil Gupta. 2002. Spatializing states: Toward an ethnography of governmentality. *American Ethnologist* 29, no. 4:981–1002.

Feyzioglu, Tarhan, Vinaya Swaroop, and Min Zhu. 1998. A panel data analysis of the fungibility of foreign aid. *World Bank Economic Review* 12, no. 1:29–59.

Fisher, William F. 1997. Doing good? The politics and anti-politics of NGO practices. *Annual Review of Anthropology* 26, no. 1:439–464.

Foucault, Michel. 1990. *Politics, philosophy, culture: Interviews and other writings, 1977–1984.* New York and London: Routledge.

Frank, Andre Gunder. 1967. *Capitalism and underdevelopment in Latin America: Historical studies of Chile and Brazil.* New York: Monthly Review Press.

Frankenberg, Ruth. 1993. *White women, race matters: The social construction of white women.* Minneapolis, MN: University of Minnesota Press.

Friedman, Johnathon. 1994. *Cultural identity and global process.* Thousand Oaks, CA: Sage Press.

Galaty, John G. 1988. Scale, politics and cooperation in organizations for East African development. *Who shares: Co-operatives and rural development.* Dehli: Oxford University Press.

Gardner, Katy. 1997. Mixed messages: Contested "development" and the "plantation rehabilitation project." In *Discourses of development: Anthropological perspectives.* Oxford, UK: Berg.

Gardner, Katy and David Lewis. 1996. *Anthropology, development and the post-modern challenge.* Chicago, IL: Pluto Press.

Gardner, Katy and David Lewis. 2000. Dominant paradigms overturned or "business as usual"? Development discourse and the White Paper on International Development. *Critique of Anthropology* 20, no. 1:15–29.

Garrison, L. 1998. Aid: Perception and reality. Notebook, Choice. 26.

Gaventa, John. 2004. Towards a participatory governance: Assessing transformative possibilities. In *Participation: From tyranny to transformation?* New York: Zed Books.

Getu, Makonen. 2001. Poverty alleviation and the role of microcredit in Africa. In *Faith in development: Partnerships between the World Bank and the churches of Africa.* Oxford, UK: Regnum Books International.

Gifford, Paul. 1994. Recent developments in African Christianity. *African Affairs* 93:513–534.

Gladwin, Christina, ed. 1991. *Structural adjustment and African women.* Gainesville: University of Florida Press.

Grant, R. and J. Nijman. 1998. Foreign aid regime in flux: Crisis or transition. In *The global crisis in foreign aid.* Syracuse, NY: Syracuse University Press.

Greene, Anne. 1993. *The Catholic Church in Haiti: Political and social change*. East Lansing, MI: Michigan State University Press.

Grillo, R. D. 1997a. Discourses of development: The view from anthropology. In *Discourses of development: Anthropological perspectives*. Oxford, UK: Berg.

Grillo, R. D. and R. L. Stirrat. 1997b. *Discourses of development: Anthropological perspectives*. Oxford, UK: Berg.

Gronemeyer, Marianne. 1992. Helping. *The development dictionary*. London: Zed.

Guillaumont, Patrick and Lisa Chauvet. 1999. *AID and performance: A reassessment*. Clermont-Ferrand, France: CERDI.

Guyer, Jane and Pauline Peters. 1987. Introduction (Special issue on conceptualizing the household: Issues of theory and policy in Africa). *Development and Change* 18:197–214.

Harding, Sandra. 1986. *The science question in feminism*. Ithaca, NY: Cornell University Press.

Haynes, Jeff. 2001. Transnational religious actors and international politics. *Third World Quarterly* 22, no. 2:143–158.

Hefferan, Tara. 1998. *A study in terror: State-sponsored sexualized violence in Haiti 1991–1994*. M.A. Thesis, University of Denver.

Heinl, Robert Debs, Nancy Gordon Heinl, et al. 1996. *Written in blood: The story of the Haitian people, 1492–1995*. Lanham, MD: University of America.

Hickey, Sam and Giles Mohan. 2004. Towards participation as transformation? Critical themes and challenges. In *Participation: From tyranny to transformation?* New York: Zed Books.

Hoben, Allen. 1982. Anthropologists and development. *Annual Review of Anthropology*, 11:349–375.

HOP (Haiti Outreach Project) n.d. Facts about Haiti. Grand Rapids: Grand Rapids Diocese.

Jenkins, Henry. 1998. *The children's culture reader*. New York: New York University Press.

Kapur, Promilla. 2000. The principle of fundamental oneness. In *The lab, the temple, and the market: Reflections at the intersection of science, religion, and development*. Bloomfield, CT: IDRC/Kumarian.

Kaufmann, Daniel. 1997. Corruption: The facts. *Foreign Policy,* 107:114–131.

Kempa, Michael, Clifford Shearing, and Scott Burris. n.d. Changes in governance: A background review. Prepared for the Salzburg Seminar on the Governance of Health. Available online.

Korten, David. 1990. *Getting to the 21st century: Voluntary action and the global agenda.* Bloomfield, CT: Kumarian Press.

Kothari, U. and M. Minogue 2002. The political economy of globalization. In *Development theory and practice: Critical perspectives.* Basingstoke, NH: Palgrave.

Kuper, Adam. 1998. *The invention of primitive society.* London and New York: Routledge.

Lacy, Anita and Suzan Ilcan. 2006. Voluntary labor, responsible citizenship, and international NGOs. *International Journal of Comparative Sociology* 47, no. 1:34–69.

Langness, L. L. 1993. *The study of culture.* Novato, CA: Chandler & Sharp Publishers.

Lewis, David and Tina Wallace. 2000. *New roles and relevance: Development NGOs and the challenge of change.* Bloomfield, CT: Kumarian Press.

Little, Peter D. 2000. Recasting the debate: Development theory and anthropological practice. *NAPA Bulletin* 18, no. 1:119–131.

Little, Peter D. and Michael Painter. 1995. Discourse, politics, and development: A response to "The making of development anthropology." *American Ethnologist* 22, no. 3:602–609.

Long, Andrew. 1992. Goods, knowledge and beer: The methodological significance of situational analysis and discourse. In *Battlefields of knowledge: The interlocking of theory and practice in social research and development.* London and New York: Routledge.

Long, Norman. 1992. From paradigm lost to paradigm regained? The case for an actor-oriented sociology of development. In *Battlefields of knowledge, the interlocking of theory and practice in social development.* London and New York: Routledge.

Long, Norman. 2000. Exploring local/global transformations: A view from anthropology. In *Reconfiguring modernity and development from an anthropological perspective.* London and New York: Routledge.

MacDonald, Laura. 1995. A mixed blessing: The NGO boom in Latin America. *NACLA Report on the Americas* 28:30–35.

Martin, Emily. 2001. *The woman in the body: A cultural analysis of reproduction.* Boston, MA: Beacon Press.

Martinussen, John. 1999. *Society, state, and market: A guide to competing theories of development.* London: Zed Books.

Maternowska, Catherine M. 1996. Coups d'état and contraceptives: A political economy analysis of family planning in Haiti. Ph.D. Dissertation, Columbia University.

Mathieu, Suze Marie. 2001. The transformation of the Catholic Church in Haiti. Ph.D. Dissertation, Indiana University.

Mayotte, Judith. 1998. Religion and global affairs: The role of religion in development. *SAIS Review* 18, no. 2: 65–69.

McCollum, Chris. 2002. Relatedness and self-definition: Two dominant themes in middle-class Americans life stories. *Ethos* 30, no. 1:113–140.

McGlone, Mary M. 1997. *Sharing faith across the hemisphere.* Washington, DC: United States Catholic Conference.

Merlingen, Michael. 2003. Governmentality: Towards a Foucauldian framework for the study of IGOs. *Cooperation and Conflict: Journal of the Nordic International Studies Association* 38, no. 4:361–384.

Mintz, Sidney. 1985. *Sweetness and power.* New York: Transaction Books.

Mohan, Giles and Sam Hickey. 2004. Relocating participation within a radical politics of development: Critical modernism and citizenship. In *Participation: From tyranny to transformation?* New York: Zed Books.

Mohanty, Chandra Talpade. 1997. Under Western eyes: Feminist scholarship and colonial discourses. In *The women, gender, and development reader.* New York: Zed Books.

Moore, Sally Falk. 2001. The international production of authoritative knowledge: The case of drought-stricken West Africa. *Ethnography* 2, no. 2:161–189.

Morgan, Lynn M. 1987. Dependency theory in the political economy of health: An anthropological critique. *Medical Anthropology Quarterly* 1, no. 2:131–154.

Morton, A. L. n.d. "Haiti: NGO Sector Study." World Bank Technical Paper 8.

Morris, C. R. 1997. *American Catholic: The saints and sinners who built America's most powerful church*. New York: Times Books.

Moser, Caroline. 1993. *Gender planning and development: Theory, practice and training*. London and New York: Routledge.

Myrdal, Gunnar. 1968. *Asian drama: An inquiry into the poverty of nations*. Harmondsworth, UK: Penguin.

NCCB (National Conference of Catholic Bishops). 1997. *Economic justice for all: Pastoral letter on Catholic social teaching and the U.S. economy, 10th anniversary edition*. Washington, DC: United States Catholic Conference.

Nederveen Pieterse, Jan. 2000. After post-development. *Third World Quarterly* 21, no. 2:175–191.

Nicholls, David. 1986. Cultural dualism and political domination in Haiti. In *Dual legacies in the contemporary Caribbean*. London: Frank Cass.

Nijman, Jan. 1998. United States foreign aid. *The global crisis in foreign aid*. Syracuse, NY: Syracuse University Press.

Nordstrom, Carolyn. 2004. *Shadows of war: Violence, power, and international profiteering in the twenty-first century*. Berkeley: University of California Press.

North-South Institute. 1996. Civil society: The development solution? Working Paper presented at the Civil Society Seminar, Institute of Development Studies. June.

Nuijten, Monique. 1992. Local organization as organizing practices: Rethinking rural institutions. In *Battlefields of knowledge: The interlocking of theory and practice in social research and development*. London and New York: Routledge.

Oatcs, M. J. 1992. Economic change and the character of American Catholic philanthropy 1790–1940. In *Religion, the independent sector, and American culture*. Atlanta, GA: Scholars Press.

Occhipinti, Laurie A. 2005. *Acting on faith: Religious development organizations in northwestern Argentina.* Lanham, MD: Lexington Books.

Office of the Press Secretary. 2001. Executive Order: Establishment of White House Office of Faith-Based and Community Initiatives. January 29. Available online.

Organization of Overseas Development Cooperation (OECD). 2006. Glossary of statistical terms: Official development assistance. Available online.

Overseas Development Institute (ODI). 1994. *Aid in transition.* ODI Briefing Paper 4/94. Available online.

Paley, Julia. 2002. Toward an anthropology of democracy. *Annual Review of Anthropology* 31:469–496.

Parish Twinning Program of the Americas (PTPA). n.d. Building parish to parish relationships: People reaching out to people. Nashville, TN: PTPA.

Parpart, Jane L. 1995. Deconstructing the development "expert": Gender, development and the "vulnerable groups." In *Feminism, postmodernism, development.* New York: Routledge.

Peoples, James G. 1978. Dependence in a Micronesian economy. *American Ethnologist* 5, no. 3:535–552.

Peet, Richard and Elaine Hartwick. 1999. *Theories of development.* New York: Guilford Press.

Peet, Richard and Michael Watts. 1996. Liberation ecology: Development, sustainability, and environment in an age of market triumphalism. *Liberation ecologies: Environment, development, social movements.* London and New York: Routledge.

Perry, James L. 2004. Civic service in North America. *Nonprofit and Voluntary Sector Quarterly*, Supplement to 33, no. 4:167s–183s.

Peters, Pauline E. 2000. *Development encounters: Sites of participation and knowledge.* Cambridge, MA: Harvard Institute for International Development, Harvard University.

Plotnicov, Leonard. 1990. *American culture: Essays on the familiar and unfamiliar.* Pittsburgh: University of Pittsburgh Press.

Poppendieck, Janet. 1998. *Sweet charity? Emergency food and the end of entitlement.* New York: Viking.

Posey, Darrell A. 1985. Native and indigenous guidelines for new Amazonian development strategies: Understanding biodiversity through ethno ecology. In *Change in the Amazon basin: Man's impact on forests and rivers.* Manchester, UK: Manchester University Press.

Rahnema, M. 1992. Poverty. In *The development dictionary.* London: Zed Books.

Rew, A. 1997. The donors' discourse: Official social development knowledge in the 1980s. In *Discourses of development.* Oxford, UK: Berg.

Richards, Paul. 1985. *Indigenous agricultural revolution.* London: Hutchinson.

Riddell, Roger C. and Mark Robinson. 1995. *Non-governmental organizations and rural poverty alleviation.* Oxford: Oxford University Press.

Rist, Gilbert. 1997. *The history of development.* London: Zed Books.

Robinson, Randall. 2004. When the major powers stage a coup. In *Let Haiti live.* Coconut Creek, FL: EducaVision.

Rostow, Walt Whitman. 1960. *Stages of economic growth: A non-communist manifesto.* Cambridge: Cambridge University Press.

Rutherford, Blair and Rinse Nyamuda. 2000. Learning about power: Development and marginality in an adult literacy center for farm workers in Zimbabwe. *American Ethnologist* 27, no. 4:839–854.

Rylko-Bauer, Barbara, Merrill Singer, and John Van Willigen. 2006. Reclaiming applied anthropology: Its past, present, and future. *American Anthropologist* 108, no. 1:178–190.

Sachs, Wolfgang. 1992a. *The development dictionary.* London: Zed Books.

Sachs, Wolfgang. 1992b. Introduction. *The development dictionary.* London: Zed Books.

Salomon, Lester M. 1993. The global associational revolution: The rise of the third sector on the world scene. *Occasional paper 15.* Baltimore, MD: Institute of Policy Studies.

Salomon, Lester M. 2001. An "associational" revolution. *The Courier.* June. Available online.

Schmidt, Hans. 1995. *The United States occupation of Haiti 1915–1934.* New Brunswick, NJ: Rutgers University Press.

Selinger, Leah. 2004. The forgotten factor: The uneasy relationship between religion and development. *Social Compass* 51, no. 4:523–543.

Sen, Amartya. 1999. *Development as freedom.* New York: Knopf.

Sen, Gita and Caren Grown. 1987. *Development, crises, and alternative visions: Third world women's perspectives.* New York: Monthly Review Press.

Shaw, Russell. 2005. Attacking a saint. *Arlington Catholic Herald.* Available online.

Sherman, Amy L. 1997. *The soul of development: Biblical Christianity and economic transformation in Guatemala.* New York: Oxford University Press.

Slater, David. 1992. Theories of development and the politics of the post-modern: Exploring a border zone. *Development and Change* 23:283–319.

Smith, Carol A. 1978. Beyond dependency theory: National and regional patterns of development. *American Ethnologist* 5, no. 3: 574–617.

Smith, Jennie Marcelle. 2001. *When the hands are many: Community organization and social change in rural Haiti.* Ithaca, NY: Cornell University Press.

St. Robert. 2003. *The joy of giving: A directory of our parish family, our programs, and ministry opportunities.* Ada, MI: St. Robert of Newminster Parish.

Svensson, Jakob. 1997. *When is foreign aid policy credible? Aid dependence and conditionality.* Policy Research Working Paper. Washington, DC: World Bank.

Tomalin, Emma. 2006. Religion and a rights-based approach to development. *Progress in Development Studies* 6, no. 2:93–108.

Townsend, Janet G. 1999. Are non-governmental organizations working in development a transnational community? *Journal of International Development* 11, no. 4: 613–623.

Tripp, Linda. 1999. Gender and development from a Christian perspective: Experience from World Vision. *Gender and Development* 7, no. 1:62–68.

Truman, H. S. 1949. President Truman's four point message. *The history of development: From Western origins to global faith.* New York: Zed Books.

Tsele, Molefe. 2001. The role of Christian faith in development. In *Faith in development: Partnerships between the World Bank and the churches of Africa.* UK: Regnum Books International.

Tvedt, Terje. 2001. *Angels of mercy of development diplomats: NGOs and foreign aid.* Trenton, NJ: Africa World Press.

United Nations. 2005. UN millennium development goals. Available online.

United Nations. 2006. Background. Available online.

United Nations Development Programme (UNDP) 2004. Human development report. *United Nations Development Programme.*

United Nations International Report. 1995. Emergency economic recovery program, 1:A1 (3 April 1996.)

U.S. Census Bureau. 2000. *Census 2000 summary file 3 (SF3)-Sample data.* Available online.

Van de Walle, Nicholas. 2001. *African economies and the politics of permanent crisis.* New York: Cambridge University Press.

Ver Beek, Kurt Allen. 2000. Spirituality: A development taboo. *Development in practice* 10, no. 1:31–43.

Verna, Chantalle Francesca. 2000. Beyond the immigration centers: A history of Haitian community in three Michigan cities, 1966–1998. M.A. Thesis, Michigan State University.

Villarreal M. 1992. The poverty of practice: Power, gender and intervention from an actor-oriented perspective. In *Battlefields of knowledge: The interlocking of theory and practice in social research and development.* London and New York: Routledge.

Wade, Robert. 1985. The market for public office. *World Development* 13, no. 4:467–497.

Walch, Timothy. 1989. *Catholicism in America: A social history.* Malabar, FL: Robert E. Krieger.

Wallerstein, Immanuel. 1974. *The modern world system, capitalist agriculture and the origins of the European world economy in the sixteenth century.* New York: Academic Press.

Walter, Tony and Grace Davis. 1998. The religiosity of women in the modern west. *The British Journal of Sociology* 49, no. 4:640–666.

Weber, Max. 1958. *The Protestant ethic and the spirit of capitalism.* New York: Charles Scribner's Sons.

Williamson, J. 1993. Democracy and the "Washington Consensus." *World Development* 21, no. 8:1329–1336.

Wolf, Eric. 1982. *Europe and the people without history.* Berkeley: University of California Press.

World Bank. 1994. The Carribean region: A review on World Bank assistance. Country assistance evaluation, operations evaluation department.

World Bank. 1997. *Global development finance.* Washington, DC: World Resources Institute.

World Bank. 1998a. *Assessing aid: What works, what doesn't and why?* Washington, DC: Oxford University Press.

World Bank. 1998b. Haiti: The challenges of poverty reduction. Volume II. Report 17242-HA. Poverty Reduction and Economic Management Unit and Caribbean Country Management Unit Latin America and the Caribbean Region.

Wuthnow, R. 2004. *Saving America? Faith-based services and the future of civil society.* Princeton, NJ: Princeton University Press.

Young, Kate. 1993. *Planning development with women: Making a world of difference.* London: Macmillan.

Zaidi, S. A. 1999. NGO failure and the need to bring back the state. *Journal of International Development* 11, no. 2:259–271.

Zweig, Michael. 1991. Economics and liberation theology. In *Religion and economic justice.* Philadelpia: Temple University Press.

Index

Also from Kumarian Press...

International Development: .

Reducing Poverty, Building Peace
Coralie Bryant and Christina Kappaz

Buddhism at Work: Community Development, Social
Empowerment and the Sarvodaya Movement
George Bond

Development and Advocacy
Edited by Deborah Eade

Southern Exposure: International Development and the Global
South in the Twenty-First Centry
Barbara P. Thomas-Slayter

New and Forthcoming:

Humanitarian Alert: NGO Information and Its Impact on US
Foreign Policy
Abby Stoddard

Born of War: Protecting Children of Sexual Violence Survivors in
Conflict Zones
Edited by Charli Carpenter

NGOs in International Politics
Shamima Ahmed and David M. Potter

Everywhere/Nowhere: Gender Mainstreaming in Development
Agencies
Rebecca Tiessen

Visit Kumarian Press at www.kpbooks.com or call toll-free
800.289.2664 for a complete catalog

green
press
INITIATIVE

Kumarian Press, located in Bloomfield, Connecticut, is a forward-looking, scholarly press that promotes active international engagement and an awareness of global connectedness.